The Constitutional Theory of the Federation and the European Union

The Constitutional Theory of the Federation and the European Union

SIGNE REHLING LARSEN

is a Fellow by Examination in Law at Magdalen College at the University of Oxford

OXFORD
UNIVERSITY PRESS

OXFORD
UNIVERSITY PRESS

Great Clarendon Street, Oxford, OX2 6DP,
United Kingdom

Oxford University Press is a department of the University of Oxford.
It furthers the University's objective of excellence in research, scholarship,
and education by publishing worldwide. Oxford is a registered trade mark of
Oxford University Press in the UK and in certain other countries

First Edition published in 2021

Impression: 4

Published in the United States of America by Oxford University Press
198 Madison Avenue, New York, NY 10016, United States of America

British Library Cataloguing in Publication Data

Data available

Library of Congress Control Number: 2020947859

ISBN 978–0–19–885926–0

DOI: 10.1093/oso/9780198859260.001.0001

Printed and bound by
CPI Group (UK) Ltd, Croydon, CR0 4YY

For Hjalte

Preface

This book is concerned with the constitutional theory of federations, in general, and the European Union (EU), in particular. It aims to show that the federation is a discrete political form on a par with, though distinct from, the other two forms of political association of modernity, namely the empire and the state. The federation is a political union of states founded on an interstate agreement of a constitutional nature, a federal compact, that does not absorb the Member States into a new state. The book further maintains that the constitutional nature of the EU, shrouded with mystery in the literature, is that of a federation. The federal constitutional nature of the EU has not been adequately appreciated because the scholarly debate on both federalism and European integration is dominated by the constitutional imagination of the state and the idea of sovereignty. This book is an attempt to break away from the state-centric world view, but crucially without leaving the world of political jurisprudence. The federation is a genuine form of *political* association, with an outside and an inside, and it is therefore not a form of 'cosmopolitan' constitutionalism.

This book has been written between three cities: London, Copenhagen, and Florence. In each place, there are a number of people I would like to thank. The book is based on my doctoral dissertation from the LSE, which I defended in September 2018. I would like to express my gratitude to Martin Loughlin and Mike Wilkinson, who were the best supervisors and mentors I could possibly have hoped for. Their distinct approaches to scholarly work in general, and to constitutional theory in particular, have been immensely influential for this book. I would also like to thank a number of people at the LSE Law Department who were kind enough to read parts of my dissertation and provide insightful comments during my doctorate: Damian Chalmers, Jan Komárek, Tom Pool, and Floris de Witte. Finally, I would like to extend my gratitude to my two examiners, Jo Murkens and Alexander Somek, whose perceptive remarks and critique have informed the revision of the dissertation into a monograph.

I finished my dissertation during a visit to iCourts, University of Copenhagen. I would like to thank iCourts in general and Mikael Rask Madsen and Jan Komárek (again) for providing a wonderful environment to round up the thesis. I would also like to thank Poul Kjær and the Department of Management, Politics and Philosophy at Copenhagen Business School for hosting me during the summer of 2019. It was in Copenhagen that I first met Kalypso Nicolaïdes, who I would like to thank for her perceptive reading of parts of the manuscript and for motivating me to write a book that could also speak to scholars beyond the discipline of law.

I hope I have succeeded in that. I would also like to thank the reviewers at Oxford University Press for their helpful suggestions and comments. The editorial team at the Oxford University Press, in particular Brianne Bellio, Jamie Berezin, and Iona Jacob together with the design team, deserve my gratitude for all their support and hard work in making this book a reality.

I finished the manuscript during a Max Weber Fellowship at the European University Institute in Florence that was in part spent in Copenhagen because of the outbreak of the Covid-19 pandemic. Nevertheless, both before and during this crisis, colleagues at the EUI were immensely helpful and supportive. I would like to thank Jorge Díaz Ceballos, Anca Cretu, Paul Dermine, Gábor Halmai, and Michał Ziółkowski for reading and commenting on parts of the manuscript. Bob Roth was an excellent editorial assistant and Alyson Price and Jen Moore provided invaluable help with the language. Needless to say, all mistakes in the book are mine entirely.

Last but not least, I would like to thank my parents, Maria and Øjvind, for their support over these last few years when I started an academic career and became a parent at the same time. I dedicate this book to my husband, Hjalte, who means the world to me.

Table of Contents

Table of Cases

THE COURT OF JUSTICE OF THE EUROPEAN UNION

THE GERMAN CONSTITUTIONAL COURT

THE DANISH SUPREME COURT

THE UK SUPREME COURT

THE US SUPREME COURT

Table of Legislation

List of Abbreviations

BVerfG	Bundesverfassungsgericht
ECB	European Central Bank
ECJ	European Court of Justice
ECSC	European Coal and Steal Community
EDC	European Defence Community
EEC	European Economic Community
EFSF	European Financial Stability Facility
EFSM	European Financial Stabilisation Mechanism
EMU	Economic and Monetary Union of the European Union
EPC	European Political Community
EU	European Union
EUCFR	The Charter of Fundamental Rights of the European Union
EURATOM	European Atomic Energy Community
ESCB	European System of Central Banks
ESM	European Stability Mechanism
GATT	General Agreement on Tariffs and Trade
GG	Grundgesetz für die Bundesrepublik Deutschland (German Basic Law)
IMF	International Monetary Fund
MoU	Memorandum of understanding
NAFTA	North American Free Trade Agreement
NATO	North Atlantic Treaty Organization
OEEC	Organisation for European Economic Co-operation
OMT	Outright Monetary Transactions Program
PSPP	Public Sector Purchase Programme
QE	quantitative easing
SEA	Single European Act
WTO	World Trade Organization

Introduction

The legal and political nature of the EU remains an enigma for academics and the general public alike. For many years, the latter could happily ignore the question of what the EU really is, yet the multiple crises characterizing the last decade of European history—the Eurozone crisis, the refugee crisis, the rise of authoritarianism in Poland and Hungary, and Brexit—have prompted a new interest in the EU. For example, one of the most googled questions in the UK after the result of the Brexit referendum was announced in the early hours of 24 June 2016 was: 'What is the EU?'[1] Within academia, the constitutional nature of the EU has been debated for decades without ever solving the mystery, and, for some time, the tacit consensus was to avoid the issue altogether by declaring the EU to be unique or 'sui generis'. While the sui generis thesis might have been a viable position in times of relative stability, the government of the Eurozone crisis, significantly extending the powers of the executive branch of government at both Union and Member State level, and relying on governmental instruments of dubious legality forces us to confront the question: *With what right are the citizens and states of Europe governed?* To answer the fundamental questions raised by the last decade of European politics, it is necessary to address the question of the constitutional nature of the EU.

This book takes up the challenge of developing a constitutional theory for the EU. The point of departure, contrary to what is maintained by the sui generis thesis, is that from the perspective of constitutional theory the EU is neither unique nor unprecedented. The EU, this book maintains, is a union of states of a special kind, a federal union, or what this book calls a *federation*. That is, *a political union of states founded on an interstate agreement of a constitutional nature, a federal compact, that does not absorb the Member States into a new state.* The book argues, further, that the federation is a discrete form of political association on a par with, though distinct from, the other political forms of modernity, that is, the *empire* and the *state*. As such, the EU is not unique in world history. Multiple manifestations of this political form predate the EU, most importantly the antebellum United States, the nineteenth-century German Confederation, and the Swiss Confederation before the constitution of a federal state in 1848.

To be sure, it is not submitted that there are no unique aspects of the EU's constitution or its law and politics, all actual political associations are unique in one

[1] Brian Fung, 'Britons are frantically Googling what the EU is after voting to leave it' *Independent* (London, 24 June 2016).

The Constitutional Theory of the Federation and the European Union. Signe Rehling Larsen, Oxford University Press (2021).
 DOI: 10.1093/oso/9780198859260.003.0001

way or another, but these singular features do not make the EU any less a federation. Germany, France, and the UK all have unique constitutional attributes and are constitutionally very different from one another, but they are no less states because of that. The same applies to federations, including the EU. A study of the constitutional nature of the EU must abandon the sui generis thesis and start to think of the EU in the context of what it is comparable to in constitutional terms, namely, federations, that is, federal unions of states.

The political form of the federation, however, has largely been forgotten. The encounter with the EU, perhaps the only true federation of the contemporary world, will therefore 'naturally' lead us to think that it is unique. Nevertheless, the description of the EU as sui generis is problematic not only because of its historical and theoretical inaccuracy. More importantly, by insisting on the EU's uniqueness, the sui generis thesis constitutes only a superficial break with the categories of the state that continue to dominate the constitutional debates on federalism and demand that all federal polities fall within one of two categories: either a confederation of sovereign states (*Staatenbund*) or a sovereign federal state (*Bundesstaat*). In this way, it perpetuates the political theory of the state that has hindered the development of a genuine constitutional theory of the federation as a discrete political form.

The political form of the state has been so successful in dominating how we conceive of political life in general, and political and public law theory in particular, that it has become difficult for us to imagine any other form of political association. The state is a historical type, and yet, more often than not, it is treated as the universal or essential form of political association. This book demonstrates the limitations of the theory of the state and its application by providing a constitutional theory of the federation as a discrete political form and by showing how the legal and political nature of the EU can be explained by it.

I. Federalism and the EU

This book is far from the first study of the EU in light of federalism. Multiple volumes have been dedicated to the subject, exploring in detail questions and problems relating to the (optimal) division of powers between different levels of government in federal and multi-layered polities, the legal and regulatory instruments of federal- and multi-level governance, and the legitimacy of federalism in general and the EU in particular.[2] Though the literature on federalism and the EU

[2] See especially Kalypso Nicolaïdes and Robert Howse (eds), *The Federal Vision: Legitimacy and Levels of Governance in the United States and the European Union* (OUP 2001); Anand Menon and Martin A Schain (eds), *Comparative Federalism: The European Union and the United States in Comparative Perspective* (OUP 2006).

is rich in breadth and depth, the questions of *constitutional theory* remain underdeveloped thanks to the conceptual framework the literature overwhelmingly takes as its point of departure.

The literature on federalism and the EU is characterized by two different approaches, neither of which allows for the development of a genuine constitutional theory of the federation as a discrete form of political association. Most of the literature sets out with a flawed 'statist' understanding of a federation as a federal state (*Bundesstaat*) that it juxtaposes with a confederation of states (*Staatenbund*). On this basis, the general argument is that the EU transcends the 'federal-confederal' axis, it is neither a federal state nor a confederation of states, and for that reason it is a sui generis association characterized by its own unique brand of federalism.[3] The EU is in this way understood as an entity that does not conform to the political form of the state,[4] but the literature does not provide a genuine constitutional theory that can account for this. It therefore characterizes the EU as 'quasi-federal',[5] an 'incomplete federation',[6] a 'federation in the making',[7] a 'postmodern confederation',[8] or simply a 'unique form of union the like of which we have never seen before'.[9]

Despite its attempts to go beyond the theory of the state, this literature manages only a superficial break because, above all, it continues to think of the foundations of public authority based on the theory of the state: either *one* federal state or a confederation of *several* states. This book, in contrast, develops a genuine constitutional theory of the federation as a discrete political form that can answer the question of the foundations of authority in the EU and account for its constitutional nature beyond the distinction between 'federal' and 'confederal'.

[3] Joseph HH Weiler, 'Federalism without Constitutionalism: Europe's Sonderweg' in Kalypso Nicolaïdes and Robert Howse (eds), *The Federal Vision: Legitimacy and Levels of Governance in the United States and the European Union* (OUP 2001); Vivien Schmidt, 'Federalism and State Governance in the European Union and the United States: An Institutional Perspective' in Kalypso Nicolaïdes and Robert Howse (eds), *The Federal Vision: Legitimacy and Levels of Governance in the United States and the European Union* (OUP 2001); Anand Menon and Martin A Schain, 'Introduction' in Anand Menon and Martin A Schain (eds), *Comparative Federalism: The European Union and the United States in Comparative Perspective* (OUP 2006).

[4] A few scholars employ a less rigorous definition of the federal state and present the argument that the EU is 'a species of a federal state', see David McKay, *Federalism and European Union: A Political Economy Perspective* (OUP 1999) 35.

[5] Guy Peters, 'Federalism and Public Administration: The United States and the European Union' in Anand Menon and Martin A Schain (eds), *Comparative Federalism: The European Union and the United States in Comparative Perspective* (OUP 2006).

[6] John Erik Fossum and Markus Jachtenfuchs, 'Federal Challenges and Challenges to Federalism. Insights from the EU and Federal States' (2017) 24 Journal of European Public Policy 470.

[7] Kalypso Nicolaïdes and Robert Howse, 'Introduction' in Kalypso Nicolaïdes and Robert Howse (eds), *The Federal Vision: Legitimacy and Levels of Governance in the United States and the European Union* (OUP 2001) 8.

[8] Daniel J Elazar, 'The United States and the European Union: Models for Their Epochs' in Kalypso Nicolaïdes and Robert Howse (eds), *The Federal Vision: Legitimacy and Levels of Governance in the United States and the European Union* (OUP 2001) 42.

[9] Michael Burgess, *Federalism and European Union: The Building of Europe, 1950–2000* (Routledge 2000) 42.

Another part of the literature is more concerned with federalism understood as a set of principles for the exercise of dispersed or decentralized governmental powers in and beyond the state. Within this literature, the questions of the foundations of authority and the legal and political nature of the EU are de-emphasized.[10] In a similar manner to the literature on multi-level governance,[11] the focus is on the legal and regulatory characteristics of federal governance, its institutional dynamics, and its positive or normative legitimacy.[12] Instead of asking about the foundations of authority, this literature is concerned with the question of whether EU law and government can be justified with reference to a set of normative criteria such as 'good governance'.[13] The substitution of the question of political right[14] with a normative approach of moral justification characterizes most legal and political theories of European integration and EU law.[15]

In contrast, this book does not provide a normative appraisal of the EU. The book does not aim to answer the questions of whether the federation is a desirable form of political association, whether the EU meets certain normative benchmarks, or whether it should or could be reformed in order to do so. Instead, the book is an exercise in political jurisprudence[16] and it is concerned with 'constitutional imagination'.[17] Constitutions influence how we understand the foundations of public power and the political worlds we inhabit. As such they have a 'world making capacity'.[18] This book explores the constitutional imagination of the federation and of

[10] Alberta Sbragia, 'The United States and the European Union: Comparing Two Sui Generis Systems' in Anand Menon and Martin A Schain (eds), *Comparative Federalism: The European Union and the United States in Comparative Perspective* (OUP 2006).

[11] Gary Marks, Liesbet Hooghe, and Kermit Blank, 'European Integration from the 1980s: State-Centric v. Multi-level Governance' (1996) 34 Journal of Common Market Studies 341; Markus Jachtenfuchs, 'The Governance Approach to European Integration' (2001) 39 Journal of Common Market Studies 245.

[12] Daniel R Kelemen, *The Rules of Federalism: Institutions and Regulatory Politics in the EU and Beyond* (Harvard University Press 2004); Fritz W Scharpf, 'Democratic Legitimacy Under Conditions of Regulatory Competition: Why Europe Differs from the United States' in Kalypso Nicolaïdes and Robert Howse (eds), *The Federal Vision: Legitimacy and Levels of Governance in the United States and the European Union* (OUP 2001); Nicole Bolleyer, *Intergovernmental Cooperation: Rational Choices in Federal Systems and Beyond* (OUP 2009); Marc Landy and Steven M Teles, 'Beyond Devolution: From Subsidiarity to Mutuality' (OUP 2001).

[13] Christian Joerges and Renaud Dehousse, *Good Governance in Europe's Integrated Market* (OUP 2002).

[14] Martin Loughlin, *Foundations of Public Law* (OUP 2012) 1–13.

[15] See, for example, Richard P Bellamy, *A Republican Europe of States: Cosmopolitanism, Intergovernmentalism and Democracy in the EU* (CUP 2019); Jürgen Habermas, *The Crisis of the European Union—A Response* (Polity Press 2012); Erik Oddvar Eriksen and John Erik Fossum, 'Europe in Search of Legitimacy: Strategies of Legitimation Assessed' (2004) 25 International Political Science Review 435; Andrew Moravcsik, 'Federalism in the European Union: Rhetoric and Reality' in Kalypso Nicolaïdes and Robert Howse (eds), *The Federal Vision: Legitimacy and Levels of Governance in the United States and the European Union* (OUP 2001); Giandomenico Majone, 'Europe's "Democratic Deficit": The Question of Standards' (1998) 4 European Law Journal 5; Andreas Føllesdal and Simon Hix, 'Why There Is a Democratic Deficit in the EU: A Response to Majone and Moravcsik' (2006) 44 Journal of Common Market Studies 533.

[16] Martin Loughlin, *Political Jurisprudence* (OUP 2017).

[17] Martin Loughlin, 'The Constitutional Imagination' (2015) 78 The Modern Law Review 1.

[18] ibid.

the EU. It aims to understand with reference to what principles and ideas authority is claimed and public power is exercised in the federation in general and in the EU in particular. It provides an analysis of the principles and types of authority that distinguish the federation from other forms of political association. The aim is to arrive at a coherent interpretation of the federation as a discrete political form and compare it with the EU. In this way, the book is analytical rather than normative.

II. The Constitutional Theory of the Federation

This book develops a constitutional theory of the federation in order to understand the foundations of authority in the EU. The constitutional theory of the federation, however, is under-researched and for that reason, the book is not merely an exercise in 'applying' a pre-given theory to the case of the EU. The great bulk of academic literature on federalism treats the federation as a species of the state. For that reason, it is concerned with the governmental structure of the federal state rather than the constitutional theory and public law of the federation as a union of states.[19] An important exception is Olivier Beaud's *Théorie de la fédération*, which is dedicated exclusively to the development of a constitutional theory of the federation as a discrete legal and political form.[20] Though *Théorie de la fédération* is inspired by the problem of the constitutional nature of the EU, Beaud does not apply his theory to the EU in any systematic manner[21] and the book ends on the following note: 'We see that there is still ample material for another book, just as there is a need for another to answer the inaugural question of this work: *is the European Union a federation?*'[22] This book answers that question in the affirmative.

Notwithstanding the significant contributions of *Théorie de la fédération*, the constitutional theory of the federation remains underdeveloped. Important constitutional questions such as those relating to emergency politics, constitutional guardianship, and constitutional identity have been touched upon only to a very limited degree by previous scholars of the theory of the federation. In order to answer the question initially raised by Beaud, this book therefore investigates underexplored aspects of the constitutional theory of the federation. The book aims to show both how the theory of the federation can provide an answer to the

[19] For an overview of the classical literature see Michael Burgess, *In Search of the Federal Spirit: New Theoretical and Empirical Perspectives in Comparative Federalism* (OUP 2012); Michael Burgess and Alain-G Gagnon (eds), *Comparative Federalism and Federation* (Harvester Wheatsheaf 1993); Arthur Benz and Jörg Broschek, *Federal Dynamics Continuity, Change, and the Varieties of Federalism* (OUP 2013).

[20] Olivier Beaud, *Théorie de la fédération* (Presses universitaires de France 2007) [Theory of the Federation].

[21] See, however, Olivier Beaud, 'Histoire. Fédération, l'Europe écrit ton nom' *Libération* (Paris, 25 January 1995).

[22] Beaud (n 20) 425, my translation, italics added.

question of the constitutional nature of the EU and, at the same time, how the EU can contribute to the development of the theory of the federation. Through a comparison of the constitutional praxis and history of the German Confederation, the antebellum United States and the EU, the book develops under-theorized aspects of the theory of the federation. There is thus a certain deliberate circularity to the methodology employed: the theory of the federation sheds light on the EU, and the EU provides an important case study for the theory of the federation. In this way, the book tells two interwoven tales. One is about the constitutional nature of the EU and the history of European integration. The other is about the federation as a discrete political form characterized by its own virtues and vices. At the heart of both of these tales is an attempt to break free from the state-centric world view that has made it impossible to understand the nature of the federation as a discrete political form and, as a consequence of that, the constitutional nature of the EU.

A few scholars have initiated the work of investigating the foundations of authority of the EU on the basis of a theory of the federation as a discrete form of political association. This book is not a critique of any of these scholars, but rather a complement to their work. Robert Schütze has demonstrated that EU constitutional law is a concrete manifestation of a federation and he has written extensively on the legal transformation of the EU in comparison to the early history of the United States, with a special focus on the development of the internal market as a federal market.[23] His interest in the subject, however, is more that of a constitutional lawyer than a constitutional theorist, and he does not develop a detailed constitutional theory of the federation. Kalypso Nicolaïdes and Sergio Fabbrinni have also suggested that we should conceive of the EU as a *federal union* rather than a *federal state*.[24] Nevertheless, they are more interested in (normative) questions of legitimacy and institutional design than the questions of constitutional theory. In *Union of States: The Theory and Practice of Confederations*, Murray Forsyth presents an overview of the history of federal political thought, develops the idea of the economic union as a federal 'subspecies', and demonstrates how the political theory of the federation applies to the then European Economic Community (EEC).[25] Nevertheless, the discussion of the EEC is limited to one chapter, and as

[23] Robert Schütze, *European Constitutional Law* (CUP 2015); Robert Schütze, *From Dual to Cooperative Federalism: The Changing Structure of European Law* (OUP 2013); Robert Schütze, *From International to Federal Market: The Changing Structure of European Law* (OUP 2017).

[24] Kalypso Nicolaïdes, 'Constitutionalizing the Federal Vision?' in Anand Menon and Martin A Schain (eds), *Comparative Federalism: The European Union and the United States in Comparative Perspective* (OUP 2006); Kalypso Nicolaïdes, 'Conclusion: The Federal Vision Beyond the Federal State' in Kalypso Nicolaïdes and Robert Howse (eds), *The Federal Vision: Legitimacy and Levels of Governance in the United States and the European Union* (OUP 2001); Sergio Fabbrinni, *Which European Union: Europe after the Eurozone Crisis* (CUP 2015); Sergio Fabbrini, 'Intergovernmentalism in the European Union. A Comparative Federalism Perspective' (2017) 24 Journal of European Public Policy 580.

[25] Murray Forsyth, *Union of States: The Theory and Practice of Confederations* (Leicester University Press 1981).

such it does not provide a comprehensive account of the EEC as a federation. In his magnum opus *Unionsbürger: Europas föderale Bürgerrecht in vergleichender Sicht,* Christoph Schönberger provides a comprehensive comparative study of EU citizenship based on the principles of federal citizenship law and as such it sheds light on a core pillar of the constitutional theory of the federation and the EU as a manifestation thereof.[26] The focus is more or less exclusively on federal citizenship, and for that reason Schönberger's work does not exhaust the need for the development of a general constitutional theory of the EU as a federation.

III. The Structure of the Book

The book is divided into five chapters. Chapter 1 is concerned with the constitutional nature of the EU and the federation as a discrete political form. The chapter shows how the federation can provide an answer to the enigma of the legal and political nature of the EU, namely, that it does not fit the theory of the state because it cannot be explained either by public law or by international law. The chapter argues that the legal and political form of the EU is that of a federation: a discrete legal and political form on a par with, though distinct from, the two other political forms of modernity, the state and the empire. It is maintained that while the federation is founded by a compact or treaty between the federating states, it does not belong to the world of international law because the federation leads to a constitutional change in the contracting states by constituting among them a new political and public law entity, the Union, through which they henceforth govern themselves as 'Member States'. A federation is characterized both by the *birth* of a new union and the *transformation* of the contracting states. It is further argued that the federation is incompatible with the concept of sovereignty and for that reason a genuine constitutional theory of the federation as a discrete political form has to be developed as a public law form without recourse to the concept of sovereignty.

Following the development of the general principles of the constitutional theory of the federation, the book goes on to discuss the origins and telos of the federation as a political form in general and the EU in particular. Chapter 2 maintains that states decide to come together in a federation when they, for one reason or another, are incapable of maintaining their own political existence and autonomy. The medieval and early modern federations were constituted between smaller states and free cities in order to protect or liberate themselves from an empire by fusing their military power. They were defence federations. With the coming of

[26] Christoph Schönberger, *Unionsbürger: Europas föderales Bürgerrecht in vergleichender Sicht* (Mohr Siebeck 2005) [Union Citizen: Europe's Federal Citizenship-law in Comparative Perspective]. See also Christoph Schönberger, 'Die Europäische Union als Bund' (2004) 129 Archiv des öffentlichen Rechts 81 [The European Union as a Federation].

the industrial revolution, political economy and the construction of larger internal markets became crucial if states wanted to maintain their political autonomy. One way this was achieved was through *empire* (internal market creation by domination), another was through *federation* (internal market creation through free and equal contract). Federations that have economic government/welfare, and importantly the creation of an internal market, as their primary aim are termed economic federations or welfare federations.

European integration is a response to both the decline of the European maritime empires and the internal markets they provided for the European imperial metropoles, and to the legal and political collapse of the European states in the interwar period dominated by the experience of fascism and Nazism. In the new world dominated not by Europe, but by the great powers of the Cold War, European and American elites alike agreed that a European federation was the only way to stabilize Western Europe, and the Western European states, from the multiple threats to their political existence and autonomy. European integration is thus a response to the decline of empire and state failure. It is born out necessity in order for the Western European states to maintain themselves politically. The chapter shows that the post-WWII period is characterized by attempts to constitute both a defence federation and an economic federation in Western Europe but that only the latter was successful. The chapter concludes that the EU remains an economic federation with defence as a subsidiary aim.

Chapter 3 is concerned with the foundations and principles for the exercise of public power in the federation, that is, the principles of federal public law. The chapter maintains that the federation has a unique structure of public law that differs from that of the state. In contrast to the state, the key concept of the public law of the federation is not sovereignty. The federation is a union of states, a double political existence, with a dual governmental apparatus composed of the Union institutions and the governmental institutions of the Member States. Neither of these governmental structures fits the theory of state. The Union institutional framework is not a new omni-competent 'super-state'. It is characterized by the principles of teleology and specialization. That is, the Union has limited powers to achieve the aims specified in the federal compact. Nor are the Member States of the federation states in the 'classical sense'. Being a Member State entails a process of state transformation. The chapter shows that the 'constraints' of member-statehood are not purely external to the Member States and imposed by Union law. Rather, the constitutional orders of the Member States and the constitutional order of the Union are intertwined, albeit in different ways. The chapter shows that the EU Member States are characterized by different 'varieties of constitutionalism' and for that reason they have internalized the demands of EU membership in different ways.

The federation is born out of the impotence or collapse of the state as a political form. Nevertheless, Chapter 4 argues, the federation is itself characterized by internal contradictions that constantly threaten its survival. The federation is simultaneously committed to preserving the autonomy and diversity of its Member States *and* committed to constituting an 'ever closer union' between its peoples. The federal balance between these two contradictory ends can be maintained when there is relative constitutional homogeneity between the Member States. In the case of the EU, the constitutional homogeneity is that of 'constrained democracy'. However, the Member States have internalized this constitutional identity to varying degrees. This means that the federal balance, known in the EU as 'constitutional tolerance', can in no way be taken for granted. In order to preserve the federal balance, federations tend to claim the right to intervene in the internal constitutional affairs of its Member States if they diverge significantly from the constitutional identity of the Union. Notwithstanding the importance of such interventions for the stability and survival of a federal union, such interventions, like the EU's potential actions against the rise of 'illiberal democracy' in Poland and Hungary, are controversial because they threaten the political autonomy of its Member States.

Chapter 5 is concerned with the emergency government of the Eurozone. It is argued that the government of the Eurozone crisis can be understood according to the theories of constitutional defence and emergency government in the federation. The chapter maintains that the reason the government of the Eurozone crisis does not conform to the theory of the 'state of exception' is that the EU is a federation and not a state. The chapter first develops a theory of federal constitutional defence based primarily on the theory and praxis of the antebellum United States (the doctrine of states' rights), on the one hand, and the nineteenth-century German Confederation (the theory of federal execution and federal intervention), on the other. Based on these theories of federal constitutional defence, the chapter analyses both 'Euro-crisis law' and the contestation of the emergency government of the Eurozone crisis by EU Member States.

Competing claims to constitutional defence can always be put forward in a federation in the name of the people as one or the people(s) as many; in the name of the '*union* of states' or in the 'union of *states*'. Authority in a federation can be wielded legally, and ultimately extra-legally, in the name of the security of the individual Member States and for the wellbeing of their citizens, *and* in the name of the security of the Union and for the wellbeing of its citizens. With regard to the Eurozone crisis, the question of ultimate authority has been raised judicially by challenges to the European Court of Justice and the European Central Bank by the German Constitutional Court.[27] The federal balance on which the EU, as all federal unions of states, relies is therefore under threat. Whether a nullification crisis can be avoided remains to be seen. Independently of how the battle of courts and

[27] C-62/14 *Gauweiler and Others* [2015] ECLI:EU:C:2015:400; C-493/17 *Weiss and Others* [2018] ECLI:EU:C:2018:1000; BVerfG, Judgment of the Second Senate of 21 June 2016—2 BvR 2728/13; BVerfG, Judgment of the Second Senate of 05 May 2020—2 BvR 859/15.

central banks turns out, it is clear that the political autonomy of, especially, the deficit Member States from a more material perspective has been eroded. Emergency politics introduces a strong element of reason of state that *de facto* if not *de jure* erodes the political autonomy of its Member States by reducing them to administrative dependencies. For that reason, emergency government presents a threat to the survival of the federation as a political form and hence to the EU's current constitutional character and the constitutional balance on which the Union relies.

1
Constitutional Nature

The debate on the constitutional nature of the EU and the foundation of its authority is long and there is still no consensus in the field. Authority has been contested with regard to the EU, and earlier the European Economic Community (EEC), ever since the European Court of Justice (ECJ) declared direct effect and supremacy of European law in *Van Gend en Loos*[1] and *Costa v E.N.E.L.*[2] What is contested are not so much the doctrines of supremacy and direct effect *eo ipso* but their foundations and hence their scope and the ultimate laws and institutions they are governed by and subjected to. The central tension in this debate is between the scholars who emphasize Member State sovereignty and those who emphasize the constitutional status of EU law.

Scholars who emphasize Member State sovereignty tend to understand the foundation of EU authority along the lines of public international law, arguing that the authority of EU law is rooted in national constitutions and that the Member States are the 'masters of the treaties'.[3] Within this field, most scholars would not dispute the primacy of EU law *eo ipso* but its source and hence its limitations. The argument presented is that the foundation of EU law is an interstate agreement and the EU therefore—however complex—must be understood as a treaty organization governed by and subject to public international law. The EU, in this view, remains international and administrative rather than constitutional.[4]

Other scholars emphasize the supranational level of the governmental structure of the Union, arguing on the basis of the autonomy of the EU legal order, the development of EU fundamental rights legislation, the doctrine of implied powers, preemption, the fidelity principle, and EU citizenship that the EU must be understood as a constitutional order in its own right with an autonomous source of authority.[5]

[1] Case C-26/62 *NV Algemene Transport- en Expeditie Onderneming van Gend & Loos v Netherlands Inland Revenue Administration* [1963] ECR 1.

[2] Case C-6/64 *Flaminio Costa v E.N.E.L.* [1964] ECR 585.

[3] Dieter Grimm, 'Sovereignty in the European Union' in Jeffrey Ellsworth and Johan Van der Walt (eds), *Constitutional Sovereignty and Social Solidarity in Europe* (Nomos 2015); Theodor Schilling, 'The Autonomy of the Community Legal Order: An Analysis of Possible Foundations' (1996) 37 Harvard International Law Journal 389.

[4] Bruno De Witte, 'The EU as an International Legal Experiment' in Joseph HH Weiler and Gráinne De Búrca (eds), *The Worlds of European Constitutionalism* (CUP 2012); Dieter Grimm, 'Treaty or Constitution? The Legal Basis of the European Union after Maastricht' in Erik Oddvar Eriksen, Agustín Menéndez, and John Erik Fossum (eds), *Developing a Constitution for Europe* (Routledge 2004); Peter L Lindseth, *Power and Legitimacy Reconciling Europe and the Nation-State* (OUP 2011).

[5] Ulrich Haltern and Joseph HH Weiler, 'Constitutional or International? The Foundation of the Community Legal Order and the Question of Judicial Kompetenz-Kompetenz', *The European Courts*

The Constitutional Theory of the Federation and the European Union. Signe Rehling Larsen, Oxford University Press (2021).
 DOI: 10.1093/oso/9780198859260.003.0002

Most scholars reject the case for EU statehood,[6] and argue instead that the EU is characterized by constitutional pluralism balancing the claims to authority of the EU with those of the Member States.[7] Some scholars see the EU as epitomizing 'post-national constitutionalism'[8] and global trends of constitutionalism beyond the state.[9] These scholars reject the foundational approach to authority in favour of a freestanding approach,[10] stressing constitutionalism as a normative order that constitutes a shared 'grammar of legitimacy'.[11] In this view, the EU is merely a stepping stone to a global order governed by the Universalist principles inherent in constitutionalism. The most influential position within EU constitutional theory, however, cautions against the comparison of the EU with other manifestations of 'governance beyond the state' and highlights the unique position of the Union.[12] In this view, the EU is a sui generis association characterized by a unique principle of constitutional tolerance that does not apply beyond the EU.[13] That the EU is sui generis is, of course, another way of saying that its constitutional nature remains an enigma; that it is neither fish nor fowl.[14]

Contrary to the dominant position in the field, this book argues that the idea of the EU as sui generis—that is, that the legal and political form of the EU is unprecedented—is incorrect. Rather, the book maintains, the legal and political nature of the EU can be explained by the constitutional theory of the federation.

and National Courts—Doctrine and Jurisprudence (Hart Publishing 1998); Joseph HH Weiler, 'In Defense of the Status Quo, Europe's Constitutional Sonderweg' in Joseph HH Weiler and Marlene Wind (eds), *European Constitutionalism Beyond the State* (CUP 2003); Mattias Kumm, 'Beyond Golf Clubs and the Judicialization of Politics: Why Europe Has a Constitution Properly so Called' (2006) 54 The American Journal of Comparative Law 505; Ingolf Pernice, 'Multilevel Constitutionalism in the European Union' (2002) 27 European Law Review 511; Armin von Bogdandy, 'The Prospect of a European Republic; What European Citizens Are Voting On' (2005) 42 Common Market Law Review 913.

6 See, however, G Federico Mancini, 'Europe: The Case for Statehood' (1998) 4 European Law Journal 14.

7 Neil MacCormick, 'Beyond the Sovereign State' (1993) 56 The Modern Law Review 1; Neil Walker, 'Constitutional Pluralism Revisited' (2016) 22 European Law Journal 333. See also Matej Avbelj and Jan Komárek, *Constitutional Pluralism in the European Union and Beyond* (Hart Publishing Limited 2012).

8 Neil Walker, 'Postnational Constitutionalism and the Problem of Translation' in Joseph HH Weiler and Marlene Wind (eds), *European Constitutionalism Beyond the State* (CUP 2003).

9 Mattias Kumm, 'How Does European Union Law Fit into the World of Public Law' in Jürgen Neyer and Antje Wiener (eds), *Political Theory of the European Union* (OUP 2010).

10 Michael A Wilkinson, 'Political Constitutionalism and the European Union' (2013) 76 The Modern Law Review 191.

11 Daniel Halberstam, 'Local, Global and Plural Constitutionalism' in Joseph HH Weiler and Gráinne De Búrca (eds), *The Worlds of European Constitutionalism* (CUP 2012); Kumm (n 9).

12 Joseph HH Weiler, 'Prologue: Global and Pluralist Constitutionalism—Some Doubts' in Joseph HH Weiler and Gráinne De Búrca (eds), *The Worlds of European Constitutionalism* (CUP 2012); Kalypso Nicolaïdes and Robert Howse, 'Legitimacy and Global Governance: Why Constitutionalizing the WTO Is a Step Too Far' in Roger B Porter and others (eds), *Efficiency, Equity and Legitimacy: The Multilateral Trading System and The Millennium* (Brookings Institute Press 2001).

13 Weiler (n 12) 13.

14 James Bohman, 'Reflexive Constitution-Making and Transnational Governance' in Erik Oddvar Eriksen (ed), *Making the European Polity: Reflexive Integration in the EU* (Routledge 2005) 33.

The EU, this book argues, is a *territorially bounded political association* of a special kind, a *federation,* that is, a federal union of states. The book takes its point of departure in the fact that 'people are organized into territorially-bounded units within which authoritative governing arrangements have been established. This is a distinctive way of being and acting in the world, the world of the political'.[15] As such, this book is an exercise in 'political jurisprudence', albeit of a different form of political association than the state.

There is a long tradition of political jurisprudence concerned with the task of describing an autonomous legal and political form irreducible to the other main political forms of modernity, the *state* and the *empire.* This tradition of legal and political thought includes figures such as Althusius, Pufendorf, Madison, Hamilton, Calhoun, Webster, de Tocqueville, Waitz, Le Fur, and Seydel. This 'federal canon' of political thought—less read than the state-centric canon of Bodin, Hobbes, Locke, Rousseau, and Hegel—was born out of an attempt to understand political associations, historical or contemporaneous, that could not comfortably be understood on the basis of the theory of the state. The most important examples of such political associations are the Old Swiss Confederation (1291–1798), the Restored Swiss Confederation (1815–48), the United Provinces of the Netherlands (1579–1795), the German Confederation (1815–66), and the antebellum United States of America (1777–Civil War). In this book, I rely on works from the federal canon of legal and political thought and draw on important examples from the earlier federal unions of states, most extensively the German Confederation and the United States.

This book is especially indebted to four legal and political theorists: Olivier Beaud, Christoph Schönberger, Murray Forsyth, and Carl Schmitt.[16] These scholars use different terms: *fédération, Bund, confederation, union of states*, and *federal union.*[17] Nevertheless, they all describe the same phenomenon, namely, a *political union of states founded on a constitutional compact.* They have, with utmost clarity, given accounts of the legal and political theory of the federation as a political association in its own right, without falling into the 'statist trap' that tends to reduce the federation to either a loose alliance of *sovereign states* exclusively

[15] Martin Loughlin, *Political Jurisprudence* (OUP 2017) 1.

[16] Carl Schmitt, *Constitutional Theory* (Jeffrey Seitzer ed, Duke University Press 2008); Olivier Beaud, *Théorie de la fédération* (Presses universitaires de France 2007); Murray Forsyth, *Union of States: The Theory and Practice of Confederations* (Leicester University Press 1981); Christoph Schönberger, *Unionsbürger: Europas föderales Bürgerrecht in vergleichender Sicht* (Mohr Siebeck 2005); Christoph Schönberger, 'Die Europäische Union als Bund: Zugleich ein Beitrag zur Verabschiedung des Staatenbund-Bundesstaat-Schemas' (2004) 129 Archiv des öffentlichen Rechts 81.

[17] I use the terms 'federation', 'federal union', and 'union of states' interchangeably. In spite of the fact that the only Anglophone author of the four (Forsyth) uses the term 'confederation', I have chosen not to adopt it. The reason is not that it is historically or theoretically inadequate to describe the phenomenon in question *eo ipso*, but that it is associated with the flawed distinction between *Staatenbund* and *Bundesstaat* that has hindered a genuine understanding of the constitutional theory of the federation (see *Chapter 1:I:A*).

governed by international law or a *sovereign federal state* exclusively governed by public law. They agree that the federation is a discrete form of political association with its own legal and political theory that cannot be understood on the basis of the theory of the state. The federation calls into question the state-centric categories we tend to think of all political life in, most importantly, the idea of sovereignty.[18] The political form of the state has been so influential—politically and theoretically—that we no longer understand political forms that question its basic assumptions. The categories of the state have blinded us to federalism and so, in the name of theory, we have denied the reality existing before our eyes.[19]

I. The Federation as a Political Form

Besides the EU, the political form of the federation is neither a part of our lived experience nor of our political imagination. To understand the EU for what it truly is, we therefore need to retrieve the lost meaning of the federation as a discrete form of political association. That we have forgotten the federation as a political form, however, does not mean that we have stopped using the words 'federalism' and 'federation'. They just mean something else in the contemporary political vocabulary. To understand the constitutional theory of the federation we must first isolate the federation as a discrete form of political association from other traditions in federal thought that are more prevalent today before we can give a positive definition. We must, in other words, provide a negative definition of the concept of the federation.

A. The Negative Definition of the Federation

To understand the federation as a discrete form of political association we must first isolate it from federalism as a Universalist ideology centred on the ideas of global or cosmopolitan constitutionalism and governance.[20] Federalism in this context refers to the 'constitutionalization of world society', manifest historically in the project of the League of Nations and in the contemporary world in the United Nations.[21] This is an aspirational idea that was historically presented during the

[18] The problem of sovereignty in a federal union of states will be discussed in the final section of this chapter (V).

[19] Schönberger, *Unionsbürger* (n 16) 45ff; Forsyth (n 16) x.

[20] David Held, *Democracy and the Global Order from the Modern State to Cosmopolitan Governance* (Wiley 2013); Ernst-Ulrich Petersmann, 'The WTO Constitution and Human Rights' (2000) 3 Journal of International Economic Law 19; Ernst-Ulrich Petersmann, 'European and International Constitutional Law: Time for Promoting "Cosmopolitan Democracy" in the WTO' in Gráinne De Búrca and Joanne Scott (eds), *The EU and the WTO: Legal and Constitutional Issues* (Hardt Publishing 2001).

[21] Bardo Fassbender, 'The United Nations Charter as Constitution of the International Community' (1998) 36 Columbia Journal of Transnational Law 529.

Enlightenment by l'Abbé de Saint-Pierre and Immanuel Kant and more recently in the context of the EU by Jürgen Habermas.[22] Within this strand of thought, a federation does not refer to a form of *political* association. Rather, it represents an aspiration to go beyond the political, most importantly war, as such. The EU is cherished by Habermas, not primarily as a political community in its own right, but as a stepping stone to a cosmopolitan world order based on Universalist aspirations for individual human rights and perpetual peace.[23] In contrast, the concept of the federation developed in this book is not a description of a 'world society' bound together in aspirational terms in order to secure universal human rights and perpetual peace. Rather, the concept of the federation as a political form refers to an *actual territorially bounded political association* with an outside and an inside.

Accepting that the federation is a territorially bounded political association can lead to another common misconception, namely, the equation of a federation with the empirical reality of present day consolidated federal states (federation = federal state).[24] This equation is understandable because federal states are today widespread and federal unions are not. If the EU is compared with a consolidated federal state like the contemporary United States or Germany, it is not surprising that so many scholars conclude that the EU is unique. The equation between the federation and the federal state leads to the fallacy that, since the EU is not a federal state like the United States, the EU cannot be a federation.

This way of thinking relies on a historical misconception, namely, that since the United States is a state today this must always have been the case. This is at least in part due to the general lack of appreciation in the accounts of the 'American state' of the power and authority wielded by the States—especially the so-called police powers in the early republic.[25] However, the United States was not founded as an 'American state' but as a *federal union of states* and it can be described as a federal *state*, at the very earliest, with the Reconstruction[26] after the Civil War and

[22] Immanuel Kant, 'Perpetual Peace: A Philosophical Sketch' in Hugh Barr Nisbet (tr), *Kant: Political Writings* (CUP 1991); Jürgen Habermas, *The Crisis of the European Union—A Response* (Polity Press 2012). See also Richard P Bellamy, *A Republican Europe of States: Cosmopolitanism, Intergovernmentalism and Democracy in the EU* (CUP 2019).

[23] Habermas (n 22) 54ff.

[24] For example, Preston T King, *Federalism and Federation* (Croom Helm 1982) 77 defines the federation as 'an institutional arrangement, taking the form of a sovereign state, and distinguished from other such states solely by the fact that its central government incorporates regional units in its decision procedure on some constitutionally entrenched basis'. See also Preston T King, 'Federation and Representation' in Michael Burgess and Alain-G Gagnon (eds), *Comparative Federalism and Federation: Competing Traditions and Future Directions* (Harvester Wheatsheaf 1993).

[25] For a history of the States' extensive 'police powers', see Gary Gerstle, *Liberty and Coercion: The Paradox of American Government from the Founding to the Present* (Princeton University Press 2018) ch 2. 'European history', Gerstle writes, 'has driven studies of the state for most of this subject's history, and that has meant an emphasis on the nature and activities of the central state, understood to be a unitary institution powerfully directed from a political center. The very term we use to discuss the phenomenon being analysed—"the state"—is indicative of this reliance on concepts developed for polities that could plausibly be thought to have a unitary institution of this sort' (ibid 55).

[26] Following Bruce Ackerman, the Reconstruction after the Civil War should be understood as a 'refounding' where an important shift in the source of constitutional authority from 'federal' to 'national'

was generally not described in these terms before the late nineteenth century. It is worth remembering that the very concept of the 'federal state' or the '*Bundesstaat*' was not even introduced in the intellectual history of the federation before around 1850.[27] Moreover, at that point in history it was a conceptualization of a 'mixed regime' and not a consolidated federal state as we understand it today.

In the contemporary world, federalism is often understood to refer to a specific form of state government or process where power is devolved from the central government to regions, cities or councils.[28] Federalism is thus reduced to a particular kind of devolution or decentralization.[29] In contrast, this book is concerned with the federation as a discrete form of political association rather than a form of state government or a process of devolution. And while it is indisputably the case that federal states have come into being as a result of devolution, such as India and Belgium,[30] these cases of 'holding-together federalism'[31] are left out of this study. The theory of the federation as a political form must be distinguished from the process of devolution and federal forms of government of the state.[32] The origin of the federation is *foedus*[33]—covenant, compact or treaty—requiring multiple political entities coming together in a common union and is thus distinct from a process of political devolution or decentralization of a unitary state. If the comparison of the EU with other federal polities is to be meaningful from the perspective of constitutional theory, we must compare it to that which it is comparable to, namely federal unions of states.[34]

In contrast to the federal state, the federation is a *union of states* based on a contract between them, that is, a compact or treaty. However, not all treaty

took place, see his *We the People II: Transformations* (The Belknap Press of Harvard University Press 1998) 198–200, 204, 209, 245, 269, 413.

[27] Paul Riley, 'Three 17th Century German Theorists of Federalism: Althusius, Hugo and Leibniz' (1976) 6 Publius 10.

[28] Carl J Friedrich, *Trends in Federalism in Theory and Practice* (Pall Mall Press 1968); Brian Galligan, 'Comparative Federalism' in Roderick AW Rhodes, Sarah A Binder, and Bert A Rockman (eds), *The Oxford Handbook of Political Institutions* (OUP 2006); Arend Lijphart, *Patterns of Democracy: Government Forms and Performance in Thirty-Six Countries* (Yale University Press 1999).

[29] William H Riker, 'European Federalism: The Lessons of Past Experience' in Joachim Jens Hesse and Vincent Wright (eds), *Federalizing Europe? The Costs, Benefits, and Preconditions of Federal Political Systems* (OUP 1996) 10; Michael Burgess, 'Federalism and Federation: A Reappraisal' in Michael Burgess and Alain-G Gagnon (eds), *Comparative Federalism and Federation: Competing Traditions and Future Directions* (Harvester Wheatsheaf 1993) 12.

[30] Robert Senelle, 'The Reform of the Belgian State' in Joachim Jens Hesse and Vincent Wright (eds), *Federalizing Europe? The Costs, Benefits, and Preconditions of Federal Political Systems* (OUP 2000).

[31] Alfred C Stepan, 'Federalism and Democracy: Beyond the U.S. Model' (1999) 10 Journal of Democracy 19.

[32] Beaud (n 16) 33. See also Jean L Cohen, *Globalization and Sovereignty: Rethinking Legality, Legitimacy and Constitutionalism* (CUP 2012) 86.

[33] Solomon R Davis, *The Federal Principle: A Journey Through Time in Quest of Meaning* (University of California Press 1978) 3; Beaud (n 16) 112–16.

[34] Beaud (n 16) 27; Thomas C Fischer, 'Federalism in the European Community and the United States: A Rose by Any Other Name' (1994) 17 Fordham International Law Journal 389, 391.

organizations are federations and not all interstate contracts are federal in nature. The argument that the federation is different from a consolidated federal state, like the contemporary United States, does not entail that all treaty organizations are federations. A federation is not 'merely' an interstate organization (as eg the World Trade Organization (WTO)) or even a (temporary) alliance/*Bündnis* (as eg North Atlantic Treaty Organization (NATO)).[35] These interstate organizations are contractual relationships between two or more states that obligate the contracting states in the *particular instances* described by the contract; they are 'obligatory commitments with a definable content'.[36] Notwithstanding that a contract of alliance (*Bündnisvertrage*), following Schmitt, is more significant than other interstate contracts because it affects the contracting states' *jus belli,* that is, the right to wage war,[37] this contract does not affect the sovereign status of the contracting states since they do not transfer their *jus belli* as such to a third party.[38] A state is not made 'half-sovereign' by its entrance into an alliance.[39] In most cases, neither do interstate trade organizations challenge the sovereign status of the contracting states because these organizations cannot make laws or measures that are directly binding *in* and *on* the states that created them.[40] They do not fundamentally alter the principle of the political autonomy and self-determination of the contracting states.[41]

The most significant remaining obstacle to a positive definition of the federation is an academic distinction originating in the German debates on federalism from the 1870s onwards on the basis of which all federations still tend to be perceived and classified: the distinction between *Bundesstaat* ('federal state') and *Staatenbund* (translated as either 'state federation' or, unfortunately, 'confederation').[42] This distinction was coined by Georg Waitz in *The Nature of the Federal State* [*Das Wesen des Bundesstaates*] in 1853. Nevertheless, it was only later, perhaps with the publication of Max von Seydel's *The Concept of the Federal State* [*Der Bundesstaatbegriff*] in 1872, that it got the meaning with which it is currently associated.[43]

The distinction between *Bundesstaat* and *Staatenbund* relies on the assumption that all actual federations can be made sense of as *either* one sovereign state *or* many sovereign states; *either* public law subject *or* international law relationship;

[35] Olivier Beaud, 'La répartition des compétences dans une Fédération. Essai de reformulation du problème' (2016) 16 Foundations of Public Law 179, 182.

[36] Schmitt (n 16) 282–83. See also Schönberger, '... Bund' (n 16) 111.

[37] According to Schmitt, *Constitutional Theory* (n 16) 282–83, the right to wage war constitutes the decisive expression of the political existence of the state.

[38] ibid 282–83. See also Forsyth (n 16) 14.

[39] Schmitt (n 16) 282–83; Forsyth (n 16) 14.

[40] Schmitt (n 16) 282–83; Forsyth (n 16) 14; Schönberger, *Unionsbürger* (n 16) 155–57.

[41] Forsyth (n 16) 13–14.

[42] Carl F Friedrich, 'Federal Constitutional Theory and Emergent Proposals' in Arthur W MacMahon (ed), *Federalism: Mature and Emergent* (Doubleday & Company 1955) 510–11; Robert Schütze, *From Dual to Cooperative Federalism: The Changing Structure of European Law* (OUP 2013) 31ff.

[43] Rupert Emerson, *State and Sovereignty in Modern Germany* (Yale University Press 1928); Dieter Grimm, *Sovereignty: The Origin and Future of a Political and Legal Concept* (Columbia University Press 2015).

either constitution *or* treaty. The problem with this distinction is that while it presents deceptively clear alternatives, it also makes it impossible to understand the legal and political reality of the federation. It achieves jurisprudential clarity but ignores reality. Schmitt presents an explicit argument for the inadequacy of this distinction. The theory of the federation, he writes, must be developed independently of the distinction between *Staatenbund* and *Bundesstaat:*

> [This distinction] presents seemingly clear and striking alternatives, yet ones that are in fact logically peculiar or impossible. The *Staatenbund* should be a purely international law relationship, in contrast to a *Bundesstaat*, which is an unadulterated public law subject. The one rests on an international law *treaty*, the other has a public law *constitution*; the one is legal relationship, the other is legal subject, etc. With such schematic and convenient formulas, the common fundamental concept of the entire problem is left out of account … Today, this simple method is no longer possible.[44]

The theory of the federation has developed in order to describe political associations that could *not* be explained by the theory of the state. In contrast, the distinction between *Bundesstaat* and *Staatenbund* is created as an attempt to make the political non-state entity of the federation—*Bund*—conform to the theory of the state. But actual federations do not conform to the neat division into *either* one sovereign state (*Bundesstaat*) *or* an association of sovereign states (*Staatenbund*).[45] This distinction, following Schmitt, endeavours to solve the problem of the political form of the federation by evading it.[46] The attempt to 'solve' the problem of the federation by literately 'attaching' the concept of the state to the federation—either 'state-federation' (<u>Staaten</u>*bund*) or 'federal state' (*Bundes*<u>staat</u>)—is therefore not satisfactory.

In his discussion of the constitutional nature of the EU, Joseph Weiler accepts the rigid distinction between 'federal' (*Bundesstaat*) and 'confederal' (*Staatenbund*) and, on that basis, mistakenly identifies the EU as 'sui generis': 'Architecturally, the combination of a "confederal" institutional arrangement and a "federal" legal arrangement seemed for a time to mark Europe's *Sonderweg*—its special way and

[44] Amended translation of Schmitt (n 16) 384. For the original, see Carl Schmitt, *Verfassungslehre* (10th edn, Duncker & Humblot 2010) 366. Arguments for the inadequacy of the *Staatenbund–Bundesstaat* distinction have also been presented by Beaud (n 16) 97; Beaud (n 35) 184–85; Schönberger, '… Bund' (n 16) 82ff; Schönberger, *Unionsbürger* (n 16) 145–46.

[45] Murray Forsyth, 'The Relevance of Classical Approaches' in Joachim Jens Hesse, Vincent Wright, and Wright Hesse (eds), *Federalizing Europe? The Costs, Benefits, and Preconditions of Federal Political Systems* (OUP 1996) 32.

[46] Schmitt (n 16) 390. See also Ernst Rudolf Huber, *Deutsche Verfassungsgeschichte seit 1789*, vol 1: Reform und Restauration 1789 bis 1830 (Verlag W Kohlhammer 1957) 644–45.

identity'.[47] This mistaken conclusion of the EU's uniqueness is bound to be made if the distinction between *Bundesstaat* and *Staatenbund* is applied.

In fact, the prevalence of the flawed distinction between *Bundesstaat* and *Staatenbund* is, following Forsyth, an important reason why the EEC/EU has not been understood in federal terms. He gives the example of the adherence to this distinction by the first President of the Commission, Walter Hallstein.[48] If, on the one hand, Hallstein argued, a confederation was defined by its lack of the possibility of legislating directly for the individual members of the union, the EEC was indisputably 'more' than a confederation. On the other hand, the EEC was also clearly not a state and was for that reason not a federal state. 'What was the Community then?' Forsyth writes, 'Hallstein was wary of calling it a federal body, and preferred to refer to it simply as a "Community," but he also interestingly termed it a "union of states." '[49]

The allure of the distinction between *Staatenbund* and *Bundesstaat* is that it protects the neat division between international law and public law on which the theory of the state relies. It makes it possible to think of the public power and authority of any given federation as being founded on *either* a treaty *or* a constitution, *either* a creature of international law *or* a creature of public law. The problem is—as illustrated by Hallstein's and Weiler's problems of fitting the EEC in either category—that the reality of the federation contradicts the dichotomy between *Staatenbund* and *Bundesstaat*. The federation is not a subspecies of the state, but rather a discrete political form. In order to understand the federation, we must therefore, in the words of Beaud, leave 'the orbit of the state'.[50]

B. The Positive Definition of the Federation

A federation can be positively defined as follows: *A federation is a permanent union of two or more states that rests on a free agreement of all Member States with the common goal of self-preservation. This agreement politically changes the constitutional status of the Member States in relation to their common aim.*[51] I will now explicate the meaning of this definition.

From a purely formalistic view it is difficult to distinguish the federation from the family of 'international organisations' because it always relies on an agreement between its Member States, a treaty or compact.[52] This interstate agreement,

[47] Joseph HH Weiler, 'Federalism without Constitutionalism: Europe's Sonderweg' in Kalypso Nicolaïdes and Robert Howse (eds), *The Federal Vision: Legitimacy and Levels of Governance in the United States and the European Union* (OUP 2001) 58.

[48] Forsyth (n 45) 32.

[49] ibid.

[50] Beaud (n 16) 37, 65. See also Schönberger, '... Bund' (n 16) 87.

[51] Schmitt (n 16) 383–84.

[52] Beaud (n 16) 261.

however, is also a constitution because it gives birth to a new political existence and transforms its Member States' constitutions politically.[53] The federation relies on a 'status contract' (*Statusvertag*) that encompasses the Member States in their entirety and gives them a new status.[54] A status contract, following Schmitt, differs from other contracts by founding

> an enduring life relation that takes into account the person in his *existence* and incorporates the person into a total order, which exists not only in definable individual relations and which cannot be set aside through voluntary termination or renunciation. Examples of such a status contract are engagement and marriage, the establishment of civil servant relationships, and in other legal orders, vassalage contracts and covenants (conjugations), etc.[55]

A federation rests on a status contract between its Member States that establishes a new *comprehensive status* encompassing the Member States in their entirety and, beyond the merely individual, contractual obligations, alters them fundamentally by giving them a new status.[56] In this way, the federation establishes a *constitution in the positive sense*. The federal compact or treaty is an independent constitutional order contracted in perpetuity that simultaneously is a component of the constitutions of all the Member States.[57]

That the federation is contracted in 'perpetuity' does not necessarily mean that it lasts forever. The 'permanence' is part of the *intention* of the federal compact. A status contract is *meant* to bind the contracting partners 'forever more'. That the federal compact, in actual historical cases, tends *not* to bind the contracting partners 'forever more' is another matter. To illustrate the meaning of 'permanence' we can look at another, more common status contract: marriage.[58] While the average length of marriage in the UK and Wales among opposite-sex couples who divorced in 2018 was 12.5 years,[59] it is not possible to go into a predetermined time-limited marriage. There is no such thing as a wedding vow declaring: 'I take you to be my wedded wife/husband for the next 12.5 years.'

[53] Huber (n 46) 661.

[54] '*The genuine constitutional contract is always a status contract.* The general constitutional contract presupposes several political units as contractual parties, which, as such, have a political status. In its content inheres the founding of a new status for all states participating in the agreement' (Schmitt (n 16) 117).

[55] ibid 118.

[56] ibid 119.

[57] ibid 385.

[58] For a comparison of marriage as a status contract with the federal compact as a status contract, see Christopher Hughes, *Confederacies: An Inaugural Lecture Delivered in the University of Leicester 8 November 1962* (Leicester University Press 1963) 12.

[59] Statistical Bulletin: 'Divorces in England and Wales: 2018. Annual divorce numbers and rates, by duration of marriage, sex, age, previous marital status, and to whom granted and reason' (Office for National Statistics, released 29 November 2019).

Similarly, in political history, city states, republics, empires, nation-states and federations alike have come into being and collapsed but in their foundational intention they tend to be in 'perpetuity' or 'permanent'. Schmitt therefore qualifies the idea of the federation as a permanent constitutional order as follows:

> The federal compact/treaty [*Bundesvertrag*] aims to establish a *permanent order*, not just a provisional regulation. That also follows from the concept of a *status* because a merely provisional individual regulation that can be promulgated and defined cannot establish status. So every federation is an 'eternal one', in other words, a federation is counted on for the long term.[60]

Federal compacts tend, therefore, to be of 'unlimited duration'. This is also the case with the EU Treaties[61] and was expressed by the ECJ in *Costa* in the following manner:

> The transfer by the States from their domestic legal system to the Community legal system of the rights and obligations arising under the Treaty carries with it a *permanent* limitation of their sovereign rights, against which a subsequent unilateral act incompatible with the concept of the Community cannot prevail.[62]

The status contract on which the federation relies leads to a political change in the constitutions of its Member States. Nevertheless, this *constitutional change* of the Member States does not necessarily entail a change of their *constitutional law*.[63] The constitutional change regards something far more important, namely, '*the concrete content of the fundamental political decisions on the entire manner of the existence of the state*'.[64] There is, following Schmitt, a fundamental distinction between a constitution and constitutional laws. The constitution is not the sum of the constitutional laws.[65] The constitution—in its *positive sense*—consists of the fundamental political decision(s) on the political form and the fundamental structure of the state; its 'identity' or 'mode of being'. In this way, Schmitt exemplifies, the fundamental decision on democracy is encapsulated in the preamble to the Weimar Constitution: 'the German people provided itself with a constitution', 'state authority derives from the people', and 'the German Reich is a republic'.[66] In the

[60] Amended translation of Schmitt (n 16) 385. For the original, see Schmitt (n 44) 137.

[61] As is currently reflected in Article 53 of the Consolidated version of the Treaty on European Union [2016] OJ C202/13 (hereafter TEU) and Article 356 of the Consolidated version of the Treaty on the Functioning of the European Union [2016] OJ C202/47 (hereafter TFEU) both stating that 'This Treaty is concluded for an unlimited period'.

[62] *Costa v E.N.E.L.* (n 2) emphasis added.

[63] Huber (n 46) 661.

[64] Schmitt (n 16) 384, emphasis added.

[65] ibid 75.

[66] ibid 77–78.

current German Basic Law, the 'identity'—meaning the fundamental political decision made by the German constituent power—is encapsulated, or so the German Constitutional Court argues, in Articles 1 and 20 of the German Basic Law, together with Article 79(3) (the so-called eternity clause) that makes the two first provisions unamendable by law.[67] The constitution in its positive sense, however, is a dynamic entity, subject to reinterpretation, and can therefore never be fully absorbed by a written constitution, not even by an 'identity clause'.[68]

In less legalistic constitutional settlements than the German Basic Law, it will be more difficult to pinpoint the constitution in its positive sense in any one text or, perhaps, in any text at all. That does not mean that these less legalistic constitutional settlements are without a constitution in its positive sense. The constitution in the positive sense is the body of principles characterizing the fundamental structure and manner of the existence of the state in its entirety.[69] It relates to *the fundamental characteristics of how a political association governs itself*. The federal compact leads to a change in this identity and it is for this reason that the federation ought to be understood as constitutional in nature. Following Schmitt, the legal foundation of the validity of a federal constitution is the political will of the contracting states and the existence of the federation that rests on it.[70] The constitutional nature of a federation is determined by the political change of its Member States and the concrete existence of a new political being, the common Union. Independent of whether this is discernible from a purely legal analysis, the federation is of a constitutional nature because it changes its Member States politically by virtue of their membership in the new common Union.

Juristically, it is indisputable that the EU relies on a treaty. From a purely legalistic perspective, the EU is therefore a treaty organization and, as such, it belongs to the world of international law, as Bruno de Witte has correctly pointed out.[71] Nevertheless, it is wrong to conclude, on that basis, that it is without a constitution according to the theory of the federation. Politically, it is not meaningful to understand the EU as 'merely' a creature of international law because the EU has subordinated its constituent units in a way that has changed the fundamental state structure and constitutional identities of the contracting states and their relations *inter se*: 'Once they have come together in a federal union, the Member States are no longer truly sovereign states, nor are they strangers to one another'.[72]

[67] The German Basic Law, 23 May 1949, last amended on 28 March 2019 <https://www.btg-bestellservice.de/pdf/80201000.pdf> accessed 27 May 2020.

[68] Marco Goldoni and Michael A Wilkinson, 'The Material Constitution' (2018) 81 The Modern Law Review 567.

[69] Schmitt (n 16) 119.

[70] 'If a constitution rests on agreement [*Vereinbarung*] or contract [*Vertrag*], then the *legal foundation of its validity* is the *political will* of the allied partners [*Bundesgenossen*] and the *existence* of the federation that rests on it', see ibid.

[71] De Witte (n 4).

[72] Beaud (n 16) 230, my translation.

The creation of the EU has led to a *political change in the constitution of the Member States* and it is this *constitutional change*—a change that affects the very identity of the contracting states—that distinguishes the EU from being 'merely' a creature of public international law: 'if the federation is neither an alliance nor an international organisation, it is because it is a political entity'.[73] Jacques Chirac, therefore, (unknowingly) described the constitutional nature of the EU when he was asked about whether the Constitutional Treaty[74] was a constitution or a treaty: 'Legally a treaty, but politically a constitution', he said.[75] Like other federations, the EU is founded on an interstate agreement of constitutional nature, a 'constitutional treaty' (*Verfassungsvertrag*).[76] This concept is not an oxymoron, in contrast to what is often maintained because of the prevalence of the statist categories.[77] Following the theory of the federation, Dieter Grimm's analysis that the EU cannot have an autonomous constitutional order because it relies on a treaty is therefore incorrect.[78]

II. The Federal Founding

A. *Bundesvertrag* and *Verfassungsvertrag*

The federal constitution is a *contractual* constitution because it presupposes two or more states, each of which containing within them one subject of the constituent power.[79] The federation rests on a *constitutional contract* between the subjects of the constituent powers of all the Member States.[80] *Within* the modern state, a constitution will, in Schmitt's view, always be a one-sided decision by the sovereign people (or prince) as the sole carrier of the constituent power.[81] The federal constitution is in this way a contract *between* two or more subjects of the constituent power entered into on a free and equal basis.[82] Whereas the constitution of a state (ideal-typically) is born out of an exercise of *will*, the constitution of a federation is

73 ibid 262, my translation.

74 Formally the Draft Treaty establishing a Constitution for Europe [2003] OJ C 169/1.

75 Jacques Chirac as cited by Christopher J Bickerton, *European Integration: From Nation-States to Member States* (OUP 2012) 42.

76 That the Constitutional Treaty was rejected does not change the constitutional validity of this claim. The Treaty of Rome, or so it will be argued, had all the core characteristics of a constitutional treaty (*Chapter 2:III:A*).

77 Beaud (n 16) 80. Following Schönberger, the notion of a 'constitutional treaty/compact/contract' (*Verfassungsvertrag*) is a perfect expression of the foundational principles of a federation ('… Bund' (n 16) 113).

78 Grimm (n 4).

79 Schmitt (n 16) 113.

80 ibid 383–85.

81 It should be noted that this view is contested in constitutional theory, see Andrew Arato, *Post Sovereign Constitution Making: Learning and Legitimacy* (OUP 2016) 121ff.

82 Schmitt (n 16) 97.

born out of a *compact* between its Member States. The constitution of a federation is therefore both a 'federal compact' (*Bundesvertrag*) and a 'constitutional contract' (*Verfassungsvertrag*).[83] There are no perfect English terms, but a federal and constitutional 'covenant', 'compact', 'contract' or 'treaty' are all possible. This book, for the most part, uses the term 'compact', from the Latin *compacisci*, to make a covenant with someone.[84] The federation is a form of secular 'covenant', the political-theological root of which is a covenant between God and men: a sacred eternal union founded on an act of faith and a solemn oath.[85] Both compact and covenant convey the core of the federal founding, namely, an agreement that both constitutes a new community and transforms the contracting parties by giving them a new status.

An example of such a federal compact is the constitution of the United States: first the 1777 Articles of Confederation and later the 1787 Constitution. That this is the case is somewhat obscured by the 'national' historical interpretation of the United States that maintains that the United States was founded by an exercise of sovereign will by the people understood as the 'American nation'. This allows for a disregard of the validity of the states' rights arguments that came to be associated with the question of slavery and the defeated Southern confederates in the Civil War.[86] Nevertheless, the radical revolutionary doctrine of popular sovereignty, the theoretical underpinnings of the revolution, was originally understood as '*the people organized as states*, not the people organized in a nation known as the "United States"'.[87] This radical doctrine, however, was quickly co-opted by

[83] Schönberger, '... Bund' (n 16) 112; Schmitt (n 16) 114.

[84] For a discussion, see Olivier Beaud, 'The Founding Constitution. Reflections on the Constitution of a Federation and Its Peculiarity' (2017) 17: Thinking about Federalism(s) Jus Politicum. Beaud suggests that 'federative compact' and 'constitutional compact' are the best English terms. See also Donald S Lutz, 'From Covenant to Constitution in American Political Thought' (1980) 10 Publius 101, 106ff.

[85] For the significance of the covenant in political thought, see Daniel J Elazar's four-volume study in *The Covenant Tradition in Politics*: Daniel J Elazar, *Covenant and Polity in Biblical Israel: Biblical Foundations and Jewish Expressions* (Transaction Publishers 1995); Daniel J Elazar, *Covenant and Commonwealth: From Christian Separation through the Protestant Reformation* (Transaction Publishers 1996); Daniel J Elazar, *Covenant and Constitutionalism: The Great Frontier and the Matrix of Federal Democracy* (Transaction Publishers 1998); Daniel J Elazar, *Covenant and Civil Society: The Constitutional Matrix of Modern Democracy* (Transaction Publishers 1999).

[86] For the historical development of the states' rights argument, see Richard E Ellis, *The Union at Risk: Jacksonian Democracy, States' Rights and the Nullification Crisis* (OUP 1989).

[87] Merrill Jensen, *The Articles of Confederation: An Interpretation of the Social-Constitutional History of the American Revolution, 1774–1781* (The University of Wisconsin Press 1970) 165. See also ibid 56: 'In their relations with one another the colonies had developed attitudes that can best be described by the term "nationalistic". In spite of social, racial, and economic affinities and the cohesive force of the British connection, they had become practically independent political entities. Each delegate thought of his own colony as his country, as an independent nation in its dealing with England and with its neighbors, with whom relations were often as not unfriendly. It is this simple fact that is too often overlooked. Instead of lamenting the absence of "national feeling", one must recognize that it was there in an intense form, but in the form that is illustrated by the attitude of John Adams when he wrote of Massachusetts Bay as "our country". Essentially, then, the delegates to the first Continental Congress came as ambassadors of twelve distinct nations (or of certain groups within those nations), and most of them came voluntarily as a result of certain forces at work within the colonies and of a common external

conservatives who argued in favour of a centralized authority with reference to Congress as a representative of the collective capacity of the people of the thirteen states.[88] At the time of ratification of the 1787 Constitution, the 'people' did still not unambiguously refer to the (new) 'American nation' rather than 'the people organized as states'; as the contemporary interpretation of 'We, the people' often suggests. The original draft of the preamble to the 1787 Constitution reads:

> We, the people of the States of New Hampshire, Massachusetts, Rhode-Island and Providence Plantations, Connecticut, New-York, New-Jersey, Pennsylvania, Delaware, Maryland, Virginia, North-Carolina, South-Carolina, and Georgia, do ordain, declare and establish the following constitution for the government of ourselves and our posterity.[89]

Nevertheless, because of the uncertainty regarding which states would ratify the constitution, the enumeration of the individual states was removed.[90] The contractual basis is not altered by the fact that the Founding Fathers broke with the Articles of Confederation in their decision that the Constitution could rest on the ratification of nine out of thirteen states. As is clear from Article 7 of the Constitution, a hypothetical ratification of the Constitution by nine states would bind *only* these nine states and not the remaining four: 'The Ratification of the Conventions of nine States, shall be sufficient for the Establishment of this Constitution *between the States so ratifying the Same*'.[91] It was not possible (at least not formally) for a majority of the states to enforce the Constitution against a minority of the states.

In Federalist 39, Madison argued that the Constitution was to be ratified directly by 'the people themselves', by which he meant via a referendum and not by the legislative authority. It was, in other words, to be ratified not by the *constituted power* but by the *constituent power*. Nevertheless, the Constitution was not founded on the constituent power of the American nation expressing its unitary sovereign *will*, in Madison's interpretation. Rather, the foundational act establishing the Constitution of the United States was a *compact* between the people of the United *States*. The contractual nature of the foundational act was, according to Madison, expressed in the single consideration that the constitution was ratified by the will of the people—*not* as one nation—but as a

force: the threatening power of Great Britain, which was taking the form of increasingly forceful attacks upon colonial liberties'.

[88] ibid 168.

[89] See the first draft of the report of the Committee of Five of the Federal Convention, 1787, Library of Congress control number 90898130.

[90] Max Farrand, *The Framing of the Constitution of the United States* (Yale University Press 1913) 190–91; Schütze (n 42) 24 n 36.

[91] Article VII of the 1787 Constitution of the United States, emphasis added.

> result from the UNANIMOUS assent of the several States that are parties to it, differing no otherwise from their ordinary assent than in its being expressed, not by the legislative authority, but by that of the people themselves. Were the people regarded in this transaction as forming one nation, the will of the majority of the whole people of the United States would bind the minority, in the same manner as the majority in each State must bind the minority; and the will of the majority must be determined either by a comparison of the individual votes, or by considering the will of the majority of the States as evidence of the will of a majority of the people of the United States. Neither of these rules have been adopted. *Each State, in ratifying the Constitution, is considered as a sovereign body, independent of all others, and only to be bound by its own voluntary act.*[92]

A federal constitution, ideal-typically, is thus a compact between several states, entered into on a free and equal basis. All federations are founded on a free and equal contract between the federating states. The notion of a 'free and equal contract' is exclusively concerned with the question of the relationship *between* the federating states and not the internal relationship between governors and governed *within* the federating states. A federation is, in other words, not necessarily a union of democratic or republican states founded on an act or acts of the constituent power of the people. Historically, there are several examples of federal unions of *internally* 'unfree and unequal' states. While the founding of the United States is a helpful ideal type of a federal founding, it is also easy to overgeneralize its meaning. The US Constitution had a 'popular founding' but that is not the case for all federations.

The German Confederation of 1815–66 provides a good example of a non-democratic/non-republican federation not constituted by or in the name of the people(s). On the contrary, the German Confederation was a counter-revolutionary federation. With the exception of the four 'free cities' (Bremen, Frankfurt, Hamburg, and Lübeck), the German Confederation of 1815 was a federal union of monarchs (*Monarchenbund*), founded on a constitutional compact between the monarchs of the German states and two foreign monarchs: the King of Denmark on behalf of Lauenburg and Holstein and the King of the Netherlands on behalf of Luxemburg and Limburg.[93] The federation is therefore not necessarily founded by an act of popular constituent power.

The principle of the free and equal contract means that a federal union of states cannot be founded by an act of force or domination by one state over another. The origin of a federal union is *foedus*[94] (covenant, treaty, compact) and not *imperium*

[92] Federalist 39 (Madison) in *The Federalist Papers* (Lawrence Goldman ed, OUP 2008) 190, emphasis added.

[93] See the Constitution of the German Confederation (*Deutsche Bundesakte*) (1815), Article 1 <http://www.documentarchiv.de/nzjh/dtba.html> accessed 2 March 2018. From 1837, the King of Great Britain was also a contracting party because of the personal union between Great Britain and Hannover.

[94] Davis (n 33) 3; Beaud (n 16) 112.

(command). With regard to its founding, the *freedom* of the states in their decision to come together in a common union is what distinguishes the political form of the federation from the political form of another kind of union of states, namely, the *empire*: 'The federation is a free union of states whereas the empire is a coercive union of states. The federation stems from a mutual agreement, most often formalised (a federal covenant), whereas the empire rests on pure fact, the conquest of a state or country, or coercion'.[95]

In contrast to the empire, the federation does not commence by an act of violence, force or domination.[96] The federation 'cannot be the result of force or coercion imposed from above and sustained by the threat of military power'.[97] A federation is based on the free consent of the contracting parties in order to perpetuate their political existence as free and equal members of a common union. The constitution of the common union by the federal compact does, for that reason, neither eliminate the constitutions of the Member States nor their political existence.[98] A federation is created in order to perpetuate the political existence of its Member States as equal members of a common union. The federation can, and often will, be a community of 'natural unequals' in the sense that it is composed of Member States with radically different size, wealth, influence, and power. Nevertheless, as is the case of a political community composed of individuals, the federal union is meant to *create equals out of unequals*.[99]

B. Europe's First Constitution

The EU differs in several important ways from the ideal-typical example of the Constitution of the United States because of the historical circumstances in which the project was created. The constitutional history of the EU will be discussed at length in Chapter 2, but two important differences have to be discussed immediately because they are central to why the constitutional and federal nature of European integration, and especially of the early period, is often disregarded. First, the absence of 'extraordinary politics' in the ratification of (early) European Treaties and, second, the absence of explicit constitutional language.

[95] Beaud (n 16) 107–8, my translation. See also Olivier Beaud, 'Federation and Empire: About a Conceptual Distinction of Political Forms' in Amnon Lev (ed), *The Federal Idea: Public Law between Governance and Political Life* (Hart Publishing 2016).

[96] Beaud (n 35) 180; William H Riker, *Federalism: Origin, Operation, Significance* (Little, Brown and Company 1964) 4–5, 12.

[97] Burgess (n 29) 6.

[98] Schmitt (n 16) 123.

[99] 'We are not born equal; we become equal as members of a group on the strength of our decision to guarantee ourselves mutually equal rights', see Hannah Arendt, *The Origins of Totalitarianism* (Harvest Books 1994) 301.

The constitutional project of the 1787 Constitution of the United States is that of the modern republican revolution bringing to life the notion of the constituent power of the people, which could express itself in acts of extraordinary politics.[100] The constituent power became understood as the source of power and freedom that could be harnessed for the creation of new constitutional orders.[101] In contrast to this revolutionary constitution-making, the post-WWII European constitutions, following Arendt, were written by experts 'as puddings made from a recipe' and imposed after the revolutions had failed: 'Their purpose was to stem the tide of revolution, and if they too served to limit power, it was the power of the government as well as the revolutionary power of the people whose manifestation had preceded their establishment'.[102] Despite still speaking in the language of 'We, the people', the constituent power of the people was generally perceived as something dangerous that ought to be constrained.[103] The general fear of 'people power' manifested itself in a general scepticism of plebiscites, especially in Germany, where the Basic Law of 1949 was not ratified via a referendum. With regard to the ratification of European Treaties in the early post-WWII years, Charles de Gaulle was the only contemporary leader who seemed to have an appetite for ratifying European Treaties by referenda.[104] The original European Treaties, in contrast to the 1787 Constitution of the United States, were not ratified by referenda but by acts of parliament and, in formal terms in the BENELUX countries, by royal assent. Nevertheless, the European Treaties have been *attributed* to expressions of the will of the peoples of Europe—in the same way as the German Basic Law has been attributed to the will of the German people—irrespective of how they were ratified. Dieter Grimm, for example, has argued that when a Member State

[100] Andreas Kalyvas, *Democracy and the Politics of the Extraordinary: Max Weber, Carl Schmitt, and Hannah Arendt* (CUP 2008).

[101] As Hannah Arendt pointed out, the revolutionary concept of the constituent power does not necessarily entail a doctrine of popular sovereignty. In *On Revolution,* Arendt argued that an important reason for the success of the American Revolution, and the failure of its counterpart in France, was its rejection of the idea of popular sovereignty, manifest in the American exceptionalism consisting of the federal nature of the Confederation, and the pre-given republican institutional structure, manifest, most importantly, in the town halls, see Hannah Arendt, *On Revolution* (Penguin 2006) 144, 154, 172–74, 190.

[102] ibid 135.

[103] Christoph Möllers, '"We Are (Afraid of) the People": Constituent Power in German Constitutionalism' in Martin Loughlin and Neil Walker (eds), *The Paradox of Constitutionalism: Constituent Power and Constitutional Form* (OUP 2008); Jan-Werner Müller, *Contesting Democracy: Political Ideas in Twentieth-Century Europe* (Yale University Press 2011).

[104] Referenda 'on Europe', however, have been held in most EU countries over the years. In the first round of enlargements, referenda on membership were held in 1972 in France (accepting the enlargement of the EEC) and in Ireland, Denmark, and Norway (the latter rejecting membership). Germany, however, still outlaws referenda. Except for Portugal, Bulgaria, and Cyprus, all acceding Member States have had referenda on membership in the EEC/EU. The UK has held two referenda on whether the UK should remain or leave the EU: first in 1975 and again in 2016, where the 'leave' won by 51.9 per cent of the vote with a turnout of 72.2 per cent. For an introduction to referenda on European integration, see Sara Binzer Hobolt, *Europe in Question: Referendums on European Integration* (OUP 2009). See also Laura Tilindyte, Briefing: 'Referendums on EU issues' (PE 582.041, European Parliamentary Research Service, May 2016).

parliament ratified the Lisbon Treaty, they act in the capacity of 'representatives of their peoples. The result is attributed to the peoples. Hence, the Lisbon Treaty can be regarded as an expression of the will of the peoples of the Member States'.[105] A similar understanding of the source of constitutional authority of EU law was expressed by Advocate General Maduro in *Kadi*: the Treaty, he argues 'is not merely an agreement between states but an agreement between the *peoples* of Europe' that creates a 'municipal legal order of transnational dimension, of which it forms the "basic constitutional charter"'.[106] By ratifying the European Treaties the 'ordinary' representatives of the peoples of Europe did something 'extraordinary', of fundamental constitutional significance and, in that sense, they acted as 'constituent legislatures'.[107]

In contrast to the 1787 Constitution of the United States, the European Treaties include constitutional vocabulary only to a very limited degree. The reason for this absence has to do with the genesis of the project of European integration. The 1787 Constitution of the United States was born out of the revolutionary development of what started out as a (modest) political project of amending the Articles of Confederation, whereas the EEC was born out of the collapse of a much grander constitutional project for a United Europe that spoke in crystal clear constitutional language (*Chapter 2:II*). In the 1957 Treaty of Rome, all the constitutional vocabulary of the newly collapsed constitutional projects of the European Defence Community and the European Political Community was left out, with the exception of the most important aim of European integration of clear political and constitutional significance, namely, the aim of 'an ever closer union among the peoples of Europe'. This constitutional aim became a key point of reference in the legal construction of European authority in the years to come through the process of 'integration through law'.[108] A precedent of constitution-making through the 'back door' or 'by stealth' was established, which has haunted the project of European integration ever since. For example, the Lisbon Treaty ratified most of the content of the Constitutional Treaty but left out the constitutional vocabulary. Irrespective of the absence of constitutional language in the Treaties, the project of European integration has established a constitution in the *positive sense*. It has united its Member States into a new, concrete political order and created institutions capable of legislating directly for its citizens leading to political change in the constitutions of the Member States. The development of the constitutional logic of the EEC/EU thus

[105] Grimm (n 3) 48.

[106] Opinion of Mr Advocate General Poiares Maduro delivered on 16 January 2008, Case C-402/05 *Yassin Abdullah Kadi and Al Barakaat International Foundation v Council of the European Union and Commission of the European Communities* [2008] ECR 2008 I-06351, para 21.

[107] Jon Elster, 'Legislatures as Constituent Assemblies' in Joakim Nergelius (ed), *Constitutionalism: New Challenges—European Law from a Nordic Perspective* (Brill Nijhoff 2008).

[108] Daniel Augenstein, *'Integration through Law' Revisited: The Making of the European Polity* (Ashgate 2012).

adheres to the core principles of the federation that will be discussed in the next section, namely, the double constitutional moment of 'birth and transformation'.

III. Birth and Transformation

A. The Double Constitutional Moment

The federal treaty or compact differs from treaties of international law because it binds not merely the states but also the peoples in an 'ever closer union'. A federation is simultaneously a union of states and peoples (*'Staaten- und Völkerverbindung'*).[109] By entering into the federal compact, a new constitutional unity encompassing all the contracting states and their citizens is born. The federal compact is at the same time an interstate treaty and the foundation for the new federal legal order: 'The federal compact is at the same time treaty *and* constitution'.[110] The federal compact transforms the identity of the contracting states by the establishment of a new political relation of governors and governed that is not 'international' in nature. For republican and democratic states, this new relationship is (actively) established by a compact between the popular constituent powers of the Member States. The federal constitution is, in this way, a contract between all the peoples and states of the Union. The federal compact thus lies in between an interstate contract and a 'social contract' between individuals.[111]

The constitution of a federation is characterized by a double constitutional moment of *transformation* and *birth*: the transformation of the contracting states and the birth of a new 'federal existence'.[112] When coming together in a common union, the contracting states give birth to a new political unity encompassing themselves and their citizens in their entirety.[113] However, the act of coming together in a common union also changes the *status*, or 'statehood', of the founding states by transforming them into *Member States* belonging to the union at large.[114] The Member States make a constitutional decision to 'open their statehood'.[115] The change in status is manifest in that the contracting states, by coming together in a common political union, no longer have a purely 'external relation' to one another of international law. Their relation is primarily an 'internal relation' governed by

109 Beaud (n 16) 271.

110 'Der Bundesvertrag is beides zugleich, Vertrag *und* Verfassung', see Schönberger, '... Bund' (n 16) 112. See also Huber (n 46) 661–62.

111 Forsyth (n 16) 15–16; Beaud (n 16) 271; Schönberger, '... Bund' (n 16) 111.

112 Beaud (n 16) 132; Schmitt (n 16) 398–99.

113 Schönberger, '... Bund' (n 16) 111.

114 Schmitt (n 16) 117; Schönberger, '... Bund' (n 16) 111; Huber (n 46) 661–62; Beaud (n 16) 205.

115 This idea has been clearly expressed by Ipsen in the context of the constitutional foundations of the EEC. See the section on 'Die Öffnung der Staatlichkeit als Verfassungsentscheidung' in Hans Peter Ipsen, *Europäisches Gemeinschaftsrecht* (Mohr 1972) 52–53.

the public law of the Union.[116] Moreover, the birth of the new constitutional order changes the status of the contracting states, in that it bypasses the contracting states' monopoly of public power within their own territories and over their populations by establishing a direct link with the Member States' citizens. It is this double moment that makes the federal compact *constitutional* and distinguishes it from other interstate contracts.

The change from independent state to Member State has two dimensions in the context of the EU, *interstate* and *intrastate*. These dimensions, however, are inextricably linked to one another. The *interstate transformation* is manifest in a change of the mutual relationship between the Member States and a change in the relationship between the Member States and non-EU states. The relationship between the Member States is changed by the establishment of a common union. After the contracting states have established among themselves a common union, the states no longer (primarily) relate to one another via international law: 'the Member States of a federation are no longer foreign countries to one another. They no longer have the relationship described by classical international law as impermeable entities vis-à-vis one another'.[117] In contrast, they appear in front of each other as equal Member States, with equal rights, of a common union.[118] Their mutual relations, cooperation, and conflict are mediated via EU institutions and EU law. Any agreement concluded by the Member States *inter se* has to conform to EU law.[119] Though the Member States, in a sense, remain autonomous, they are at the same time interdependent.

The Member States can, furthermore, no longer treat the nationals of other EU Member States as aliens.[120] Like other federal unions, the EU breaks with the opposed distinctions of the nation-state between national and alien, inclusion and exclusion, and introduces in its place a tertiary distinction between citizen of a Member State, citizen of the Union, and non-Union foreigner.[121] The category of Union citizenship allows a citizen of one Member State to become 'quasi-citizen' of another Member State. The 'quasi'-citizenship of the federation can be termed 'interstate citizenship',[122] in that it differs from the citizenship of a nation-state and a consolidated federal state. The core of 'interstate citizenship' is that, as a matter of

116 Schmitt (n 16) 397; Beaud (n 16) 206; Forsyth (n 16) 48; Huber (n 46) 662–63.

117 Schönberger, '. . . Bund' (n 16) 116, my translation. See also Schönberger, *Unionsbürger* (n 16) 113.

118 Member State equality is a core principle of EU law, see Article 4(2) TEU.

119 Case C-546/07 *Commission v Germany* [2010] ECR I-00439. This is even the case for agreements between Member States *inter se* predating the establishment of the EEC in 1957. See Allan Rosas, 'The Status in EU Law of International Agreements Concluded by EU Member States' (2011) 34 Fordham International Law Journal 1319.

120 Olivier Beaud, 'The Question of Nationality within a Federation: A Neglected Issue in Nationality Law' in Randall Hansen and Patrick Weil (eds), *Dual Nationality, Social Rights and Federal Citizenship in the U.S. and Europe: The Reinvention of Citizenship* (Berghahn Books 2002) 318–19; Schönberger, *Unionsbürger* (n 16) 55, 63, 97; Schönberger, '. . . Bund' (n 16) 116.

121 Beaud (n 120) 317.

122 Schönberger, *Unionsbürger* (n 16) 64, 99; Beaud (n 16) 222–25.

Union law, the Member States have a duty to treat the citizens of the other Member States—subject to certain limits[123] and conditions[124]—as they treat their own. Schönberger uses the concept '*Indigenat*', which originally described the fundamental principle of federal citizenship in the North German Confederation of 1867.[125] The common '*Indigenat*' granted a right of a citizen of one Member State to be treated as a 'non-alien' in another Member State, that is, the right to be treated equally with the 'natives' (*indigena, Eingeborener*) in the other Member States.[126] Article 3(1) of the North German Constitution reads:

> In the entire extent of the federal area there exists a common *Indigenat* with the effect that the national (subject, state-citizen) of any constituent state must be treated as a non-alien in any other constituent state, and accordingly must be admitted under the same conditions as an indigenous person for the purposes of settled residence, economic activity, public offices, acquisition of land, acquisition of the right of state-citizenship and the enjoyment of all other civil rights, also that he or she is to be treated equally with regard to prosecution and legal protection.[127]

The EU Treaties guarantee EU citizens the right to move and reside freely within the EU,[128] the right to vote and stand for municipal elections in the Member State that the EU citizen chooses to reside in,[129] and the right to consular and diplomatic protection.[130] The substantial rights of EU citizenship, however, are derived primarily from the principle of non-discrimination.[131] When residing in Member States other than their own, the citizens of an EU Member State have the right to equal treatment with the nationals of the Member State they reside in within most

[123] As is the case of EU citizenship, comprehensive political rights were excluded from the rights associated with the common *Indignat* in the North German Confederation. In the German case, a *politische Indigenat* was first comprehensively included with the Weimar Constitution, see Schönberger, *Unionsbürger* (n 16) 107–9.

[124] The right to make use of the rights associated with federal citizenship, the common *Indigenat*, is often subject to the border-crossing citizens not being a social burden on their host Member State. This is, at least to some extent, still the case for EU citizenship. This was also the case for federal citizenship in the North German Confederation until 1870 (ibid 105). In the US, it was only with *Edwards v California* 314 U.S. 160 (1941) that state law prohibiting a non-resident US indigent citizen from entering the state was struck down as unconstitutional (ibid 76). In Switzerland, it was decided only in 1976 that the cantons had a duty to care for resident poor natives of the other cantons (ibid.). This is discussed in more detail in Chapter 2:III:A.

[125] Schönberger, *Unionsbürger* (n 16) 100ff.

[126] ibid.

[127] ibid 100–1. Translation as by Jeremy B Bierbach, 'Who's Afraid of Union Citizenship?' (2009) 5 European Constitutional Law Review 517, 519.

[128] Article 21 TFEU.

[129] Article 22 TFEU.

[130] Article 23 TFEU.

[131] Article 18 TFEU.

areas of state life (political rights being the main exception).[132] This principle of horizontal mutual recognition is equivalent to that of *Indigenat*. As in other federations, 'interstate citizenship' of the EU is based on the principle of *horizontal mutual recognition*.[133] The status of interstate citizenship, in the case of the EU as in other federations, is not based on international law but on the public law of the Union.[134] In the relationship between the Member States *inter se*, the distinction between 'inside' and 'outside' of international law is no longer applicable in the same way.

Furthermore, the relationship between Member States and non-EU states is changed. Where the Treaties provide for it or where it is necessary in order to obtain an objective of the Treaties, the Union can make international agreements that are binding and directly applicable to the Member States as well as to the Union institutions.[135] Furthermore, by being a part of a common union, the Member States' relationship and agreements with non-EU states cannot be against the interest of the Union.[136] Before undertaking any actions on the international scene that could affect the interest of the Union, the EU Member States are obliged to consult the other Member States in the European Council or the Council of the European Union.[137] If the Member States conclude agreements of international law with third countries, these agreements will be understood by the Union as forming part of domestic law and they will therefore have to yield to Union law in case of conflict.[138] A hierarchy is thereby established between the Member States' *internal* relations *inter se* as governed by the Union, which enjoys primacy over the Member States' *external* relationship with non-EU third countries. Commitments made by EU states within international law can, as a rule, not be honoured if they conflict with the internal commitments of the Union.[139]

The *intrastate transformation* is manifest in the alteration of the relationship between the contracting states and their own citizens, which happens as a consequence of the establishment of a common union. The governmental apparatus of the EU can, as pointed out by Weiler, be distinguished from other structures of 'governance beyond the state' because it has imposed its norms, not so much *on* the

132 The principle of non-discrimination is key to understanding the intermediary status of citizenship in federations, see Beaud (n 16) 223–24; Schönberger, *Unionsbürger* (n 16) 69; Schönberger, '... Bund' (n 16) 116.

133 Schönberger, '... Bund' (n 16) 116–17; Schönberger, *Unionsbürger* (n 16) 93–94.

134 Beaud (n 16) 225.

135 Article 261 TFEU. See also Rosas (n 119) 1309.

136 Article 24(3) TEU: '[The Member States] shall refrain from any action which is contrary to the interests of the Union or likely to impair its effectiveness as a cohesive force in international relations'. This was also the case for the German Confederation, see Huber (n 46) 604.

137 Article 32 TEU.

138 Rosas (n 119) 1313.

139 The main exceptions are international agreements predating the establishment of the EEC *and* the Member States' accession to the Union (Article 351 TFEU). That being said, following *Kadi* (n 103) para 5, Article 351 TFEU (ex-Article 307 TEC) cannot be invoked to disapply the foundational principles of the Union hereunder fundamental rights.

Member States as *in* the Member States.[140] Through the preliminary reference procedure, the EU has, by way of the confluence of the principles of direct effect and supremacy, bypassed the principle of *state responsibility* pertaining to public international law.[141] The individual citizens are directly governed as subjects of rights by the European legal order.[142]

The direct governmental link between Union institutions and the citizens of its Member States is not a unique feature of EU law but a fundamental character trait pertaining to most federations.[143] The direct link between the Member State citizens and the legal order of the Union shows the shortcomings of the statist distinction between international law and public law pertaining to the distinction between *Staatenbund* and *Bundesstaat* respectively. Notwithstanding that the EU is founded on a contract of international law (a *Staatenbund* principle) it has established a direct governmental link with the citizens of its Member States and exercises public power under a system of internal public law (a *Bundesstaat* principle). The EU, as other unions of states, carries characteristics of both a *Staatenbund* and a *Bundesstaat.* A federal union of states is, in Madison's words, a 'mixed regime' with both 'national' and 'federal' characteristics.[144]

As in the case of Union citizenship in other federations, EU citizenship is a fundamental challenge to the relationship between governors and governed *within* the Member States, in that the state monopoly of force over its citizens is no longer in place. In the 'mixed regime' of the EU, the 'inter-state privileges' of EU citizenship allows EU citizens to 'escape' their own states, if they so wish, and enjoy equal treatment with nationals in whichever Member State they choose to reside in.[145] EU citizens are endowed with rights that they can claim against their own states and governments; most fundamentally and radically, the rights of free movement and non-discrimination. Through EU law, citizens of the Union can emancipate themselves from their states because they have a real possibility, through EU law, of enjoying the rights of 'quasi-citizens' in another state. The relationship between governors and governed is fundamentally altered because the governed belong equally to another constitutional order on whose protection they can rely against their own states and other states of the Union.

140 Joseph HH Weiler, 'Van Gend En Loos: The Individual as Subject and Object and the Dilemma of European Legitimacy' (2014) 12 International Journal of Constitutional Law 94.

141 ibid.

142 *Vand Gend en Loos* (n 1).

143 Schönberger, '... Bund' (n 16) 92.

144 See Federalist 39 (n 92) 190. See also Martin Diamond, 'The Ends of Federalism' (1973) 3 Publius 129, 133; Martin Diamond, '"The Federalist" on Federalism: "Neither a National nor a Federal Constitution, but a Composition of Both"' (1977) 86 The Yale Law Journal 1273.

145 Floris De Witte, 'Emancipation through Law?' in Loïc Azoulai, Etienne Pataut and Ségolène Barbou (eds), *Constructing the Person in EU Law: Rights, Roles, Identities* (Hart Publishing 2016) 21–22. For a similar argument with regard to the early history of the United States, see Gerstle (n 25) 70: 'As long as one could choose one's state, one could live as one wished'.

B. The Double Political Existence

The *political change* in the constitutions of the Member States, which brings the federation beyond international law, consists in the constitution of a new permanent constitutional order that simultaneously encompasses the Member States in their entirety and makes up a part of the individual Member States' constitutions. The double constitutional moment of birth and transformation is therefore inherently connected. It is the creation of a public law framework consisting of governors and governed, with a (nascent) political identity of its own, that leads to a political change in the constitutions of the Member States. The constitutional change of the Member States consists in the establishment of a *permanent order* that includes the Member States in a *common political existence*.[146] The federation is characterized by a *double political existence*, namely, those of the Member States and that of the Union as a whole. 'Existing alongside one another in every federation are two types of political existence', Schmitt writes, 'the collective existence of the federation and the individual existence of the Member States'.[147] The federation is (paradoxically) a political unity that is composed of other political unities.[148]

In the case of the EU, this double political existence has been written into the preamble of the EU Treaties from Rome to Lisbon as the political aim (*finalité politique*) of the Union: 'Determined to lay the foundations of an *ever closer union* among the *peoples* of Europe'.[149] From the perspective of the theory of the federation, it is crucial that this common political existence does not eliminate the existence of the individual Member States: 'Both types of political existence must continue to coexist as long as a federation is to remain in place'.[150] The 'ever closer union' is not supposed to eliminate the constitutional existence of a multiplicity of peoples: 'The collective existence of the federation must not subsume the individual existence of the Member States, nor can the existence of the Member States subsume that of the federation'.[151]

The double political existence of the federation can be illustrated with the example of federal citizenship. In contrast to the unitary nature of citizenship in a nation-state, federal citizenship is by definition dual: federal citizenship implies '*dual citizenship of the same person at the state and the federal level*'.[152] Whereas dual citizenship is an anomaly in the nation-state, it is the norm in the

146 Beaud (n 16) 30–31, 103.

147 Amended translation of Schmitt (n 16) 388. For the original, see Schmitt, *Verfassungslehre* (n 44) 371.

148 Beaud (n 16) 103; Forsyth (n 16) 7.

149 Treaty establishing the European Community [1992] OJ C224/6, emphasis added.

150 Schmitt (n 16) 388. See also Beaud (n 120) 319.

151 Amended translation of Schmitt (n 16) 388. For the original, see Schmitt, *Verfassungslehre* (n 44) 371.

152 Christoph Schönberger, 'European Citizenship as Federal Citizenship: Some Citizenship Lessons of Comparative Federalism' (2007) 19 European Review of Public Law 66. See also Beaud (n 120) 317; Schönberger, *Unionsbürger* (n 16) 43, 67.

federation because the citizens of the Member States also are citizens of the federation.[153] They belong simultaneously to two political entities: a Member State and the Union. With the birth of the federation, a new status comes into being, federal citizenship, through which the citizens of the Member States become direct subjects of federal authority.[154] Within their respective jurisdictions, the Union and the Member States create rights and obligations for their citizens.[155] The establishment of federal citizenship constitutes the establishment of a nascent 'people' or 'nation', albeit *not* an exclusive nationality that abolishes the nationality of the individual Member States. The establishment of federal citizenship does not imply the abolition of the original status of Member State citizenship. Citizenship of a federation and citizenship of its Member States exist alongside one another. In EU law, this principle is expressed in Article 9 of the TEU: 'Citizenship of the Union shall be additional to national citizenship and shall not replace it'. This dual political existence is what characterizes the political form of the EU as a federal union of states.

IV. The Twin Sources of Governmental Authority

A. The Union and the Member States

Since the federal compact entails a double constitutional moment, giving birth to a new constitutional order and transforming the constitutions of the Member States, the federal constitution has two sources for its authority: the new federal political existence and the transformed contracting states that have become Member States. This is manifest in the dual nature of the federal constitution, the content of which is simultaneously the federal compact/treaty and a part of the constitutions of the Member States.[156] The constitution of the federation, in this way, includes all its Member States in a common whole and makes up a part of their constitutional orders. In contrast to the authority of a state that ultimately relies on its unitary political existence expressed in the will of the people or the prince, the federation, being a double political existence, has twin sources of public power: the political existence of the Union and the political existence of its Member States. Governmental authority in a federation can be wielded legally—and ultimately extra-legally—in the name of the security of the Member States and for the wellbeing of their citizens

[153] Beaud (n 120) 43, 67, 317.

[154] William J Schrenk, 'Citizenship and Immigration' in Carl J Friedrich and Robert R Bowie (eds), *Studies in Federalism* (Little, Brown and Company 1954) 635.

[155] ibid.

[156] Schmitt (n 16) 385.

and in the name of the security of the Union as a whole and for the wellbeing of its citizens.[157] That is, authority can be wielded in the name of the people as one or the peoples as many; in the name of the *union* of states or the union of *states.*

From the acknowledgement of the dual political existence of the federation, the question of their relationship *inter se* presents itself: is either the Union or its Member States subordinated to the other part? From the perspective of the theory of the federation, this question must be answered in the negative: 'The Member States are not simply subordinated, subjects of the federation, nor is the federation subordinated to and subject to them. *The federation exists only in this existential connection and in this balance*'.[158] In contrast to a state, a federation is characterized by a double political existence where neither the Union nor the Member States are subordinated to each other. For that reason, the different public powers in the federation constantly have to be balanced and coordinated (*Chapter 4:I*).

The limitation of the statist distinction between *Staatenbund* and *Bundesstaat* becomes especially clear when we consider the relationship between the different constitutional orders of a federation. From the perspective of the statist distinction, it is only possible to think in terms of hierarchy: *either* the Member States are the source of authority *or* the Union is the source authority. Following the classical distinction, a convenient hierarchy is thereby established emanating *either* from the top (*Bundesstaat*) *or* from the bottom (*Staatenbund*). The federation is thereby made comprehensible to the general theory of the state. The same logic of hierarchy is predominant in the debate on the foundations of EU authority where scholars will adopt a 'particularistic' or 'monocular view' favouring *either* the Union *or* the Member States in order to establish a hierarchical relationship between them.[159] From the particularistic perspective, it is thus possible to construct an EU-centred or a state-centred hierarchy (depending on one's 'ideological preference'[160]). The problem is that this conceptualization, from an empirical point of view, is an adequate description of only the weak alliance and the centralized federal state.[161] A hierarchical relationship between the Union and the Member States does not apply to federal unions of states.

[157] Ernst Rudolf Huber, 'Bundesexekution und Bundesintervention: Ein Beitrag zur Frage des Verfassungsschutzes im Deutschen Bund' (1953) 79 Archiv des öffentlichen Rechts 1. For a further discussion, see Chapter 4:IV and Chapter 5.

[158] Amended translation of Schmitt (n 16) 388, emphasis added. For the original, see Schmitt, *Verfassungslehre* (n 44) 371. See also Schönberger, *Unionsbürger* (n 16) 183; Schönberger, '... Bund' (n 16) 98.

[159] MacCormick (n 7) 5; Walker (n 7) 337–41.

[160] Walker (n 7) 337–41; Neil Walker, 'Late Sovereignty in the European Union' in Neil Walker (ed), *Sovereignty in Transition* (Hardt Publishing 2003) 11.

[161] Schönberger, '... Bund' (n 16) 97.

B. Constitutional Pluralism

Constitutional pluralists have long argued that the EU is not characterized by the unitary hierarchical structure of the state. Following constitutional pluralism, the EU is characterized by a plurality of constitutional orders and claims to foundational authority—that of the Union and those of the Member States—that are in a heterarchical and interactive relationship with one another.[162] As pointed out by Alexander Somek, there is a fundamental resemblance between constitutional pluralism and the theory of the federation:

> Had those who introduced the notion of constitutional pluralism to European Union law either read Schmitt's *Constitutional Theory* or remembered, from their reading, his perceptive remarks on the theory of the federal system, they might have addressed pluralism by using the characterisation that Schmitt had prepared for its occurrence.[163]

What constitutional pluralism has identified is a fundamental aspect of the constitutional theory of the federation. However, by describing the EU as a new and sometimes unique form of constitutionalism, constitutional pluralism—like the sui generis thesis—unfortunately obscures the federal nature of the EU.[164] That being said, constitutional pluralism succinctly describes some of the fundamental problems relating to the relationship between the multiple constitutional orders of a federation in the context of the EU and is therefore of great importance to a federal study of the EU.

Constitutional pluralism suggests that, within the scope of their respective jurisdictions, the different constitutions will be interpreted as the highest source of law by their highest decision-making authority.[165] That is, within the domestic constitutional orders a domestic court or political institution has the final authority to interpret the domestic constitution and within its jurisdiction the domestic constitution is the highest source of law. Similarly, the ECJ has the final authority to

[162] Neil MacCormick, *Questioning Sovereignty: Law, State, and Nation in the European Commonwealth* (OUP 1999); Neil MacCormick, 'The Maastricht-Urteil: Sovereignty Now' (1995) 1 European Law Journal 259; Walker, 'Late Sovereignty in the European Union' (n 160); Neil Walker, 'The Idea of Constitutional Pluralism' (2002) 65 The Modern Law Review 317. For an introduction to the debates about constitutional pluralism, see also Avbelj and Komárek (n 7).

[163] Alexander Somek, 'Monism: A Tale of the Undead' in Jan Komárek and Matej Avbelj (eds), *Constitutional Pluralism in the European Union and Beyond* (Hart Publishing 2012) 355. See also Cohen (n 32) 83.

[164] Robert Schütze, 'Federalism as Constitutional Pluralism' in Jan Komárek and Matej Avbelj (eds), *Constitutional Pluralism in the European Union and Beyond* (Hardt Publishing 2012) 211; Schütze (n 42) 50–51.

[165] MacCormick, 'The Maastricht-Urteil' (n 162) 264; Mattias Kumm, 'Rethinking Constitutional Authority: On the Structure and Limits of Constitutional Pluralism' in Matej Avbelj and Jan Komarék (eds), *Constitutional Pluralism in the European Union and Beyond* (Hart Publishing 2012).

interpret Union law and within its jurisdiction the EU Treaties will be the highest source of law. Within each constitutional order, the highest decision-making authority will claim *Kompetenz-Kompetenz*:

> It is for the European Court of Justice to interpret in the last resort and in a finally authoritative way the norms of Community law. But equally, it must be for the highest constitutional tribunal of each Member State to interpret the interaction of the validity in the given state system.[166]

If the multiple constitutional orders were completely independent of one another, the lack of hierarchy would be unproblematic. In that case, they would merely be coexisting parallel legal orders. However, the legal orders, constitutional pluralism continues, though independent of one another, are also overlapping and interacting. The problem then is *how* to decide on the borderline or scope of the two constitutional orders. In case of a conflictual overlap, the question is *what* constitution would prevail and *who* would settle that question?

Constitutional pluralism and the theory of the federation agree that there is no legal answer to this question. Or, more precisely, there are two valid mutually exclusive legal answers based in, respectively, the EU Treaties and the constitutions of the Member States as ultimate sources of authority. On the basis of the authority granted by the Treaties and with reference to the uniform and efficacious application of EU law,[167] the ECJ has continuously asserted its right[168] to decide on the validity of EU law[169] and the legality of all acts of the EU institutions,[170] including the EU Treaties that constitute the Union and confer competence upon it, and thereby the right to decide upon the boundaries of EU authority. The ECJ thus claims *Kompetenz-Kompetenz* with regard to EU law. However, this claim to authority has generally not been accepted by national constitutional courts. With reference to the principle of conferral[171] and their own constitutions, the national constitutional courts have argued that, ultimately, they are the guardians of the boundaries of EU authority. The most vocal proponent of this argument is the German Constitutional Court that, with reference to German constitutional law

[166] MacCormick, 'The Maastricht-Urteil' (n 162) 264; Daniel Halberstam, 'Systems and Institutional Pluralism' in Matej Avbelj and Jan Komárek (eds), *Constitutional Pluralism in the European Union and Beyond* (Hart Publishing 2012) 97ff; Miguel Poiares Maduro, 'Three Claims of Constitutional Pluralism' in Matej Avbelj and Jan Komárek (eds), *Constitutional Pluralism in the European Union and Beyond* (Hart Publishing 2012) 70.

[167] Case C-11/70 *Internationale Handelsgesellschaft v Einfuhr und Vorratsstelle für Getreide und Futtermittel* [1970] ECR 1125.

[168] Case C-314/85 *Foto-Frost v Hauptzollamt Lübeck-Ost* [1987] ECR 4199.

[169] Following Article 19 TEU, the ECJ is entrusted with the authority to decide on all issues relating to the application and interpretation of EU law.

[170] Following the Annulment procedure (Article 263 TFEU) it is within the jurisdiction of the ECJ to review the legality of all acts of EU institutions, including legislative acts.

[171] Article 5(1)–(2) TEU.

and the principle of conferral, has maintained that it has the ultimate authority to determine the boundaries of Union competencies and the legality of EU law.[172] The EU, the German Constitutional Court has argued, has not been endowed with *Kompetenz-Kompetenz*. Furthermore, all German state institutions have a duty not to apply EU law, which the German Constitutional Court deemed to be *ultra vires*.[173] Despite being bound by the principle of fidelity,[174] the ultimate loyalty of German institutions, the German Constitutional Court argues, resides not with the EU but with the German state.

The question of where *Kompetenz-Kompentenz* resides in the EU is especially salient in Germany and perhaps this has to do with the German debate on federalism and sovereignty that took place in late nineteenth century. In this debate, the question of *Kompentenz-Kompetenz* became understood as the deciding issue of where sovereignty lies in a federal polity, which again would determine its constitutional nature.[175] If the federal level (*Bundesebene*) was endowed with *Kompetenz-Kompentenz*, the *Bund* would really be a *Bundesstaat*: a *sovereign* federal state. Contrariwise, if the Member States were endowed with *Kompetenz-Kompetenz*, the *Bund* would really be a *Staatenbund*: an alliance of *sovereign states*. In other words, the question of *Kompetenz-Kompetenz* became the means by which all federal unions could be brought to conform to the political form of the state, be that one or many, *Bundesstaat* or *Staatenbund*.

Nevertheless, in the EU, as in other federal unions, there is, as we have seen, no *legal* solution to the question of where *Kompetenz-Kompetenz* lies. There are always two valid legal answers based, on the one hand, in the constitution of the Union, and, on the other hand, in the constitutions of the Member States. The legalistic *Kompetenz-Kompetenz*-test of federal unions can only be applied if the claims of either the Union or the Member States are ignored; that is, the problem can only legally be 'solved' by a gross reduction of reality.

Kompetenz-Kompetenz remains contested in the EU. What is less clear is what that means for the question of where—and whether—sovereignty persists in the EU. The question of sovereignty in the federation is much broader in scope than the question of a jurisdictional hierarchy between the federation and the Member States and much older than the concept of *Kompetenz-Kompetenz*.

[172] See, eg, BVerfG, Judgment of the Second Senate of 30 June 2009—2 BvE 2/08 (*the Lisbon decision*). See also the recent cases from the German Constitutional Court on the ECB's OMT and QE programmes: BVerfG, Judgment of the Second Senate of 21 June 2016—2 BvR 2728/13 and BVerfG, Judgment of the Second Senate of 05 May 2020—2 BvR 859/15. These cases are discussed in further detail in Chapter 5:III.

[173] See, eg, BVerfG, Judgment of the Second Senate of 05 May 2020—2 BvR 859/15, para 234.

[174] Article 4(3) TEU.

[175] Dieter Grimm, 'Was the German Empire a Sovereign State?' in Sven Oliver Müller and Cornelius Torp (eds), *Imperial Germany Revisited: Continuing Debates and New Perspectives* (Berghahn Books 2011); Grimm (n 3) 45.

V. The Question of Sovereignty

A. The Legal and Political Conceptions of Sovereignty

The (primarily) German debate on *Kompetenz-Kompetenz* takes its point of departure in a *legal conception of sovereignty* stressing authority and competence.[176] Although this conception of sovereignty dominates legal scholarship, it provides only a partial understanding of the concept. Together with the legal conception of sovereignty there is also a *political conception of sovereignty*, stressing power and capacity, that tends to be ignored or suppressed by lawyers.[177] Nevertheless, the foundation of the legal order of the state, and hence the legal definition of sovereignty, is the political power of the people, and hence the political conception of sovereignty. Sovereignty thereby simultaneously expresses *legal competence* and *political right*,[178] with the latter being the foundation of the former. The political conception of sovereignty expresses foundational sovereignty or what George Lawson described as 'real' majesty, namely 'the power to constitute, abolish, alter, reform forms of government'.[179] The foundations of the authority of the state are ultimately *not legal but political*,[180] or in the terminology of Emmanuel Sieyès, the foundation of *constituted power* is *constituent power*.[181]

Sovereignty emerged in the modern world as the foundational concept of the public law of the state to describe the autonomy of the realm of *the political* from religion and private power.[182] In response to the collapse of the medieval order of feudalism, sovereignty became the key concept of the new political form of the state, which was characterized by the triadic unity of one people, one territory, and one ruling authority, enjoying autonomy from outside intervention. It became the key to understanding the autonomy and legal supremacy of the state to govern itself unilaterally from within and the autonomous relationship between the states.[183] In this way, sovereignty became the key concept for both public law and public international law.[184] The concepts of state and sovereignty are as intimately linked to each other as two sides of the same coin.

[176] Martin Loughlin, *The Idea of Public Law* (OUP 2003) 78.

[177] ibid.

[178] Martin Loughlin, 'The Erosion of Sovereignty' (2016) 45 Netherlands Journal of Legal Philosophy 57, 60.

[179] George Lawson, *Politica Sacra et Civilis* (Conal Condren ed, CUP 1992) 47.

[180] Schmitt (n 16) 125.

[181] Emmanuel Joseph Sieyès, 'What Is the Third Estate?' in *Political Writings: Including the Debate between Sieyès and Tom Paine in 1791* (Hackett Pub Co 2003); Schmitt (n 16) 97ff; Loughlin (n 176) 99–113.

[182] Loughlin (n 176) 73–79.

[183] Martin Loughlin, 'Political Jurisprudence' (2016) 16 Jus Politicum: Martin Loughlin's Foundations of Public Law. A Critical Review 15.

[184] Bardo Fassbender, 'Sovereignty and Constitutionalism in International Law' in Neil Walker (ed), *Sovereignty in Transition: Essays in European Law* (Hardt Publishing 2002) 115.

Sovereignty is the supreme expression of the public power and the authority of the state, and the sovereign represents the personification of the state. It describes a political relationship between the sovereign and the subjects, yet sovereignty is not vested in either.[185] Sovereignty is *relational*. The public power of the state is vested in the institutional apparatus of the state and not in the individual holding office and is thus official rather than personal.[186] Sovereignty expresses the supreme authority of the state to make law and, as such, sovereignty underpins the modern idea of law.[187] The public power of the state is a product of *political power* that is channelled through the institutionalization of authority.[188] Because sovereignty signifies the institutionalization of public authority and, at the same time, is founded on a political relationship, there is a tension between the legal and political conceptions of sovereignty mentioned above.[189] Nevertheless, what unites them is the idea that sovereignty signifies the ultimate power or authority of the state as a political association to self-legislate and decide on its own destiny. Authority and power, competence and capacity are inextricably linked to one another.

In the context of the EU, the political conception of sovereignty is employed by national constitutional courts, importantly the German Constitutional Court,[190] and by 'statist' scholars such as Dieter Grimm. Their argument is that the EU derives its power and authority not from an autonomous political existence ('the people of Europe') but rather from the Member States and, for that reason, the EU does neither have a truly autonomous existence nor a genuine constitution.[191] The notion of a constitution, in this view, is inextricably linked to the idea of the state as a political form at the heart of which is a political conception of sovereignty.

B. The Antinomy of Sovereignty

This book also takes its point of departure in the idea of the *autonomy and primacy of the political*, that is, the idea that the foundation of a constitutional order and public power in general is a political relationship.[192] Only political associations have constitutions in the public law sense of the term. Nevertheless, statist scholars like Grimm are wrong in their assessment that the EU is without a constitution. The reason for that is that *the state is not the only type of political association of*

[185] Loughlin (n 176) 83.
[186] ibid 79, 83.
[187] Loughlin (n 178) 58.
[188] Loughlin (n 176) 78.
[189] ibid.
[190] BverfG, *Brunner v The European Union Treaty* [1994] 1 CMLR 57 (the Maastricht decision).
[191] Dieter Grimm, 'The Constitution in the Process of Denationalization' (2005) 12 Constellations 447, 459. See also Martin Loughlin, 'Constitutional Pluralism: An Oxymoron?' (2014) 3 Global Constitutionalism 9.
[192] Loughlin (n 176) 81; Martin Loughlin, 'In Defence of Staatslehre' (2009) 48 Der Staat 1–27; Hannah Arendt, *The Human Condition* (University of Chicago Press 1998) 8–9, 175–78.

modernity. The EU is a manifestation of the federation, which is a discrete political form that cannot be understood on the basis of the general theory of the state, hereunder the concept of sovereignty. For that reason, the federation has a constitutional theory of its own. This chapter has laid out the key features of this constitutional theory: the federal compact is the constitutional foundation of the federation (II); the federation is characterized by the principles of birth and transformation (III); and the federation has twin sources of governmental authority, namely the political existence of the Union and the Member States that stand in a heterarchical relationship to one another (IV).

To be sure, it is not argued that *federalism*, understood as a principle for the exercise of dispersed public authority or devolution, is necessarily incompatible with sovereignty. Rather, the argument is that there is an antinomy between sovereignty and the *federation as a discrete political form*. There is a fundamental antinomy between *both the legal and the political conceptions of sovereignty* and the federation. The federation calls into question the ultimate power and authority of the state, not merely with regard to ultimate legal competence—that is, *Kompetenz-Kompetenz*—but also with regard to *political right*.

Chapters 4 and 5 demonstrate that, even with regard to questions of constitutional change or situations of exceptional crises or emergency, it is not clear whether the Member States of a federation in general and (all) the Member States of the EU in particular retain ultimate power and authority. Even in these borderline cases where, Schmitt tells us, 'real' sovereignty emerges[193]—that is, in the extraordinary moments where an authoritative decision is made—political authority is fundamentally contested, dispersed or undecided in the federation. Within a federal union there is never any fully autonomous constitutional order[194] and there are no 'internal affairs' of the Member States that cannot potentially be understood as a matter of common security.[195] For that reason, as Chapter 5 demonstrates, federal emergency politics is a form of 'mixed emergency rule' that tends to involve multiple actors and multiple claims to emergency authority.

As valuable as the concept of sovereignty is to understand the state as a political form, it only leads to confusions and misunderstandings when it comes to the federation. Sovereignty is impossible to reconcile with the legal and political reality of the federation: founded, as it is, on a constitutional compact, and characterized by a double political existence and a plurality of partly overlapping constitutional orders that stand in a heterarchical relationship to one another. The implications of the constitutional theory of the federation as a discrete political form are that the ideas of the autonomy of the political and a constitution, in particular in cases like

[193] Carl Schmitt, *Political Theology: Four Chapters on the Concept of Sovereignty* (University of Chicago Press 2010) 13. See also Giorgio Agamben, *State of Exception* (University of Chicago Press 2005) 24–26.
[194] David McKay, *Federalism and European Union: A Political Economy Perspective* (OUP 1999) 16.
[195] Beaud (n 16) 301.

the EU, have to be decoupled from the political form of the state and the notion of sovereignty.

In his influential book *Questioning Sovereignty*, Neil MacCormick concluded with regard to the EU that 'there now coexist these two entities or sets of entities, the states of Europe, now not-fully-sovereign states, and the European Union, still a non-sovereign Union'.[196] However, the concept of sovereignty cannot allow this to be the case because, as Martin Loughlin puts it, 'sovereignty divided is sovereignty destroyed'.[197] Its fundamental binary logic demands that sovereignty must lie *either* with the Union *or* with the Member States. For that reason, it is not possible to understand the federation in terms of sovereignty.[198] The principle of sovereignty contradicts the principles of the federation.[199]

C. Bracketing Sovereignty

The antinomy between sovereignty and the federation in general and the EU in particular has been dealt with in a variety of different ways by scholars. However, most of the attempts fall within one of the following two unsatisfactory categories. On the one hand, there is a cluster of theories that 'resolve' the antinomy by denying the existence of the federation and reducing it to the political form of the state: either *Staatenbund* or *Bundesstaat*. These theories of the 'sovereignty hunters' are preoccupied with finding the 'locus of sovereignty', which must lie *either* with the Union *or* the Member States.

Both the American debate between Calhoun and Webster[200] over the constitutional nature of the United States prior to the Civil War and the German debates over the constitutional nature of the German Confederation (1815–66), the North German Confederation (1867–70) and the German Empire (1871–1918) can be read as contestations of the notion of sovereignty in order to establish its locus *either* with the Unions/Empire *or* with the individual Member States.[201] In all these debates, there was no consensus on whether the polity in question—German Confederation, the North German Confederation, the German Empire or the

196 MacCormick, *Questioning Sovereignty* (n 162) 142.

197 Loughlin (n 176) 84.

198 Beaud (n 16) 44, 57–58; Friedrich (n 42) 512; Friedrich (n 28) 8.

199 Beaud (n 16) 43.

200 The debate on the locus of ultimate authority in the United States did, of course, predate the one between Webster and Calhoun. It can be traced back to a debate at the first Continental Congress between conservatives, who only reluctantly accepted independence and argued in favour of a new centralized government, and the radicals, who with reference to the principle of popular sovereignty argued in favour of the people's right of political revolution. The radical doctrine of popular sovereignty initially signified '*the people organized as states,* not the people organized in a nation known as the "United States"' (see Jensen (n 87) 165).

201 For a summary of these debates, see Emerson (n 43) chs 2–3; Grimm (n 3) 39ff; Grimm, 'Was the German Empire a Sovereign State?' (n 175). See also, Ellis (n 86) ch 1.

United States—'really' was *one* sovereign state (*Bundesstaat*) or *several* sovereign states (*Staatenbund*). Acknowledging the division of the exercise of public power in federations, these debates tend to define sovereignty exclusively on the basis of ultimate authority understood in terms of legal competence.

The strategy of this position is generally to construct a 'sovereignty test' that will allow for the trivialization of the significance of either the Member States or the Union. Following Dieter Grimm, the German debate was closed with the answer Georg Jellinek gave, namely, that sovereignty resided with whomever held ultimate authority understood in terms of *Kompetenz-Kompetenz*.[202] Sovereign is she, the argument goes, who is endowed with the competence to decide on the extent of her own competence. In order to preserve the concept of sovereignty, this cluster of theories is forced to reduce the legal and political complexity of the federation and resolve the problem by a number of clever but arbitrary tests or by coming up with the 'proper definition'. The randomness of some of these conceptual creations led Rupert Emerson to comment that '[h]istorical and common-sense explanations having been discarded as having no necessary bearing on those of jurisprudence, the juristic imagination was free to clothe the given facts in such mystery of legal form as might be desired'.[203]

On the other hand, there is a cluster of theories that resolves the antinomy by trivializing the concept of sovereignty, reducing it to a bundle of competences, such as 'fiscal sovereignty' and 'monetary sovereignty'.[204] This allows scholars to talk about 'double sovereignty', 'pooled sovereignty', 'divided sovereignty', 'half sovereignty' or 'shared sovereignty'.[205] These theories spring from the acknowledgement of the legal and political reality of a federal union of states like the EU with multiple interacting authorities and public powers. What this cluster of theories is not interested in is sovereignty as the *ultimate* power or authority. In order to do justice to the political reality of the federation, these theories reduce the concept of sovereignty to the exercise of public power.

The problem with this position is that it trivializes the concept of sovereignty and thus 'solves' the problem by evading it. Tellingly, the most dominant contemporary version of this position has completely abandoned the concept of sovereignty and speaks instead of 'multi-level governance', concluding that the idea of the sovereign state 'is more an idealization of nineteenth-century political thought than a useful

[202] Grimm (n 3) 35. It seems to be a somewhat selective reading of German constitutional history that Jellinek 'closed the debate' since it continued even after the constitution of the Weimar Republic, see Emerson (n 43) 236–54.

[203] Emerson (n 43) 112.

[204] Claus D Zimmermann, 'The Concept of Monetary Sovereignty Revisited' (2013) 24 European Journal of International Law 797.

[205] Schütze (n 42) 72–73; John Erik Fossum and Markus Jachtenfuchs, 'Federal Challenges and Challenges to Federalism. Insights from the EU and Federal States' (2017) 24 Journal of European Public Policy 467, 477; Sergio Fabbrinni, *Which European Union: Europe after the Eurozone Crisis* (CUP 2015) xxxiii. With regard to the German Confederation, an influential theory of the 'division of sovereignty' in a federation was suggested by Georg Waitz, see Emerson (n 43) 94–96.

analytical concept for the reality of the twenty-first century'.[206] Instead of inquiring into the difficult problems related to foundations of governmental authority in Europe, the dominant strand of research is concerned with the depersonalized activity of 'governance' and normative justifications for its legitimacy or lack thereof.

These attempts to deal with the antinomy between sovereignty and the federation illustrate why sovereignty is inadequate as a concept with which to understand the federation. Sovereignty is 'like a scalpel',[207] cutting through the complex reality of the mixed nature of the federation, cleanly dividing it by the force of the binary logic of the state. At the same time, any true appreciation of the complex reality of the federation might easily lead one to trivialize or even deny sovereignty as a concept. A way out of this unsatisfactory dilemma of either reducing the federation to the political form of the state or trivializing sovereignty as a concept has been suggested by Beaud: in order to think of the federation as a political form, we must *bracket the question of sovereignty*.[208] Rather than attempting to do the impossible, namely reconciling sovereignty with the federation, or sacrificing the one for the sake of the integrity of the other, we should isolate them from each other and recognize that they each have their merits in describing ways in which political associations can be organized. Sovereignty is an obstacle for thinking of the federation and for that reason, Beaud argues 'the theory of the federation ought to be developed without recourse to the concept of sovereignty'.[209]

The fundamental incompatibility between the federation and the concept of sovereignty is precisely why the federation has to be understood as a discrete political form. While sovereignty is the preeminent concept for understanding the legal and political form of the state, it is useless when it comes to the federation. That we cannot make sense of the federation on the basis of sovereignty means that the federation cannot be conceptualized on the basis of the theory of the state. Within the federation, sovereignty is not a meaningful concept with which to understand how public power and authority are derived and exercised. Sovereignty as a concept forbids us to think of the federation as a theoretical possibility and hence, if we want to understand the federation, we must not begin with the quest for the location of sovereignty. Sovereignty is not the 'right key' for entering the political universe of the federation.[210] To understand the federation, Beaud argues, we must 'forget about sovereignty'.[211]

As will be discussed in Chapters 4 and 5, claims to sovereignty do nevertheless appear in the federation, most often when the political autonomy of the Member

[206] Markus Jachtenfuchs, 'The Governance Approach to European Integration' (2001) 39 Journal of Common Market Studies 258.
[207] Beaud (n 16) 56, my translation.
[208] ibid 38.
[209] ibid 63, my translation.
[210] ibid 59.
[211] ibid 58.

States is (perceived to be) under threat or during an existential crisis. Sovereignty is claimed when political authority is understood as being eroded or lost, or when necessity demands an extension of governmental authority to deal with an existential crisis. 'Sovereign is she who decides on the exception', as Schmitt (in)famously declared.[212] The surfacing of sovereignty in the federation thus signals crisis and conflict. As will become clear, claims to authority with reference to sovereignty are always contested and often repressed in order to preserve the political balance between the Union and the Member States. The federation is a discrete political form characterized by the *internal absence, contestation, or repression of sovereignty*.

D. Sovereignty and Political Stability

The theory of the federation is 'a pure theory of anti-sovereignty'.[213] Depending on one's view of the sovereign state, this tends to lead to opposite evaluations of the political stability of the federation as a political form. The disagreement between Schmitt and Arendt is an apt illustration.

Despite his recognition of the federation as a political association, irreducible to that of the statist distinction between *Staatenbund* and *Bundesstaat*, Schmitt viewed the federation as a mere transitory phenomenon on the road to the constitution of a nation-state characterized by complete political unity.[214] Because of its political duality and lack of hierarchy, the federation was, in Schmitt's view, a fundamentally unstable and contradictory political form that was bound to collapse into the form of the state when faced with an internal existential conflict. Only the state, Schmitt thought, could provide political stability.[215]

In complete opposition to this view, Arendt maintained that only the federation as a political form held any promise for political life and freedom in modernity, precisely because it was characterized by the internal absence of sovereignty. If the foundation of the nation-state was sovereignty, it was a foundation 'built on quicksand' because the sovereign will, if more than a legal fiction, would be ever-changing and hence incapable of providing any kind of political stability.[216] 'What saved the nation-state from immediate collapse and ruin', Arendt writes sarcastically, 'was the extraordinary ease with which the national will could be manipulated and imposed upon whenever someone was willing to take the burden or glory of dictatorship upon himself'.[217]

[212] Schmitt (n 193) 5, amended translation ('Souverän ist, wer über den Ausnahmezustand entscheidet').
[213] Riley (n 27) 18.
[214] Schmitt (n 16) 389, 404.
[215] In his later works, however, Schmitt suggested that the *Großraum*, rather than the state, was the viable political form, see Carl Schmitt, *The Nomos of the Earth: In the International Law of the Jus Publicum Europaeum* (GL Ulmen ed, Telos Press 2006).
[216] Arendt (n 101) 154.
[217] ibid.

With its triadic unity of state–people–territory, the nation-state, Arendt believed, would always lead to internal repression of minorities and external domination and expansion. Sovereignty in political life for Arendt meant nothing but tyranny.[218] The state was, in Arendt's view, a fundamentally unsustainable political form. Only the federation—founded on a constitutional compact instead of sovereign command and entailing a true division of power manifest in the multiplicity of the constituting states and in real checks and balances—could provide the constitutional conditions for political freedom in the modern world.[219]

In this book, the federation will be treated as a discrete political form with virtues and vices of its own and, in that sense, neither Schmitt's dismissiveness nor Arendt's veneration will be emulated. Because of its incompatibility with sovereignty, the federation is undoubtedly saved from some of the vices of the political form of the state. This, however, does not mean that the federation is a panacea: 'it is not a healing lotion that can be sprayed over the world',[220] as William Beveridge put it. As will become clear in Chapters 4 and 5 of this book, the federation is characterized by its own unique internal contradictions, which might lead to its collapse. Maintaining that the federation is a discrete form of political association entails a treatment of both its strength and its weaknesses on its own terms.

From a more historical perspective on European integration, Arendt's understanding was prevalent in post-WWII Europe. After WWII, as Chapter 2 will demonstrate, the nation-state was perceived to be the problem by most political elites and a European federation was understood as the solution. Whether the absence of war in Western Europe in the post-WWII era is due to European integration is impossible to answer. Whether the EU, and as such the only federal union of our times, will collapse in the near or distant future, only time will tell. We do without doubt live in a time with significant political demands for a return to the primacy of the nation as a source of authority and a resurgence in the demands for the protection of the sovereignty of the state. Whether these movements will be successful or not in reforming or abolishing the EU, the EU deserves to be treated as more than a transitory phenomenon, having been a central part of the post-WWII political and constitutional settlement for more than seven decades. To do that, we must endeavour to understand how a federation in general—and the EU in particular—comes into existence and governs itself as a political union of states on its own terms without reducing it to the categories of the constitutional theory of the state. In short, we have to endeavour to understand the federation as a political order without sovereignty.

[218] ibid 143, 173. See also Arendt (n 99) 279–90.

[219] Arendt (n 101) 142–43, 172–73, 206; Hannah Arendt, 'Parties, Movements, and Classes' (1945) 12 Partisan Review 504. See also William Selinger, 'The Politics of Arendtian Historiography: European Federation and the Origins of Totalitarianism' (2016) 13 Modern Intellectual History 417.

[220] Sir William H Beveridge, *Peace by Federation* (Federal Union 1940) 23.

2
Origins and Telos

Why do states decide to constitute among themselves a federal union? What are the origins of federations? Federations are constitutional projects and as such they are often created in order to realize or perpetuate a specific political identity or 'way of life' for their Member States. Examples are republicanism in the case of the United States (1781–) and monarchy in the case of the German Confederation (1815–66). The constitutional project that the EU is meant to help realize for its Member States is 'constrained democracy', or so it will be argued in Chapters 3 and 4. But federations are not primarily concerned with the realization of a specific vision of political life. As a general rule, states only decide to come together in a federal union because they are incapable of accomplishing separately one or more of their fundamental substantive aims: external security, internal stability, or the wellbeing of their citizens. They come together not only in order to 'live well' but out of necessity. Federations are for that reason created in order to secure one or more of the substantive aims of their Member States and thereby perpetuate their political existence. Federations and states are different forms of political association. Nevertheless, their substantive aims are expressions of the same overall principle: *Salus populi suprema lex esto.*

Federal unions of states have historically emerged among smaller states or city-states in order to secure their fundamental aims. Often this was a product of their relationship to a great neighbouring empire. The Old Swiss Confederation, usually dated from 1291, was created in order to ensure the security and stability of the Swiss cantons situated geographically on the outskirts of the Holy Roman Empire.[1] Two of the main historical cases of federations were constituted in order to break free from an empire. The United Provinces of the Netherlands was constituted in 1579 against the rule of the Spanish Empire.[2] The Confederation of the United States of America was constituted in 1777 against the rule of the British Empire.[3]

[1] For an introduction to the early history of Swiss constitutional law, see Andreas Würgler, 'Geschichte des schweizerischen Verfassungsrechts bis 1798' in Oliver Diggelmann, Maya Hertig Randall, and Benjamin Schindler (eds), *Verfassungsrecht der Schweiz* (Schulthess Verlag 2020).

[2] Jonathan Israel, *The Dutch Republic: Its Rise, Greatness, and Fall 1477–1806* (OUP 1998) chs 9–10; James D Tracy, *The Founding of the Dutch Republic: War, Finance, and Politics in Holland, 1572–1588* (OUP 2008). For a discussion of the political thought of the 'Dutch revolt', see Martin van Gelderen, *The Political Thought of the Dutch Revolt 1555–1590* (CUP 1992).

[3] See, eg, Robert Middlekauff, *The Glorious Cause: The American Revolution, 1763–1789* (OUP 1982); Merrill Jensen, *The Articles of Confederation: An Interpretation of the Social-Constitutional History of the American Revolution, 1774–1781* (The University of Wisconsin Press 1970).

The Constitutional Theory of the Federation and the European Union. Signe Rehling Larsen, Oxford University Press (2021).
 DOI: 10.1093/oso/9780198859260.003.0003

In response to the collapse of the Holy Roman Empire at the end of the Napoleonic Wars, the German Confederation (*Deutscher Bund*) was founded in order to ensure the security and stability of the German states and a smaller number of free cities, and of Europe at large.[4]

Notwithstanding that European integration has been realized through economic and not military integration, this chapter maintains that the EU at a fundamental level has origins similar to those of previous federal unions. European integration has its origins in the crisis of the European states and their fundamental inability to maintain themselves politically. The Western European states that came together in the European Economic Community (EEC), with the exception of Luxemburg, were either failed or crumbling empires. With the impeding collapse of imperial economic unions, the Western European states looked towards 'Europe'. Rather than continuing the history of empire—that is, the creation of larger internal markets via land-grabbing and domination—they created a larger internal market via mutual and equal contract: economic union by federation.

European integration was the outcome of a political vision for securing the core aims of the Western European states without dissolving their political autonomy through constituting a new 'super-state' in the post-WWII world order dominated by two non-European imperial 'super powers', the USA and the USSR. In this geopolitical context, the EEC was created in order to provide the foundation for stability and security, in a broad sense beyond military security, for the Western European states. In order to understand the project of European integration, an analysis of the political significance of its substantive aims is therefore necessary. To grasp the nature of the project of European Union, we need to understand what it was meant to achieve beyond the promise of 'peace and prosperity'.

Before we turn to a concrete analysis of the post-WWII reconstitution of Europe, the chapter lays out an overall theory of the substantive aims of the federation: the 'federal telos'. This chapter shows that federations can be subcategorized in terms of the content of their substantive aims: defence and/or welfare (economic prosperity). A defence federation is primarily concerned with military integration, whereas an economic or welfare federation is primarily concerned with economic integration and the creation of an internal market. Notwithstanding the multiple proposals for a federal European defence union after WWII, the chapter maintains that the project of European integration that was successfully established in the post-WWII era should be understood (primarily if not exclusively) in terms of an economic federation.

Nevertheless, the fundamental aims of all federal unions of states, defence federations and economic federations alike, are the same. Independently of whether

[4] Beatrice de Graaf, Ido de Haan, and Brian Vick (eds), *Securing Europe after Napoleon: 1815 and the New European Security Culture* (CUP 2019) ch 8; Thomas Nipperdey, *Germany from Napoleon to Bismarck: 1800–1866* (Princeton University Press 2014) chs 1 and 3.

a federation is primarily concerned with the government of military defence or economic life, a federation is a *political union* constituted in order to perpetuate the *political existence* of its Member States. The substantial aims vary but the fundamental aims remain political. In the words of David McKay, 'union formation is unambiguously a *political* decision'.[5]

I. The Federal Telos

A. Security and Welfare

The federal telos is the raison d'être of a federation. By 'the federal telos' is meant the purpose specific to a concrete federation, that is, the reason for which it was constituted. An investigation into the federal telos is thus concerned with understanding both the political form of the federation in general and the constitutional aims of any particular federation. 'Federation might best be understood in terms of the problems to which it has constituted a set of historically varying answers', Preston King writes. 'If we understand the problems, the understanding of structure more clearly follows'.[6] A study of the federal telos is concerned with the fundamental 'mission' the federation must accomplish if it is to be loyal to the purpose for which it was created.[7] Martin Diamond has expressed the importance of the federal telos, or the 'ends of federalism', for the study of federations in the following manner:

> it is only in the light of the ends of federalism that the nature of federalism becomes visible ... At various times, men have sought varying ends from federalism, and the variety of federal systems has resulted from that variety of ends; each actual federal system differs from all others ... by the peculiar blend of ends sought from the particular federal system.[8]

The ends of federalism vary and for that reason all actual federal unions are unique. Nevertheless, the substantive aims of federations include either *security* or *welfare*, two expressions of the general principle of 'salus populi': 'In historical retrospect it becomes apparent that states have generally moved toward federation under the compulsion of defence and economic needs'.[9]

[5] David McKay, *Federalism and European Union: A Political Economy Perspective* (OUP 1999) 35.

[6] Preston T King, 'Against Federalism' in Robert Benewick and Robert Nandor Berki (eds), *Knowledge and Belief in Politics* (St Martin's Press 1973) 153.

[7] Olivier Beaud, *Théorie de la fédération* (Presses universitaires de France 2007) 279.

[8] Martin Diamond, 'The Ends of Federalism' (1973) 3 Publius 129, 129–30.

[9] Robert R Bowie, 'The Process of Federating Europe' in Arthur W MacMahon (ed), *Federalism: Mature and Emergent* (Doubleday & Company 1955) 493.

The most common reason why states come together in a federal union is to ensure collective defence against a common enemy. Often this is a hostile neighbouring empire they can withstand only collectively.[10] Most federations are therefore *defensive* in origin.[11] The substantive aim of common security signifies that the raison d'être of the federation is that of providing common defence in order to ensure the political autonomy of its Member States. The federal aim of defence always has a double political subject: the security of the Union as a whole and the security of its individual Member States. Moreover, the federation's aim of security is directed not merely towards external threats but also towards internal threats: '*Externally,* the federation protects its members against the dangers of war and against every attack. *Internally,* the federation necessarily signifies enduring *pacification*'.[12] Together with external security the federal aim entails internal security, that is, the repression of existential conflicts *between* and internal uprisings and crises *within* its Member States.[13] The federation aims at securing a 'civil peace'.

These aims of federal security are inextricably linked to one another and mutually reinforcing. If the federation is well protected against external attacks, it will be easier for it to develop and protect itself internally. Likewise, a federation that is internally stable will be able to have stronger, unified, external protection. As Ernst Rudolf Huber puts it, 'the independence and inviolability of the individual Member States could only persist when the independence and inviolability of the Federal Union as a whole [*Bundesganzen*] were secured'.[14] This interdependence means that the common security of the federation is of interest to the security of the individual Member State and that the internal stability of the individual Member State is of interest to the security of the Union as a whole, and hence of interest to all the other Member States: 'a disequilibrium in one part of the federation may have repercussions in all the other parts'.[15] The federation is characterized by a mutualization of risk among its Member States. By coming together into a common union, all internal conflicts between the Member States, and instabilities and crises within the Member States become potential questions of common security for the Union as a whole.[16]

[10] This argument was, eg, made in Federalist 4 (Jay), see *The Federalist Papers* (Lawrence Goldman ed, OUP 2008) 22–25.

[11] Carl F Friedrich, 'Federal Constitutional Theory and Emergent Proposals' in Arthur W MacMahon (ed), *Federalism: Mature and Emergent* (Doubleday & Company 1955) 519–20; William H Riker, *Federalism: Origin, Operation, Significance* (Little, Brown and Company 1964) 12ff.

[12] Carl Schmitt, *Constitutional Theory* (Jeffrey Seitzer ed, Duke University Press 2008) 386, emphasis in original. See also Christoph Schönberger, 'Die Europäische Union als Bund: Zugleich ein Beitrag zur Verabschiedung des Staatenbund-Bundesstaat-Schemas' (2004) 129 Archiv des öffentlichen Rechts 81, 104.

[13] In the German Confederation of 1815, the federal aim was explicitly formulated as securing both external and internal security, see Ernst Rudolf Huber, *Deutsche Verfassungsgeschichte seit 1789*, vol 1: Reform und Restauration 1789 bis 1830 (Verlag W Kohlhammer 1957) 594.

[14] ibid 594, my translation.

[15] Beaud (n 7) 296, my translation.

[16] For further discussion, see Chapters 4:IV and 5.

Together with the aim of common security, some federations are constituted in order to promote the 'general welfare' or 'economic prosperity' of the community: 'The prominence of economic provisions of all successful federations demonstrates the historic importance of economic factors in persuading separate States to unite'.[17] Welfare is not understood in its twentieth-century sense of the 'welfare state' but as the government of population, infrastructure, and the economy at large, that is, political economy in a broad sense. The simple reason for the importance of the welfare aim for federal unions is that 'defence and security do not exist in a vacuum'.[18] Military protection is highly dependent on a functioning economy, a developed technology, and infrastructure.[19] 'It is no exaggeration to say', Lionel Robbins writes, 'that a federation will stand or fall by the adequacy of its economic constitution'.[20] As is the case for the state, there is a strong interdependence in the federation between the aims of security and prosperity (military protection and economic government) that few of the classical examples of federal unions escape. For that reason, the Old Swiss Confederation as well as the United Provinces of the Netherlands 'concerned themselves in practice with matters which were as much with common welfare as they were with common defence: coinage, trade, health, transport, and so on'.[21]

Common defence and general welfare were intertwined and interdependent aims of the United States of America from the very beginning. Article 3 of the 1781 Articles of Confederation is a clear example:

> The said states hereby severally enter into a firm league of friendship with each other, for their common defence, the security of their Liberties, and their mutual and general welfare, binding themselves to assist each other, against all force offered to, or attacks made upon them, or any of them, on account of religion, sovereignty, trade, or any other pretence whatever.[22]

Despite the explicit inclusion of 'mutual and general welfare' as a federal aim, the lack of federal power to give it effect led to protectionism and 'commercial wars' between the States and hence a weakening of the Union.[23] Some States erected

[17] Arthur E Sutherland, 'Commerce, Transportation and Customs' in Carl J Friedrich and Robert R Bowie (eds), *Studies in Federalism* (Boston and Toronto, Brown and Company 1954) 297.

[18] Murray Forsyth, *Union of States: The Theory and Practice of Confederations* (Leicester University Press 1981) 160–62. See also Beaud (n 7) 302; Federalist 4 (Jay) (n 10) 22–25.

[19] Sutherland (n 17) 299. See also John Fischer, 'Prerequisites of Balance' in Arthur W MacMahon (ed), *Federalism: Mature and Emergent* (Doubleday & Company 1955) 62.

[20] Lionel Robbins, *Economic Aspects of Federation* (Federal Union, MacMillan 1941) 3.

[21] Forsyth (n 18) 160. See also William H Riker, 'European Federalism: The Lessons of Past Experience' in Joachim Jens Hesse and Vincent Wright (eds), *Federalizing Europe? The Costs, Benefits, and Preconditions of Federal Political Systems* (OUP 1996) 12.

[22] Article 3 of the Articles of Confederation, emphasis added.

[23] George Van Cleve, *We Have Not a Government: The Articles of Confederation and the Road to the Constitution* (University of Chicago Press 2017) chs 4 and 9; Max Farrand, *The Framing of the Constitution of the United States* (Yale University Press 1913) ch 3.

internal trade barriers against the other States that were even higher than their external trade barriers to Britain. In Madison's eyes, these internal commercial wars led not only to negative economic outcomes but also to political strife and internal alienation of the States of the Union. The provisions for welfare in the Articles of Confederation, Madison as well as Hamilton concluded, needed to be strengthened.[24] The Annapolis Convention of 1786 was therefore concerned with the question of interstate trade. More particularly, they were commissioned to consider the trade and commerce of the United States and 'how far a uniform system in their commercial intercourse and regulations might be necessary to their common interest and permanent harmony'.[25] A central task of the Constitutional Convention held in Philadelphia the year after was to solve the problems of commerce and taxation in the Confederation after attempts at piecemeal reform over several years had failed.[26]

The interdependence of defence and welfare as federal aims can also be illustrated by the difficulties of two pure defence unions, both constituted in the last days of the Napoleonic Wars at the Congress of Vienna in 1815: the Swiss Confederation (1815–48) and the German Confederation (1815–66). The Swiss Confederation did not have the promotion of general and mutual welfare as an aim and that led to widespread discontent. For that reason, one of 'the strongest purposes of the Swiss Federal Constitution of 1848 was the elimination of the intercantonal trade barriers'.[27] The German Confederation *had* a welfare clause. Nevertheless, it was incapable of giving it effect, attributable to an internal disagreement between its two hegemonic *Länder*: Austria (favouring protectionism) and Prussia (favouring a liberal exchange economy).[28] Out of this failure, a new kind of federal union emerged between some of the Member States: the German *Zollverein* (customs union) that began functioning in 1834.[29] This economic union excluded Austria and had Prussia as its solitary hegemon. It was concerned with the government of the economy and its primary aim was the promotion of general welfare.

[24] Forsyth (n 18) 160; Sutherland (n 17) 297.

[25] Address of the Annapolis Convention, 14 September 1786 <https://founders.archives.gov/documents/Hamilton/01-03-02-0556> accessed 11 June 2020.

[26] Van Cleve (n 23) 280ff. See also Robert Schütze, 'Limits to the Union's "Internal Market" Competence(s)' in Loïc Azoulai (ed), *The Question of Competence in the European Union* (OUP 2014) 216ff.

[27] Sutherland (n 17) 299. See also Andreas Auer, 'The Constitutional Scheme of Federalism' in Alexander Trechsel (ed), *Towards a Federal Europe?* (Routledge 2006); Forsyth (n 18) 160ff; Beaud (n 7) 306–12.

[28] Emmanuel N Roussakis, *Friedrich List, the Zollverein, and the Uniting of Europe* (College of Europe 1968) 35, 42–43.

[29] For a history of the Zollverein, see William O Henderson, *The Zollverein* (CUP 1939). For a history of the ideational foundation of the Zollverein, see Arnold H Price, *The Evolution of the Zollverein: A Study of the Ideas and Institutions to German Economic Unification between 1815 and 1833* (University of Michigan Pres 1949).

B. The Economic Federation

Defence and welfare have been the interdependent aims of federal unions of states throughout most of history. Military warfare, in practice, cannot easily be separated from the government of infrastructure, health, coinage etc. Nevertheless, around the time of the industrial revolutions, the creation and government of larger internal markets and economic prosperity began to emerge as a relatively autonomous aim for which states decided to federate. This was a response to a broader shift in the understanding of the relationship between politics and economy at the time, namely, that commerce, international trade, and the access to larger internal markets became necessary for the political survival of the state:

> Economic confederation begins to crystallize into a distinct form alongside security confederation when relatively small states begin to feel their independence and statehood threatened as much by the commercial and industrial power of larger states as by their military strength.[30]

The most important examples are the Constitution of the United States of America of 1787 and the Zollverein. By granting the federal government extensive powers to regulate internal and external commerce in order to give effect to the federal aim of general welfare, the US Constitution is, in one respect, the 'true beginning' of an economic federation. In another, the Zollverein is a more ideal-typical example in that it had welfare as its exclusive aim. While the Swiss Confederation of 1815 was a pure military federation, the Zollverein was a pure economic federation.

What is important to stress is that an economic federation, or economic union, is qualitatively different from a free trade agreement. An economic union, as Murray Forsyth puts it, is 'emphatically not a means or technique for *liberalizing the external trade of states*'.[31] Rather, it is 'the transformation by mutual agreement of external trade into internal trade'.[32] By coming together in a common union, the relationships between states (external trade) is transformed into an internal matter of the federation (internal trade). Defence federations and economic federations alike are characterized by the intrinsically linked constitutional principles of *birth* and *transformation*: the birth of a new federal union and the transformation of the constituent states (*Chapter 1:III*). For the economic federations, this means that there is an intrinsic relationship between free trade internal to the union and an external protection of the union by a tariff barrier, a customs union.[33]

30 Forsyth (n 18) 173. For an intellectual history of the debates around the so-called jealousy of trade and the birth of economic nationalism, see István Hont, *Jealousy of Trade: International Competition and the Nation-State in Historical Perspective* (Belknap 2010) Introduction.

31 Forsyth (n 18) 173 emphasis in original.

32 ibid.

33 ibid. See also Robbins (n 20) 31.

The political significance of the customs union was first theorized by a contemporary protagonist of the Zollverein, Friedrich List. List maintained that, by way of the Zollverein, 'the German nation has for the first time attained to one of the most important attributes of nationality', namely, 'the internal freedom of exchange and the common external representation that was inherent in the concept of nationality'.[34] Federal unions are always characterized by an outside and an inside. In an economic union, this entails a difference between the internal regulation of economic activity between the Member States and the external relationship of the Union with other states or organizations. The aim of the economic federation is to transform the trade between states into the single internal market with a unilateral external representation and protection from foreign (economic) powers.

Notwithstanding the differences between economic federations and military federations, their cardinal telos is the same: to perpetuate the political autonomy of their Member States. At the origins of the economic union is the Member States' wish to remain politically autonomous. States come together in an economic union in order to constitute and institutionalize a common new power that will protect them from foreign powers: 'in order to preserve and secure their economic statehood each participating member has to place itself as a totality within a new overarching politico-economic body'.[35] In terms of their raison d'être, defence unions and economic unions alike are for that reason *political unions* constituted to ensure the political autonomy of their Member States.

This wish for political autonomy was a powerful reason for the 1787 Constitution of the United States, providing the federal government with more extensive powers to regulate the commerce of the United States. After winning the war against the British Empire and securing their independence, the United States was exposed to the commercial power of their former enemy without any common power of protectionism or economic regulation. The individual states of the Confederation tried to create their own protectionist policies. However, these protectionist policies had the negative effect of leading to internal strife and instability in the Union and disinclined Britain to enter into trade negotiations with the Confederation.[36]

The emergence of the Zollverein is in many ways similar to the consolidation of an economic union as part of the Constitution of the United States.[37] As was the case for the United States, military struggles exposed the German states to both the economic force of the British Empire and protectionism from their neighbouring

[34] Friedrich List, *Das nationale System der politischen Ökonomie: Volksausgabe auf der Ausgabe letzter Hand und Randnotizen in Lists Handexemplar* (Artur Sommer ed, Kyklos 1959). As translated and cited by Forsyth (n 18) 173. For a comparison of the views of Adam Smith, Alexander Hamilton, and Franz List, see Edward Mead Earle, 'Adam Smith, Alexander Hamilton, Friedrich List: The Economic Foundations of Military Power' in Peter Paret (ed), *Makers of Modern Strategy from Machiavelli to the Nuclear Age* (Princeton University Press 1986).

[35] Forsyth (n 18) 174.

[36] ibid 162–63.

[37] Roussakis (n 28) 96; Price (n 29) 28.

states, notably France and Russia.[38] This led the individual German states to engage in their own protectionist policies that harmed the other Member States of the German Confederation.[39] This dire situation led many contemporary businessmen and economists, including Friedrich List, to petition the Federal Diet in 1819 to create a German customs union within the German Confederation to protect its Member States and citizens: 'the interests of the German people are not only endangered by foreign arms', List wrote, 'foreign tariffs are the canker worms which devour German prosperity. For this reason we declare it to be the obligation of the Confederation to protect us not only by armed might, but by federal tariff'.[40]

In contrast to the United States, the German Confederation did not create an economic union within its constitution. Such attempts were pre-empted by the conservative Austria that politically as well as economically and socially belonged to the Ancien Régime. Instead, an economic union in the shape of the Zollverein emerged in the north of the German Confederation around Prussia.[41] The Zollverein was, therefore, a 'federation in a federation' (*ein Bund im Bund*).[42]

The consolidation of general and mutual welfare in the 1787 Constitution of the United States and the formation of the German Zollverein attest to the emergence of the creation and government of internal markets as a relatively autonomous aim of federal unions of states. Together with military defence, economic prosperity and stability became understood as a vital condition for the political autonomy of states and as such a substantive aim for federal unions of states.

II. The Alternative to Empire

A. Market Creation by Domination

If access and control of larger internal markets became indispensable for the perpetuation of the political autonomy of states following the industrial revolution, why were economic federations mostly if not completely absent in Europe between the Zollverein and the post-WWII era?[43] The simple answer to this question is that economic unions of states *did* exist in this period but they were *imperial*, not federal, in nature. The internal markets that the European states relied on were

38 Price (n 29) 28; Henderson (n 29) 33–34.

39 Price (n 29) 28; Henderson (n 29) 9, 21–23.

40 Excerpt from an 1819 petition to the Federal Diet drafted by Friedrich List, as cited by Forsyth (n 18) 164.

41 Huber (n 13) 796.

42 Ernst Rudolf Huber, *Deutsche Verfassungsgeschichte seit 1789*, vol 2: Der Kampf um Einheit und Freiheit, 1830 bis 1850 (Verlag W Kohlhammer 1968) 287. See also Forsyth (n 18) 167; Beaud (n 7) 311.

43 Forsyth (n 18) 177 argues that a few examples of genuine economic federations appeared between the Zollverein and the EEC, all of which involved a constellation of the BENELUX countries: the 1921 economic union between Belgium and Luxembourg, the monetary convention between the BENELUX governments in exile in 1943, and the Benelux Customs Union of 1948.

anchored in colonial expansion rather than federal compact. The 'age of empire', roughly between 1875 and 1914, was characterized by a growing interdependence of the economies of most if not all sovereign states and by the struggle between these self-same states to extend their control of the emerging world economy via imperialism: market-creation by domination.[44]

WWI, the Great War fought predominantly between the European Empires, did not lead to a stable new world order. In the territories where the newly collapsed European land empires had been (the Habsburg Empire, the German Empire, and the Ottoman Empire) proper 'nation-states' that did not belong to a greater empire were created for the first time in Europe outside the Balkans.[45] The interwar period was moreover characterized by attempts to recreate the old world economy. This proved impossible because the old hegemonic foundations (the British Empire) had been drastically weakened without a new hegemon (the United States) willing to take its place.[46] The last attempt to resurrect the old world of European empire, of market creation via domination, was the project of the Nazi *Großraum* in the interwar period that sought to substitute oversees colonies by imperial expansion within Europe itself and thereby 'make the great spaces of Eastern Europe into Germany's equivalent of the [British] Raj'.[47] For first time in history, the techniques of colonial exploitation were applied to Europeans, on European soil.[48] Following Arendt, imperialism has to be understood as a symptom of the general and systematic crisis of the European state and the political system built around it. The state could no longer live up to its most basic promises of security and stability. Having 'lost its very foundations', Arendt wrote, the national state 'leads the life of a walking corpse, whose spurious existence is artificially prolonged by repeated injections of imperialistic expansion'.[49]

In contrast to empire, an economic federation is the expansion of an internal market on the basis of free agreement between the Member States. A federation provides the possibility for the creation of a concrete economic order established not on the basis of land-grabbing but on mutual promises and pledges. Imperial expansion is a more 'frequent method of aggregation' than federation, as pointed out by William Riker, but, he continues, 'imperial expansion is costly, if, that is, the potential victims resist. So occasionally, ambitious expansionists federate rather

[44] Eric Hobsbawm, *The Age of Empire, 1875–1914* (Abacus 1994).

[45] Borislav Chernev, *Twilight of Empire: The Brest-Litovsk Conference and the Remaking of East-Central Europe, 1917–1918* (University of Toronto Press 2017).

[46] Adam Tooze, *The Deluge: The Great War and the Remaking of Global Order 1916–1931* (Allen Lane 2014).

[47] Forsyth (n 18) 175.

[48] Tony Judt, *Postwar: A History of Europe since 1945* (Vintage Books 2005) ch 1. For one of the most famous accounts of the effects of colonial exploitation, see Frantz Fanon, *The Wretched of the Earth* (Penguin 1967).

[49] Hannah Arendt, 'The Seeds of a Fascist International' in Hannah Arendt, *Essays in Understanding: 1930–1954: Formation, Exile, and Totalitarianism* (Jerome Kohn ed, Schocken Books 1994) 143. See also Sir William H Beveridge, *Peace by Federation* (Federal Union 1940).

than conquer'.[50] In this way, federalism can be understood as a historical alternative to empire: 'federalism holds out the prospects of organizing the world at large as the alternative to imperial domination'.[51] Economic federalism and imperialism alike are means for the state to access a larger internal market—by free and mutual contract or by force and violent expropriation—that will allow the state to maintain itself politically.

The autarkic European nation-state, if it ever existed, was the exception rather than the rule. Nevertheless, it is the myth of the self-sufficient nation-state that lies at the heart of much scholarship on post-WWII European integration. Instead of interpreting the EU in line with previous projects of market creation through empire and federation, the story of the post-WWII project of European integration is often interpreted as a 'conflict' or 'competition' between the Union and the Member States as the dominant forces in a zero-sum game. The rest of this chapter demonstrates that the project of European integration, like other federal unions of states, was born out of necessity in order for the European states to preserve their political existence and autonomy. In order to understand the origins and telos of European integration, we need to break away from the mythical story of the self-sufficient European states that still informs much of the debate on the project of European integration that emerged after WWII.

B. After Empires

While WWI destroyed the European land empires, WWII spelled the eminent decline of the European sea empires that would be dismantled in the years to come in the process of decolonization.[52] The foundations of the old world-order in imperial markets was crumbling. With the end of WWII, 'Europe' was no longer the centre of the world order but divided into two spheres of influence by the hegemonic powers of the new world order: the USA and the USSR. 'Europe will no longer decide Europe's destiny', the historian Arnold Toynbee wrote a few years after the war: 'Her future lies on the knees of the giants who now overshadow her'.[53]

With few exceptions (notably the United Kingdom, Ireland, Sweden, and Switzerland), at the beginning of the post-WWII era Europe was a region of more or less failed states on the fringes of emerging imperial super powers.[54] In addition

[50] Riker (n 21) 11–12.

[51] Carl Joachim Friedrich, *Man and His Government: An Empirical Theory of Politics* (McGraw-Hill 1963) 608.

[52] Timothy Snyder, 'Integration and Disintegration: Europe, Ukraine, and the World' (2015) 74 Slavic Review 695, 700.

[53] Arnold Joseph Toynbee, *Civilization on Trial* (OUP 1948) 124.

[54] See, eg, Judt (n 48) ch 1.

to the states already mentioned, only two European states were unoccupied at the end of WWII, Salazar's Portugal and Franco's Spain, both under fascist or authoritarian rule. With the dawn of the post-WWII era, most European states faced a long overdue crisis, namely, their fundamental inability to secure even the most basic aims of territorial defence and internal stability.

This crisis had its roots in the interwar period and did not evolve around one single threat or problem but several. The internal stability of the European states during the interwar period had been short-lived, leading to civil wars, rebellions and ultimately to the rise of authoritarianism, fascism, and Nazism.[55] The Great Depression had left the European states incapable of providing economic security and stable governmental regimes. The interwar period is characterized by an economic, social, as well as political collapse of the European states. 'The truth was', Hannah Arendt wrote towards the end of WWII, 'that the national State, once the very symbol of the sovereignty of the people, no longer represented the people, becoming incapable of safeguarding either its external or internal security'.[56] The most potent example is perhaps the Weimar Republic, which proved completely incapable of realizing a stable form of government.[57] This led to wide use of emergency decrees that ultimately brought the Nazis to power with the promise of 'work, freedom and bread'. A promise that was temporarily 'redeemed' by the creation of a war economy in Germany in their imperial quest for *Lebensraum* in Eastern Europe.[58]

In the immediate post-WWII era, Western European security relied on American economic and military support, importantly the Marshall Plan (1948–52) and NATO from 1949.[59] The Americans as well as Christian Democratic leaders across Western Europe, however, agreed that this could not be the permanent solution to the multiple and complex security threats that the Western European states

[55] See, eg, Robert Gerwarth, *The Vanquished: Why the First World War Failed to End, 1917–1923* (Allen Lane 2016).

[56] Hannah Arendt, 'Approaches to the German Problem' (1945) 12 Partisan Review. Reprinted in Hannah Arendt, *Essays in Understanding, 1930–1954: Formation, Exile, and Totalitarianism* (Jerome Kohn ed, Schocken Books 2005) 11. In a memorandum of advice written to Charles de Gaulle at the end of WWII, Alexandre Kojève, 'Outline of a Doctrine Of French Policy' [2004] Policy Review 3, 6 made a similar argument: 'the German example proves clearly that nowadays, a nation, no matter which one, which persists in maintaining its national political exclusivity must sooner or later cease to exists politically … the current war, conducted by Empire, signalled the last act of the great tragedy which national States have performed for five centuries'. See also Robert Howse, 'Kojève's Latin Empire' [2004] Policy Review 41.

[57] Clinton Rossiter, *Constitutional Dictatorship: Crisis Government in the Modern Democracies* (Princeton University Press 1948) 29–61.

[58] Timothy Snyder, *Bloodlands: Europe between Hitler and Stalin* (Basic Books 2010) 19; Timothy Snyder, *Black Earth: The Holocaust as History and Warning* (Tim Duggan Books 2015).

[59] Judt (n 48) 88ff.

faced. The transatlantic consensus that emerged was that Western Europe had to recover economically and be remilitarized in order to protect itself from the expansionist ambitions of the Soviet Union.[60] In the eyes of the new governments, economic security was understood to be of equal importance to military defence. The period was characterized by a general change in the understanding of security that strongly emphasized its economic dimension. A stable economy became integral to the suppression of the internal 'communist threat' in the form of either a coup d'état or a democratic majority.[61]

At the start of the Cold War, the internal 'communist threat' as well as the external threat of the Soviet Union were felt ever more acutely by the Americans and by the European Christian Democratic parties.[62] In 1948, the Communist Party assumed unlimited control of the government of Czechoslovakia, initiating four decades of Communist rule.[63] In the same year as the Prague coup, the Berlin Blockade prompted the Berlin airlift. Economic security was in this regard perceived as pivotal for the creation of stable governmental regimes that were capable of securing the obedience and loyalty of their citizens and furthermore weaken the communist parties and ideology.[64] Moreover, the outbreak of the Korean War in 1950 was widely interpreted as the prelude to a Soviet invasion of Western Europe, demanding a solution to the conundrum of how to remilitarize West Germany.[65] German rearmament was feared by many European states after WWII, especially by France, yet a weak and unarmed Germany was a threat to the new American hegemony in Western Europe.[66]

[60] Mark Gilbert, *European Integration: A Concise History* (Rowman & Littlefield Publishers 2011) 11ff.

[61] In the words of Wolfram Kaiser, *Christian Democracy and the Origins of European Union* (CUP 2007) 199: 'Western Europe had to respond to the ideological challenge of communism with its boundless promises of human welfare and its apparent technological and socio-economic advances'. In a similar manner, Gilbert (n 60) 12, writes: 'The fact that European (and American) leaders had constantly to remember in the postwar years was that for millions of Western Europeans, Soviet Russia was a model of economic modernization, not ruthless dictatorship, and in the event of economic failure in Western Europe, the USSR might exert an attraction for millions more'. Judt (n 48) 88: 'the attraction of Communism was real'.

[62] E Timothy Smith, 'United States Security and the Integration of Italy into the Western Bloc, 1947–1949' in Francis H Heller and John R Gillingham (eds), *NATO: The Founding of the Atlantic Alliance and the Integration of Europe* (MacMillan 1992); Klaus Schwabe, 'The Origins of the United States' Engagement in Europe, 1946–1952' in Francis H Heller and John R Gillingham (eds), *NATO: The Founding of the Atlantic Alliance and the Integration of Europe* (MacMillan 1992); Gilbert (n 60) 13ff.

[63] Judt (n 48) 138–39.

[64] Kaiser (n 61) 199, 223.

[65] Edward Fursdon, *The European Defence Community: A History* (Macmillan 1980) 67ff; Schwabe (n 62) 181; Judt (n 48) 151ff.

[66] Richard Griffiths, *Europe's First Constitution: The European Political Community, 1952–1954* (Federal Trust for Education and Research 2000) 55. See also N Piers Ludlow, 'European Integration and the Cold War' in Melvyn P Leffler and Odd Arne Westad (eds), *The Cambridge History of the Cold War*, vol 2: Crises and Détente (CUP 2010).

The agreement that emerged between the European and American elites was that these multiple problems and threats required a *European* solution. For the Christian democrats as well as the Americans, this meant European unification, and ultimately a European federal union or federal state.[67] The reconstitution of Europe after WWII constitutes a fundamental break with the older order of European public law; it was not sought through a 'balance of power' but by the constitution of a European federation.[68] This path was consistently defended by the Christian democrats.[69] The link between the perceived unviability of the nation-state and the project of European unification was clearly expressed, for example, in the speeches of Adenauer:

> The age of national states has come to an end. Everybody must feel that a change has taken place, that an era has vanished and that a new age is dawning in which men will look beyond the borders of their own country and work in fraternal cooperation with other nations for the true aims of humanity. Whoever fails to realize this is beyond help. This very task and the construction of a Europe dedicated to this goal afford a great mission for German youth. And when this Europe, this new Europe, is built, our young people will once more find scope for active and peaceful lives. We in Europe must break ourselves of the habit of thinking in terms of national states ... An age of peace and cooperation will dawn only when nationalist ideas are banned from politics. Here in Europe, we have made a start in that direction by building plans for European unity.[70]

Like other federal union of states, the project of European unification that emerged after WWII has to be understood on the basis of the fundamental wish for political autonomy on the part of its founding states and their incapacity to of secure this autonomy as fully independent states. This combination of a wish for autonomy and impotence in securing it led the states to constitute among themselves a common union and confer on it powers to achieve their fundamental aims. It is thus a fundamental misunderstanding to think of the EEC/EU as antithetical to the European states. Post-WWII European history is, at least in part, the story of the 'rescue of the nation-state' as correctly pointed out by Alan

[67] Antonin Cohen, 'Constitutionalism Without Constitution: Transnational Elites Between Political Mobilization and Legal Expertise in the Making of a Constitution for Europe (1940s–1960s)' (2007) 32 Law & Social Inquiry 109, 125; Gilbert (n 60) 16ff.

[68] 'A mere restoration of the nation-state system that existed before 1939 with territorial alterations would serve only to revive the causes that led to the collapse of Europe', Reginald D Lang, 'The Germanic Confederation of 1815 and a European Confederation Today' (1946) 45 South Atlantic Quarterly 434 remarked in 1946: 'Europe needs to be refounded upon a new principle and not restored upon an old one. That new principle is a confederation of Europe'. See also Beveridge (n 49).

[69] Kaiser (n 61) 284.

[70] Konrad Adenauer, *World Indivisible—With Liberty and Justice for All* (George Allen & Unwin Ltd 1956) 6–7.

Milward.[71] The new post-WWII political consensus on which the Western European states relied required European integration and the transfer of public powers to the Community: 'Without it, the nation-state could not have offered to its citizens the same measure of security and prosperity which it has provided and which has justified its survival'.[72] European integration was a key element in the reassertion of the project of the political autonomy of the state. The emergence of post-WWII European states and European integration are inherently linked to one another.

Nevertheless, the states that first came together in the EU cannot be termed 'nation-states' with ease for two reasons. First, the Original Six were not unequivocally nation-states before European integration. At the end of the war, France, the Netherlands, and Belgium were still empires (albeit in radical decline), and Germany and Italy were failed fascist imperial states.[73] In other words, apart from Luxemburg, one of the few remaining European Grand Duchies, the founding Member States of European integration were the metropoles of failed or declining empires.[74] More precisely, therefore, European integration, emerging in tandem with decolonization, made it possible for a Western Europe of non-imperial nation-states to appear for the first time in history.[75] Second, European integration entailed a radical process of state transformation to the extent that they can longer be understood as fully sovereign states.[76] Rather than sovereign 'nation-states', the post-WWII states that emerged through the dual process of decolonization and European integration were 'Member States'. As Chapter 3 will demonstrate, Member States are not states in the 'classical sense'. [77] What this means is that the 'core states' of the European project were never genuine nation-states.[78] First, they were metropoles of imperial unions and when their empires started to collapse, they became Member States of a federal union.

[71] Alan S Milward, *The European Rescue of the Nation-State* (Routledge 1992) 3, 18.

[72] ibid 3. Konrad Adenauer (n 70) 50 writes: 'It may offend our national pride, but we must admit that under present conditions none of the European nation-states could, if left to itself, guarantee its citizens' welfare, freedom and territorial integrity. The necessity for union for economic, political and military reasons is incontestable'.

[73] MacGregor Knox, *Common Destiny: Dictatorship, Foreign Policy, and War in Fascist Italy and Nazi Germany* (CUP 2000). See also Mark Mazower, *Dark Continent: Europe's Twentieth Century* (Penguin 1999) 71ff.

[74] 'Even after the end of the Second World War, the European nations that had not lost the conflict clung tightly to their colonial possessions, which they considered an extension of the *metropole*, a central component of their prestige and national identity, and vital economic "living space", not to mention strategic reserve of cheap labour', Giuliano Garavini, *After Empires: European Integration, Decolonization, and the Challenge from the Global South, 1957–1985* (OUP 2012) 8.

[75] Eastern Europe, in contrast, *had* a period of nation-states, albeit a short one, in the two decades after WWI, see Snyder, 'Integration and Disintegration' (n 52).

[76] Joseph HH Weiler, 'The Transformation of Europe' (1991) 100 The Yale Law Journal 2403; Christopher J Bickerton, *European Integration: From Nation-States to Member States* (OUP 2012).

[77] Beaud (n 7) 204.

[78] For a similar argument, see Timothy Snyder, *The Road to Unfreedom: Russia, Europe, America* (The Bodley Head 2018) 76–77: 'In history there was no era of the nation-state: generally (with exceptions such as Finland), empire ended while integration began, with no interval in between. In the indispensable cases of Germany, France, Britain, Italy, the Netherlands, Spain and Portugal there was no moment between empire and integration when the nation was sovereign and the state flourished in isolation'.

III. The Reconstitution of Europe

A. The Birth of European Integration

Proposals for European integration came in many different shapes and sizes. Some were in the form of military alliances, such as the Western Union and Western European Union. Others came in the form of 'sectoral integration', importantly the European Coal and Steel Community (ECSC) established in 1951. The ESCS at the time was understood as a step towards the goal of a true European federation but it was itself not federal in nature.[79] Despite the ECSC being created for deeply political reasons and notwithstanding that it established common institutions, purely sectoral integration, in this case the common market for coal and steel, is not federal in nature. The Zollverein was not merely 'an interstate commercial agreement' or a 'functional agency', as, for example, the Universal Postal Union, 'but an acting economic totality of states, in the same way that a classical confederation is an acting defensive totality of states'. [80] Neither sectoral integration nor alliances qualify as federations; in contrast to what is often argued, however, the economic union constituted with the Treaty of Rome *does*.

The European Economic Community (EEC) amounts to what the first section of this chapter has called an 'economic federation': a federal union of states that has welfare, economic prosperity, and the creation of an internal market, as its primary aim. Initially, however, this economic union was not meant to stand alone but to be a part of a broader project that included a European defence federation. However, because of the failure first of the European Defence Community (EDC) and the European Political Community (EPC) project, and later of the Fouchet Plan, the project of European integration that emerged had welfare/the economy as its primary if not exclusive aim, or so it will be argued. That the EU/EEC has economic integration, and not military integration, as its primary aim is one of the main reasons that the federal nature of the EU/EEC has generally been overlooked. The federal aims of welfare and the creation of an internal market remain underreached aspects of federalism and the federation.

The first proposal for a military federation in Western Europe was put forward in the 1950 Pleven Plan that proposed 'the creation, for our common defence, of a European Army under political institutions of a united Europe'.[81] The Pleven Plan envisioned that the army of a United Europe should bring about 'a complete fusion of its human and material components under a single political and military

[79] Fursdon (n 65) 58; Finn Laursen, 'Federalism: From Classical Theory to Modern Day Practice in the EU and Other Polities' in Finn Laursen (ed), *The EU and Federalism: Polities and Policies Compared* (Routledge 2011) 10.

[80] Forsyth (n 18) 168.

[81] The Pleven Plan of 1950, reprinted in Anjo G Harryvan and Jan Harst (eds), *Documents on European Union* (MacMillan Press 1997) 65–69.

European authority'.[82] This was to be realized by the EDC, the establishing treaty of which was signed in Paris in 1952.[83] An ad hoc Assembly was created in order to draw up a plan for the future federal political organization of the EDC and in 1953 it signed the draft treaty establishing the EPC that, echoing the 1787 Constitution of the United States, opened with 'We, the peoples'. Article 1 of the draft treaty of the EPC speaks unambiguously in the language of federalism: 'The Community is founded upon a *union of peoples and states*, upon respect for their personality and upon *equal* rights and duties for all. It shall be *indissoluble*'.[84]

The EPC's general aims were common security and defence, the coordination of foreign policy, contributions towards the endeavours of NATO, the Council of Europe and the European Convention for Co-operation, the protection of human rights and fundamental freedoms and finally economic and social unification of Europe through the establishment of a common market.[85] It was the Dutch politicians especially who insisted on the treaty including economic and social unification among its fundamental aims specified in the preamble.[86] A political integration of Europe, which had military integration as its exclusive object, would only to a very limited degree lead to unity between the Member States, the Dutch diplomat Johan Willem Beyen argued.[87] The Dutch politicians were not convinced that the proposals for the EPC went far enough, which prompted them to draw up a supplementary plan, the Beyen Plan.

The Beyen Plan commenced with the argument that, together with common defence, the principal aim of European integration should be 'the raising of the general standard of living of the European peoples'.[88] Echoing Franz List's argument as well as those of Madison and Hamilton, the Beyen Plan asserted that this could not be achieved in a Europe 'divided into a number of limited markets as a result of trade barriers and subject to monetary instability'.[89] The establishment of a united Europe, ultimately of a 'federal or confederal nature', the plan continued, 'should be bound up with the establishment of common bases of economic development and a merging of the essential interests referred to in the resolution'.[90] The grand project of a European military federation of the EPC and the EDC collapsed, owing to the rejection of the latter by the French Parliament in 1954. The previously relatively

[82] Pleven Plan, ibid 67.

[83] Fursdon (n 65) 150.

[84] Draft Treaty embodying the Statute of the European Community (EPC Treaty), Article 1 (Strasbourg, 11 March 1953) reprinted in *Documents on European Union* (n 81) emphasis added.

[85] EPC Treaty, Article 2 (n 84).

[86] Richard T Griffith and Alan Milward, 'The Beyen Plan and the European Political Community' in Werner Maihofer (ed), *Noi si mura: Selected Working Papers of the European University Institute* (Office for Official Publications of the European Communities 1986).

[87] Griffiths (n 66) 100.

[88] The Beyen Plan for Economic Integration, 11 December 1952, as reprinted in *Documents on European Union* (n 81) 71–74.

[89] ibid.

[90] ibid.

unpopular idea of a European economic union, however, did not fall apart as a consequence of this failure.[91] The projects of a European defence union failed, but the project of an economic federation was successfully constituted with the EEC in 1957.

B. The European Economic Federation

With the Treaty of Rome the EEC was constituted as an economic federation. 'The Community is based on a treaty which is more than a conventional interstate treaty', Forsyth writes: 'It is a constitutive treaty which, in the act of creating a new body politic, alters the constitutions of the partners to it'.[92] The Treaty of Rome has all the characteristics of a federal and constitutional compact: a treaty that leads to a political change in the constitutions of its Member States and constitutes a new political unity.[93] The EEC is thus characterized by the federal principles of *birth* and *transformation* (*Chapter 1:III*). The Treaty of Rome creates a new system of public law that is binding throughout the Union and common federal institutions capable of legislating for the citizens of the new Union 'which are also endowed with considerable discretionary powers to fulfil the general objectives of the union'.[94] As other federal unions, the EEC is imagined as a new and permanent community devoted to the 'ever closer union' of its peoples.[95]

A similar constitutional, if not federal, interpretation of the Treaty of Rome has been presented by Hans Peter Ipsen in his *Gesamtaktstheori* ('collective act theory').[96] Following Ipsen, the EEC was created by a 'collective act' (*Gesamtakt*), meaning, a common constitutional decision (*Verfassungsentscheidung*) made by the collective wills of the Member States fused into a general will (*Gemeinwillen*).[97] They thereby created an autonomous legal order with a Community public authority (*Gemeinschaftsgewalt*) distinct from, and potentially superior to, the public authorities of the Member States.[98] Community law affects the constitutional orders or the Member States qualitatively and quantitatively by the denationalization

[91] Griffiths (n 66) 102ff.

[92] Forsyth (n 18) 183. See also Robert Schütze, *From Dual to Cooperative Federalism: The Changing Structure of European Law* (OUP 2013) 58.

[93] The constitutional change in the Member States does not necessarily entail a change in constitutional law. Rather, the political change in the constitutions of the Member States entails a change in their *status* or *statehood* (see *Chapter 1:I:B*).

[94] Forsyth (n 18) 183. See also Article 189, Treaty establishing the European Economic Community (Treaty of Rome) [1992] OJ C224/6.

[95] Schönberger (n 12) 102.

[96] Hans Peter Ipsen, *Europäisches Gemeinschaftsrecht* (Mohr 1972). See also Paul Gragl, *Legal Monism: Law, Philosophy, and Politics* (OUP 2018); Heribert Franz Köck, *Der Gesamtakt in der deutschen Integrationslehre: Eine Untersuchung aus dem Grenzbereich von staatlichen Recht und Völkerrecht* (Duncker and Humblot 1978).

[97] Ipsen (n 96) 60–61.

[98] ibid 7, 62–63; Gragl (n 96) 275.

of public tasks.[99] By establishing the European Communities, Ipsen writes, the basic norms of the Member States' statehood and very existence as states are *transformed*.[100] Moreover, the Community, and Community law, Ipsen writes, sets itself above and apart from international law by its purpose and aim: 'With its aims, tasks and purposes, the European Community raises itself above other international organisations to a degree that its legal order constitutes a unique legal order'.[101]

What is important to understand with regard to the purpose and aim of the EEC is that it is not a technical tool for the promotion of free trade but a political project of federation, it 'represents the transformation of the external economic relations between a number of states into an internal market'.[102] This transformation is a process of 'enclosure' towards the outside world through the creation of a common external tariff and common commercial policies towards non-EEC states: 'It draws a boundary between insiders and outsiders, and establishes a far-reaching form of internal preference'.[103] Federations, defence unions and economic unions alike, are never global orders. They are concrete historical and territorially bounded unions of states with an outside and an inside.

The relationship between the EEC/EU and the General Agreement on Tariffs and Trade (GATT)/World Trade Organization (WTO) is a good illustration of the 'enclosure' of the EEC to the outside world. Though the EEC/EU was not a formal member of the GATT/WTO until 1995, it was recognized as the *de facto* unilateral representative of its Member States as early as two years after the Treaty of Rome came into effect.[104] As other federal unions, the EEC is characterized by a common external representation, clearly made manifest in its effective replacement of its Member States in the negotiations of international trade agreements.[105] The radical difference between the EEC/EU and the GATT/WTO is thus clear in the simple fact that while the EEC/EU could become a (*de facto*) member of GATT/WTO, the opposite scenario would never be possible.

Together with the construction of a *common exterior* representation of the Community to the outside world, the EEC creates a new *common interior* by removing barriers to the free movement of goods, services, workers, and capital

99 Ipsen (n 96) 7.

100 ibid 48. For further discussion of Member State transformation and its constitutional significance, see Chapter 3:II.

101 ibid 12, my translation.

102 Forsyth (n 18) 183. This was, eg, clearly expressed in relation to the accession of the post-fascist Mediterranean states who wanted to join the EEC for deeply political reasons (see Chapters 3:II and 4:II). See also Murray Forsyth, 'The Relevance of Classical Approaches' in Joachim Jens Hesse, Vincent Wright, and Wright Hesse (eds), *Federalizing Europe? The Costs, Benefits, and Preconditions of Federal Political Systems* (OUP 1996) 38–39.

103 Forsyth (n 102) 38–39.

104 Jacques HJ Bourgeois, 'The European Court of Justice and the WTO: Problems and Challenges' in Joseph HH Weiler (ed), *The EU, the WTO, and the NAFTA: Towards a Common Law of International Trade?* (OUP 2001) 72.

105 Robbins (n 20) 30. For a summary of the international treaties agreed by the Zollverein see Huber (n 13) 296–97.

within the Community. A crucial aspect of this, as with all economic federations, was the establishment of a customs union that removed internal tariffs and, in the words of List, 'protected' the Union by a common federal tariff to the outside.[106] The new common interior constituted by the EEC is governed by its own system of public law. In contrast to other trade organizations like the North American Free Trade Agreement (NAFTA) and GATT/WTO, the EEC/EU has never relied on the public international law principles of state responsibility and state retaliation *internally* to enforce the Treaties.[107] That the EEC is radically different from international organizations of trade liberalization is clear from the sanctions on treaty infringements it relies on.

With the creation of the EEC, the Six could no longer treat each other as *aliens*. On the contrary, they appeared in front of each other as equal Member States, with equal rights, of a new common Union through which their relations *inter se* from now on and for the most part would be governed. This is a manifestation of the *interstate* dimension of state transformation. A central part of the *interstate* dimension of state transformation relates to the altered relationship between the Member States and the nationals of other Member States they are no longer allowed to treat as aliens. This is the heart of federal citizenship; as will be shown in what follows, it was introduced with the EEC.

The federal character of the EEC is clear in its introduction of the 'true kernel of federal citizenship', namely, the right to free movement and the right to non-discrimination on the basis of nationality.[108] These two rights constitute the core of the principle of *Indigenat* that characterizes the interstate citizenship of federations.[109] When states come together in a federal union they all have their own citizenships. Once they conclude the federal compact, however, they sow the seeds for a new citizenship, a new fundamental status, for their citizens, namely federal citizenship. That the EEC does not formalize these rights in the status of legal federal citizenship is typical of young or emerging federations. In the words of Christoph Schönberger:

> Once they conclude the founding treaty of a new Union, this is also the beginning of the new federal citizenship. Usually this new status is not yet formalized and it does not yet need formalization. This is due to a simple fact: The federal

[106] Raymond Bertrand, 'The European Common Market Proposal' (1956) 10 International Organization 559.

[107] William Phelan, *In the Place of Inter-State Retaliation: The European Union's Rejection of WTO-Style Trade Sanctions and Trade Remedies* (OUP 2015) 22. See also Joined Cases C-90/63 and C-91/63 *Commission of the European Economic Community v Grand Duchy of Luxembourg and Kingdom of Belgium* [1964] ECR 625; Joined Cases C-142 and C-143/80 *Amministrazione delle Finanze dello Stato v Essevi SpA and Carlo Salengo* [1981] ECR 1413; C-38/89—*Ministère public v Guy Blanguernon* [1990] ECR I3.

[108] Christoph Schönberger, 'European Citizenship as Federal Citizenship: Some Citizenship Lessons of Comparative Federalism' (2007) 19 European Review of Public Law 68, 73.

[109] Schönberger (n 12) 116–17.

> citizenship only denotes the legal status of state citizens at the federal level; it serves as an abbreviation for the federal rights those citizens enjoy in addition to the legal position they continue to have at the state level. It is, as it were, the additional hat the State citizens wear as far as the Federation is concerned.[110]

Moreover, federal citizenship in the EEC/EU, as in other young federations, is *derived* from citizenship of one of the Member States. That is, the status of federal citizenship is acquired and lost on the basis of citizenship in one of the Member States.[111] This derivative nature of federal citizenship can even continue to be the case in a consolidated federal state. This is the case in Switzerland where Swiss citizenship is a derivative status from cantonal citizenship.[112] In the United States, state citizenship became a derivative status to federal citizenship with the 14th Amendment after the Civil War ('All persons born or naturalized in the United States, and subject to the jurisdiction thereof, are citizens of the United States and of the state wherein they reside'[113]).

That the EEC/EU citizenship does not entail (full) political rights is in no way exceptional either. Following Schönberger, the main task of young federations is to eliminate the alien status of citizens of the different Member States: 'In its beginnings, the main task of federal citizenship is to end the alien status of citizens of the sister states. ... In founding times, the dimension of political participation remains secondary compared to such more fundamental problems'.[114] The obvious objection that it cannot be understood as constituting federal citizenship because the EEC only granted these rights to economically active citizens is also dismissed by Schönberger. Federal citizenship, not merely for young federations, tends to be conditional on the mobile citizens not being a social burden for the host Member States. In the Articles of Confederation, the conditional status of free movement was expressed in Article IV, Clause 1:

> The better to secure and perpetuate mutual friendship and intercourse among the people of the different States in this Union, the free inhabitants of each of these States, paupers, vagabonds, and fugitives from justice excepted, shall be entitled to all privileges and immunities of free citizens in the several States; and the people of each State shall have free ingress and regress to and from any other State, and shall enjoy therein all the privileges of trade and commerce, subject to the same duties, impositions, and restrictions as the inhabitants thereof.

110 Schönberger (n 108) 67.
111 ibid 76.
112 ibid 62.
113 The 14th Amendment to the Constitution of the United States, Section 1.
114 Schönberger (n 108) 75.

'Poor migrants', Schönberger argues, did not enjoy the rights of the yet untitled interstate citizenship of the United States under the Articles of Confederation and they were to wait a long time to have equal rights with the well-off citizens.[115] In the United States, it was only in 1941 with *Edwards v California,* that free movement of US citizens within the United States could no longer be restricted for indigent citizens.[116] In Switzerland, the equality of indigent Swiss citizens was only fully accomplished in 1975.[117] Not merely young federations but also federations that have evolved into consolidated federal states tend to exclude 'poor migrants' from the benefits of interstate citizenship for significant periods. The EU, Schönberger argues, should rather be understood as exceptional with regard to how fast it has broken down the conditions of self-sufficiency to free movement in its case law in comparison with other young federations.[118]

C. The Project of a European Defence Federation

With the Treaty of Rome, an economic federation was successfully established between the Six. But that did not silence the question of how to establish a political framework for common European defence. After the failure of the EDC and the EPC, a number of international treaties, none of them federal in nature, were concluded in order to solve the immediate problem of security in Europe, most importantly the Western European Union (WEU) and the inclusion of West Germany in NATO on 6 May 1955. The security of Western Europe was thereby guaranteed by NATO meaning, ultimately, by the military might and nuclear guarantee of the United States.

Nevertheless, the idea of a European defence federation, or a 'political union'[119] as it became known, was not abandoned. Interestingly, it was the French who previously had brought down the EDC, led by de Gaulle, who in 1960 took the initiative on a European defence union with what became known as the Fouchet Plan.[120] Shortly after taking office in January 1959, de Gaulle made it clear that he disapproved of the contemporary organization of NATO because it did not reflect his plans for the re-establishment of France as a world power.[121] De Gaulle envisioned France, together with Britain, as a European world power independent from the

[115] ibid 68.

[116] ibid 71; Sutherland (n 17) 297.

[117] Schönberger (n 108) 71.

[118] ibid 77.

[119] From the perspective of the theory of the federation, the identification of a 'political union' with a 'defence union' is problematic because defence unions and economic unions alike are political unions whose most fundamental aim is the preservation of the political autonomy of their Member States.

[120] Anthony Teasdale, 'The Fouchet Plan: De Gaulle's Intergovernmental Design for Europe' [2016] LEQS 1; Wilfried Loth, *Building Europe: A History of European Unification* (De Gruyter 2015) 101ff.

[121] Frédéric Bozo, *Two Strategies for Europe: De Gaulle, the United States and the Atlantic Alliance* (Rowman & Littlefield Publishers 2001) 9ff; Teasdale (n 120) 9–10.

United States, with access to nuclear weapons.[122] The Fouchet Plan was de Gaulle's vision for a European defence union under French hegemony because France would be the only Member State with nuclear weapons.

The Fouchet Plan spoke in the clear language and intent of a classic defensive federation. The preamble speaks of the High Contracting Parties being resolved to lay the foundation for a common destiny 'to be henceforth irrevocably shared; resolved to this end, to give statutory form to the union of their peoples'.[123] In Title I, 'Union of the European Peoples', it is declared that 'By the present Treaty, a union of States, hereafter called "the Union", is established. The Union is based on respect for the individuality of the peoples and of the Member States and for equality of rights and obligations. It is indissoluble' (Article 1).[124] In contrast to the 'supranational' institutional structure of the EEC, embodied in the Commission and the European Court of Justice (ECJ), the Fouchet Plan imagined an 'intergovernmental' design for the Union closer to the classical federal diet, with the Council as the strongest institution taking unanimous decisions (*Chapter 3:III*).

The response to the Fouchet Plan, however, was not unequivocally applauded by the other Five.[125] The strongest opposition came from the Dutch and the Belgian governments, both of whom where critical because they saw the Fouchet Plan as a threat both to the EEC and its governmental principles of 'supranationalism' and 'independence' and the close relationship between Europe and the United States in NATO.[126] The Dutch and Belgians further believed that the United Kingdom, which had applied for membership of the EEC in August 1961, should be included in the discussions for a 'political union' of Europe.[127] While the response from the delegations of Italy, Germany, and Luxembourg was not a blank opposition, they shared the Dutch and Belgian concern regarding the weakening of NATO by the Fouchet Plan.[128] These differences of opinions were further radicalized following an intervention by the European Parliament in December 1961, arguing for the use of qualified or simple majority voting by the Council and the granting of new, significant powers to the European Parliament and the ECJ.[129]

In response to the widening chasm, the French tabled a revised version of the Fouchet Plan in January 1962, the *second* Fouchet Plan, which, to the general astonishment and anger of the Five, included no concessions but hardened the French

[122] Bozo (n 121) 34–50; Teasdale (n 120) 9–10.

[123] Negotiations on a Draft Treaty for the Establishment of a Political Union, (first Fouchet Plan), 2 November 1961, reprinted in European Parliament and Political Committee, *Towards Political Union: A Selection of Documents with a Foreword by Mr Emilio Battista* (Emilio Battista ed, General Directorate of Parliamentary Documentation and Information 1964) 11–12.

[124] ibid 12.

[125] Teasdale (n 120) 30.

[126] ibid 9, 17, 24.

[127] ibid 31.

[128] ibid 21, 29–32.

[129] ibid 36. See also the Recommendation of the European Parliament, reprinted in *Towards Political Union* (n 123) 15–17.

position significantly.[130] In response to the second Fouchet Plan, the Five quickly agreed and signed a Counter-Treaty in February 1962 for a 'European Union' of a stronger and even more explicit federal design. Article 1 of the Counter-Treaty states that, 'By the present Treaty, a union of States and of European peoples, hereafter called "the European Union", is established. The European Union is based on the principle of the equality of the rights of and obligations of its members'.[131]

The European Union proposed by the Five was much closer to the Pleven Plan than any of the Fouchet Plans. The Union's power should not prejudice the powers of the EEC, it would adopt a common defence policy within the framework of NATO, decisions in the Council would be taken by qualified majority voting, and the powers of the ECJ and the European Parliament were to be strengthened/included.[132] The proposal of the Five further entailed an automatic review of the treaty when the EEC moved to the third and last stage of its transitional development in preparation for which the Council was to draft a constitution with highly integrationist goals: the extension of qualified majority voting, the introduction of direct elections to the European Parliament, and an extension of the powers of the ECJ.[133] The German delegations had further hoped to include European citizenship as a formal status.[134]

The proposal of the Five was not acceptable to the French and despite the efforts of the Italians to reach a reconciliation, the negotiations collapsed at the last meeting in Paris on 17 April 1962. At this meeting, the Dutch and the Belgians made it clear that their price for any deal was UK membership in both the EEC and the proposed European Union.[135] No agreement was reached at this meeting and the negotiations broke down never to be resumed. Less than a year later, de Gaulle vetoed the UK's accession to the EEC. The Germans and the Italians launched a project of a less formal political union in 1964; this was again blocked by the French. When the 1966 deadline for the beginning of the third stage of the transitional development and for the wider introduction of qualified majority voting was reached, the French boycotted the meetings, initiating the 'empty chair crisis' and enforcing *de facto* Member State veto power with the Luxembourg Compromise. With the failure of the Fouchet Plan, the idea of common European defence was abandoned for a number of years. As a result, the European federation that emerged came to have welfare as its solitary aim in the broad sense defined by Article 2 of the Treaty of Rome: the establishment of the common market and economic prosperity and stability and a closer relationship between the Member States.[136]

[130] Teasdale (n 120) 36–40.
[131] Proposal of the Five, reprinted in *Towards Political Union* (n 123) 25–39.
[132] Teasdale (n 120) 41.
[133] Proposal of the Five, reprinted in *Towards Political Union* (n 123) 3–33. See also Teasdale (n 120) 41.
[134] Teasdale (n 120) 41.
[135] ibid 46–48.
[136] Article 2 of the Treaty establishing the European Economic Community (Treaty of Rome) [1992] OJ C224/6.

Before the introduction of qualified majority voting with the Single European Act (SEA), the substantive aim of welfare, the raison d'être of the EEC, was advanced primarily through the teleological interpretations of the Treaties by the ECJ. In the two years following the collapse of the Fouchet Plan, the ECJ delivered two seminal judgments: *Van Gend en Loos* and *Costa v E.N.E.L.* Because of the failures first of the EDC and later the Fouchet plan, the project of a European defence federation is rarely taken into account as the political background of the project of 'integration through law'.[137] Nevertheless, the authority of EU law claimed the early 'foundational' case law of the ECJ relies heavily on the political aim of European integration, first expressed in the Pleven Plan and the Beyen Plan, the EDC/EPC and the EEC, and reaffirmed in negotiations over the Fouchet Plan by all the Member States, including the French, and even more strongly in comments by the European Parliament.[138] The idea of a European federation was not merely a utopian project dreamed up in the minds of idealists during the war and then quickly abandoned afterwards, as the story is often told.

The EEC was never a 'mere' free trade agreement and the ECJ did not 'invent' the project of a European constitution.[139] That is not to say that the ECJ was not an activist court or that the integration through law was insignificant. Rather, the famous court cases of the ECJ should be understood as the advancement of the project of a European Constitution by a Union institution, the ECJ, in response to the political gridlock of the Member States. It is more a shift 'from politics to law' than a freestanding 'constitutionalization' of international law.[140] The idea advanced by some scholars that the 'constitutionalization of European law'[141] can be replicated in other trade agreements[142] is therefore a misunderstanding of the political and historical foundations of the project of European integration and unification.

[137] See, however, the recent legal history of European integration, importantly Cohen (n 67). For an introduction to 'integration through law', see Loïc Azoulai, '"Integration through Law" and Us' (2016) 14 International Journal of Constitutional Law 449.

[138] The experience of the failure of the EDC/EPC led to the development of a shared constitutional understanding of the ECJ during the 1950s among a transnational network of European legal actors, many of them Christian Democrats. The notion of the special nature of the community invoked in the two seminal judgments had historical roots in the European federalist ideas of the 1940s and 1950s (and the early 1960s we might add). See Morten Rasmussen, 'The Origins of a Legal Revolution: The Early History of the European Court of Justice' (2008) 14 Journal of European Integration History 97; Cohen (n 67) 125ff.

[139] Alec Stone Sweet and James A Caporaso, 'From Free Trade to Supranational Polity: The European Court and Integration' in Wayne Sandholtz and Alec Stone Sweet (eds), *European Integration and Supranational Governance* (OUP 1998).

[140] '[C]onstitutionalism without constitution', Antonin Cohen (n 67) 127 writes, 'must therefore be understood as a legal substitute for a failed political constitution in the broader context of transnational interplays between American and European lawyers'.

[141] The literature is vast. See, eg, G Mancini, *Constitutionalism and Democracy in the European Union: Collected Essays* (Hart 2000); Koen Lenaerts, 'Constitutionalism and the Many Faces of Federalism' (1990) 38 The American Journal of Comparative Law 205; Eric Stein, 'Lawyers, Judges, and the Making of a Transnational Constitution' (1981) 75 The American Journal of International Law 1.

[142] Klaus Armingeon and others, 'The Constitutionalisation of International Trade Law' in Thomas Cottier and Panagiotis Delimatsis (eds), *The Prospects of International Trade Regulation* (CUP 2011).

Europe might have been integrated 'through law' and advanced by lawyers, but that does not mean that its foundations are not political.

As a consequence of the collapse of two grand post-WWII projects for defence federations in Europe, the EDC/EPC and the Fouchet Plan, the EEC/EU has developed as a federation with welfare or the economy as its primary aim. That being said, the ideas of common European defence never completely disappeared. After the French presidency went from de Gaulle to Georges Pompidou in 1969, elected on a pro-European manifesto, the stalemate that had developed after the failure of the Fouchet Plan could be remedied. British membership of the EEC became possible. Some of the ideas expressed in the Pleven Plan and the Fouchet Plan could be taken up again in the project of European Political Cooperation that, since 1970, has been part of the informal relationship between the Member States of the EEC but separate from the legal order of the Community. [143] Before SEA, European Political Cooperation had no formal legal standing and even under SEA, it was formally separate from the EEC. It created no, or limited, formal legal obligations and since it was excluded from the jurisdiction of the ECJ, it lacked a federal enforcement mechanism.[144] Furthermore, military security and defence were not included as substantive aims of SEA.[145]

It was not before the Maastricht Treaty in 1992 that security became a substantive aim of the EU:[146] *external* security with the Common Foreign and Security Policy (CFSP) on the one hand, and *internal* security with the Police and Judicial Co-operation in Criminal Matters (PJCC) on the other. The double aims of security were constituted as respectively the second and third pillars of the EU by the Maastricht Treaty. Notwithstanding that the three pillars introduced by the Maastricht Treaty were governed by one institutional structure, it constituted only a notional entity.[147] In contrast to the first pillar of the EU, the amended European Communities, the second and third pillars were only to a limited degree governed by the institutional structure set up with the EEC.[148] They were almost exclusively

[143] For a restatement of the legacy of the Pleven Plan and the Fouchet Plan, see especially 'The European Commission on the Future of the European Community' (Brussels, 1 July 1968) and the Davignon Report (Luxembourg, 27 October 1970) both reprinted in *Documents on European Union* (n 81). See also the 'Draft Treaty establishing the European Union' ('Spinelli Draft') (Bulletin of the European Communities, February 1984, No 2. Luxembourg: Office for official publications of the European Communities) 8–26.

[144] Renaud Dehousse and Joseph HH Weiler, 'EPC and the Single Act: From Soft Law to Hard Law?' in Martin Holland (ed), *The Future of European Political Cooperation* (Palgrave 1991); Simon J Nuttall, *European Political Co-Operation* (OUP 1992); Wolgan Wessels, 'EPC After the Single European Act: Towards a European Foreign Policy via Treaty Obligations' in Martin Holland (ed), *The Future of European Political Cooperation* (Palgrave 1991).

[145] With the Single European Act, the general aim of the European Communities (EEC, ECSC, and EURATOM) and the European Political Co-operation is 'to contribute together to making concrete progress towards European unity' (Article 1 of the Single European Act [1987] OJ L169/1).

[146] Article B of the Treaty on European Union (Maastricht Treaty) [1992] OJ C191/1.

[147] Deirdre Curtin, 'The Constitutional Structure of the Union: A Europe of Bits and Pieces' (1993) 30 Common Market Law Review 17, 24.

[148] Steve Peers, *EU Justice and Home Affairs Law* (OUP 2011) 15.

governed by the European Council and the legal effect of its decisions were binding on the level of international law alone. It was therefore left up to the Member States to determine the legal effect of these decisions within domestic law. Nevertheless, since the second and third pillars relied on the first, most importantly with regard to their budgets, a clear-cut distinction between the three pillars was always dubious. With the Treaty of Amsterdam, several substantive areas of the third pillar were transferred to the first pillar.

Finally, with the Treaty of Lisbon, the Union replaced and succeeded the Community and assumed a legal personality. Not before the Lisbon Treaty did the EU truly have security as a substantive aim. That being said, the powers of the EU within common security are limited when compared with classical defence federations. Defence unions tend to have *jus belli* and guarantee the territorial integrity of its Member States. Neither of these fundamental aspects are present in the EU even after the Lisbon Treaty. National security remains a reserved competence of the Member States.[149] To this day, the EU remains an economic federation with defence and military security as a subsidiary aim.

In 2016, however, the project of a common European defence union once again gathered some momentum.[150] The growing isolationism of the United States under President Trump and the prospect of the UK (a long-time critic of stronger European defence) leaving the EU have been important motivational factors for a positive commitment of EU Member States to stronger cooperation on defence.[151] Whether these initiatives over time will lead to the establishment of a genuine European defence federation on a par with the ones proposed in the early days of European integration remains to be seen.

[149] Article 4(2) of the Treaty on European Union [2016] OJ C202.

[150] See, eg, Rome Declaration of the Leaders of 27 Member States and of the European Council (the European Parliament and the European Commission Brussels, 25 March 2017) Statements and Remarks 149/17 25/03/201.

[151] See, eg, the European Commission's White Paper on the Future of Europe: 'Reflections and scenarios for the EU27 by 2025', COM(2017)2025 (Brussels, 1 March 2017). See also 'EU to spend €1.5bn a year on joint defence' *EUobserver* (Brussels, 7 June 2017).

3
State Transformation and Teleology

The federation is a discrete political form and for that reason the foundations and principles for its exercise of public power are different from that of the state. For the state, the core concept of public law is sovereignty. Power and authority are generated in the relationship between the people and its representatives and this relationship is the foundation of the public power of the state. The federation, like the state, is a political association. Sovereignty, however, is not at the heart of its public law. Public power is exercised in the federation but we need to de-emphasize the question of sovereignty to understand the principles in accordance with which public power is wielded and regulated (*Chapter 1:V*).

The federation has its own principles for the institutionalization of public power and the activity of governing. This chapter is concerned with understanding the foundations and principles for the exercise of public power in the federation and in the EU. The aim is to understand how the federation in general—and the EU in particular—governs itself as a political order without sovereignty. The argument presented is that the federation has a public law structure that is fundamentally different from that of the state. For that reason, it is a fruitless endeavour to study the EU based on the assumption that the same logic that applies to the state will be replicated 'beyond the state' in the EU. In contrast to the state, the federation is characterized by a dual and composite governmental structure of the Union and of the Member States. Both parts of this dual governmental structure differ from that laid out in the general theory of the state.

The Union institutions do not amount to a new 'super-state'. As discussed in Chapter 2, the Member States come together in a federation in order to obtain or secure certain aims. That is the raison d'être of the federation; the federal telos. In order to achieve those aims, the Member States create federal institutions. For that reason, the authority of Union institutions is derived from, and limited in relation to, the realization of these aims. The Union's institutional structure is therefore characterized by two governmental principles that differentiate it from a state: teleology and specialization. Nor are the Member States of a federation independent sovereign states in 'the classical sense'. Becoming a Member State entails a process of state transformation and constraints on the exercise of public authority. In the context of the EU, the process of state transformation is intertwined with the emergence of the constitutional regimes of the Member States, albeit in different ways. For the 'core' EU Member States, the process of state transformation is part of the broad post-WWII political and constitutional project of 'constrained democracy'.

The Constitutional Theory of the Federation and the European Union. Signe Rehling Larsen, Oxford University Press (2021).
 DOI: 10.1093/oso/9780198859260.003.0004

For the 'evolutionary democracies' of the UK and Scandinavia, EU membership has facilitated a form of constitutional 'modernization' that, in broad terms, has aligned their constitutional regimes with those of the 'core' European states. For the post-communist Member States, the EU was a key event in their reconstitution after 1989 and it provided a mythical promise of the 'return to Europe'.

This chapter has three sections. After a preliminary discussion of the public law structure of the federation (section I), the chapter goes on to discuss, in the context of the EU, the principles for the exercise of public power by the Member States (section II) and by Union institutions (section III).

I. The Public Law Structure of a Federal Union

A. Federal Duality

The most important structural feature of federal public law is its duality. The federation has twin sources of authority (*Chapter 1:IV*) and two autonomous but interdependent 'governments'. A federation, in the words of Daniel Elazar, consists of 'self-rule plus shared rule'.[1] The federation is a community of communities or, in Montesquieu's celebrated definition, a 'society of societies'.[2] The implication for the exercise of public power is that whereas the state governs itself as a unity, the federation governs itself as a plurality. In this way, the principles for the exercise of public powers are similar in the federal union and in the federal state. They both rely on a significant division of public powers between the level of the Member States and the Union.

Nevertheless, the federal union and the consolidated federal state differ with regard to the foundations of authority. The federal union is characterized by two qualitatively distinct and autonomous sources of public power: the political existence of the Union and the political existence of the Member States, none of which are subordinated to the other (*Chapter 1:IV*). In contrast, in a consolidated federal state like the present-day United States, the question of sovereignty has been irrevocably resolved in favour of the Union over the will of the States. In the case of the United States, 'We, the people' no longer carries an ambiguity between state peoples and one nation. With the end of the Civil War, the Constitution of the United States obtained a *national* foundation. Importantly, this is manifest in the ratification of the 14th Amendment, declaring for the first time the superiority of national citizenship over state citizenship and ignoring the old federalist ratification process for constitutional amendments. As Bruce Ackerman puts it, it was made clear 'that

[1] Daniel J Elazar, *Exploring Federalism* (University of Alabama Press 1987) 12.
[2] ibid 102–3.

the will of the nation was independent of, and superior to, the will of the states'.[3] It is only with this 'refounding' that the United States can be understood as a *state* rather than as a *federal union of states*.

The federation has two distinct 'governments' that exercise public power over the same subjects and within the same territories. The structure of the constitutional framework of a federation is therefore dual, namely, the institutional structure of the Union and the institutional structure of the Member States. The federation as a concept is ambivalent; at the same time it refers to a political association, a union of states, *and* to an institutional structure, which is autonomous from the Member States.[4] The federation as a political association, a union of states, is governed by a dual governmental structure composed of the Union institutions and the institutions of the Member States. For that reason, there is an *asymmetry* between the federation as political association and the federation as institution: the federation as a union of states is governed by not only Union institutions but also by Member State institutions.

This conceptual ambivalence also applies to the EU, which simultaneously refers to the union of states and to the institutional structure that is independent of the Member States. The EU as a union of states is governed by the institutional structure of the Union (the Council, the Parliament, the Commission, the European Court of Justice (ECJ), the European Central Bank (ECB) etc) *and* the institutional structures of the Member States. As is the case for other federations, the government of the EU, as a political association, is characterized by the exercise of public power by a dual governmental structure: 'Two systems, the EU and the Member States, are established with each having a right to govern or rule'.[5] Together they make up the government of the EU as a union of states.

B. Independence and Interdependence

The dual public powers of a federation are characterized by a 'mixed autonomy' or by the principles of *independence* and *interdependence*.[6] The Member States come together in a federation to preserve themselves politically. Their statehood and autonomy are therefore not dissolved. However, it is not merely the Member States vis-à-vis the Union but also the Union vis-à-vis the Member States that has an autonomous status. The federation is characterized by a *double autonomy*: the

[3] Bruce Ackerman, *We the People*, vol I: Foundations (The Belknap Press of Harvard University Press 1991) 81.

[4] Olivier Beaud, *Théorie de la fédération* (Presses universitaires de France 2007) 103.

[5] Damian Chalmers, 'European Restatements of Sovereignty' in Richard Rawlings, Peter Leyland, and Alison L Young (eds), *Sovereignty and the Law: Domestic, European and International Perspectives* (OUP 2014) 190.

[6] Beaud (n 4) 183ff; Kenneth C Wheare, *Federal Government* (OUP 1963) 10.

autonomy of the Member States and the autonomy of the Union as a whole.[7] By coming together in a federation, the Member States give birth to a new political association that is autonomous from them. A federal union of states is different from the sum of its parts.[8]

The difference between a federation and the sum of its parts can be established not merely because many federations, including the EU, govern through majority decision or qualified majority decision within central areas of state power.[9] Even in cases where a decision is made on the basis of unanimity and all the Member States have a veto, there is a fundamental difference between a decision made by the federation and a unanimous decision of international law. The reason is that, in contrast to the latter, the former needs no ratification by the individual Member States: 'More precisely, every Member State is constitutionally (because the federal constitution is a component of its own constitution) bound directly and in public law terms by the federation decision'.[10] The federal constitutional contract gives birth to an autonomous legal order and a new source of law (*Rechtsquelle*).[11] Moreover, it institutionalizes a public authority which is autonomous from the public authorities of the Member States and directly binding on them without further ratification.

In a 1967 judgment, the German Constitutional Court interpreted the European Economic Community (EEC) and the status of Community law along those lines. The German Constitutional Court argues that the Community is neither a state nor a federal state but rather a Community of a 'special nature' committed to the process of ever-closer integration.[12] Together with the other Member States, the German Constitutional Court continues, Germany has transferred sovereign rights to the Community and a 'new public authority has thereby been created, which is autonomous and independent vis-à-vis the public authorities of each Member State'.[13] As

[7] Beaud (n 4) 185.

[8] In Chapter 1, the double constitutional moment and double political existence of the federation were described by the principles of *birth* and *transformation*: the birth of the union and the transformation of contracting states.

[9] Under the Ordinary Legislative Procedure, the Council votes by qualified majority (55 per cent of EU Member States representing 65 per cent of the EU population). When the Council votes on a proposal that is made by neither the Commission nor the High Representative, there is a higher threshold (72 per cent of EU Member States vote in favour representing at least 65 per cent of the EU population).

[10] Carl Schmitt, *Constitutional Theory* (Jeffrey Seitzer ed/tr, Duke University Press 2008) 401, amended translation. For the original, see Carl Schmitt, *Verfassungslehre* (10th edn, Duncker & Humblot 2010) 385. See also Ernst Rudolf Huber, *Deutsche Verfassungsgeschichte seit 1789*, vol 2: Der Kampf um Einheit und Freiheit, 1830 bis 1850 (Verlag W Kohlhammer 1968) 294–95; Christopher Hughes, *Confederacies: An Inaugural Lecture Delivered in the University of Leicester 8 November 1962* (Leicester University Press 1963) 13.

[11] Schmitt, *Constitutional Theory* (n 10) 399.

[12] Bundesverfassungsgericht (BVerfG), Judgment of 18 October 1967—1 BvR 248/63 and 216/6—*EEC Regulations Constitutionality Case*. See Andrew Oppenheimer (ed), *The Relationship between European Community Law and National Law: The Cases* (CUP 1994) 412.

[13] ibid 413. See also BVerfG, Judgment of 9 June 1971—2 BvR 225/69—*Alfons Lütticke GmbH*, para 137. See Oppenheimer (n 12) 418; Case C-57/65 *Alfons Lütticke GmbH v Hauptzollamt Sarrelouis* [1996] ECR Spec Ed 205.

a consequence of that, the German Constitutional Court continues, 'its acts do not require approval ("ratification") by the Member States, nor can they be annulled by those States. The EEC Treaty to a certain extent constitutes the Constitution of the Community'.[14] The Community, the German Constitutional Court states,

> forms its own legal order which is part of neither public international law nor the national law of the Member States. Community law and municipal law of Member States 'are two internal legal orders which are distinct and different from each other'.[15]

By the act of coming together in a common union, the Member States have given birth to a new legal order which, though autonomous, is not external to them. The European legal order is a new legal order *and yet it is internal to the Member States.*

The interdependence of the legal order of the Union and those of the Member States is manifest in that they are not strangers to one another and accept parts of each other's legal orders as their own. As is the case for all federations, the EU and its Member States are in an internal public law relationship to one another.[16] This interdependence has a clear institutional expression. The classical example given in EU law is that domestic courts, through the preliminary reference procedure, make up a component part of the European legal order. EU law is enforced by domestic courts acting as Union courts. Even more striking, perhaps, is the case of the central banks of the Eurozone Member States. After the creation of the European System of Central Banks (ESCB), the central banks of the Member States are completely independent of the Member States.[17] More akin to branches of the ESCB, they answer only to the ECB. The government of money, paraphrasing Madison, is a 'national' function of the 'mixed regime' of the EU.[18]

By way of another illustration, Union institutions are to a large extent made up by Member State officials. The Council of Ministers comprises ministers from each Member State (sitting in ten configurations with regard to specialization); the European Council is an assembly of the Heads of the Member States/Member State governments; and the ECJ has one judge from each Member State, appointed by common accord of the Member State governments.[19] The official personnel of the Union are to a large extent also part of Member State governments or bureaucracies. In this way, the Member States govern themselves collectively with their own representatives through the EU.

[14] *EEC Regulations Constitutionality Case* (n 12) 413.
[15] ibid.
[16] Beaud (n 4) 192.
[17] Chiara Zilioli and Martin Selmayr, *The Law of the European Central Bank* (Hart 2001).
[18] See Federalist 39 (Madison) in *The Federalist Papers* (Lawrence Goldman ed, OUP 2008) 190.
[19] Article 253 of the Consolidated Version of the Treaty on the Functioning of the European Union [2016] OJ C202/47 (hereafter TFEU).

Notwithstanding the institutional interdependence of the Union institutions and the Member States, they constitute two autonomous governmental entities characterized by different principles for the exercise of public powers. The exercise of public power by the Union and by the Member States is regulated in fundamentally different ways and for that reason there is an asymmetry between the two levels of 'government'. Nevertheless, they are similar in the sense that neither the Union nor the Member States exercise public power as sovereign states. The rest of the chapter discusses the principles for the exercise of public power by the Union and by the Member States.

II. State Transformation

A. Becoming a Member State

When relatively independent states decide to come together in a federation or accede to one (*Chapter 4:III*), they undergo a process of state transformation manifest in a change in their constitutional orders (*Chapter 1:III*). This constitutional change of the Member States is not necessarily manifest in a change in their constitutional laws. Whether discernible using a purely legal analysis or not, the constitutional change is manifest in the transformation of the Member States' constitutions in the *positive sense*, namely the fundamental characteristics of how they govern themselves as political associations (*Chapter 1:I:B*). By becoming Member States, the states of a federation are given a fundamentally new status. Notwithstanding the fundamental political change inherent in the process of state transformation, it does not eradicate the political autonomy of the Member States. In contrast to a decentralized state, the Member States are not mere administrative regions and neither does the process of state transformation deprive the Member States of their governmental, administrative, or other institutional apparatuses.[20] The Member States have a 'political dignity' that the federation is meant to protect.[21] After all, the Member States come into a common union in order to perpetuate their political autonomy. That being said, the Member States of a federation are not states 'in the classical sense'.[22]

European integration, as we saw in Chapter 2, allowed for the stabilization of the core European states after WWII. It was the 'rescue of the nation-state', in Milward's terms.[23] Nevertheless, European integration has entailed a fundamental

[20] William H Riker, 'European Federalism: The Lessons of Past Experience' in Joachim Jens Hesse and Vincent Wright (eds), *Federalizing Europe? The Costs, Benefits, and Preconditions of Federal Political Systems* (OUP 1996) 10.
[21] Beaud (n 4) 102.
[22] ibid 204.
[23] Alan S Milward, *The European Rescue of the Nation-State* (Routledge 1992).

transformation of the European states to the extent that they can no longer be understood as fully sovereign nation-states. For that reason, it is a mistake to tell the story of post-WWII Europe integration as a 'struggle over sovereignty',[24] which must lie either with the Union or with the Member States (*Chapter 1:IV*). European integration is as a process of *state transformation* from 'nation-state to Member State', as Christopher Bickerton puts it.[25] Or, in the case of most of the core Member States, the transformation of former imperial *metropoles* into Member States (*Chapter 2:II*).

The process of state transformation, as discussed in *Chapter 1:III*, has two aspects. First, the transformation of the relationship between the contracting states that have become Member States (*interstate*). Second, the transformation of the internal constitutional arrangements of the Member States (*intrastate*). At a fundamental level, the *interstate* dimension is manifest in the way that Member States no longer relate to each other, or to each other's citizens, as aliens. Their relations are henceforth (primarily) governed by the internal public law of the Union rather than international law. For that reason, the dichotomies of internal/external and national/alien pertaining to the theory of the state no longer apply to the relationship between the states in the same way. The Member States are 'sister states'; the federation is 'like a big family within which all the states are brothers and sisters'.[26] Being a Member State entails that some of its decisions must be taken as a member of a common community rather than as a fully autonomous sovereign entity. Amongst other things, this entails accepting the validity of judgments made in other Member States.[27]

The *intrastate* dimension of state transformation originates in the necessity to incorporate and accommodate the Union constitution in the constitutional orders of the Member States. The federal constitution simultaneously incorporates the Member States in their totality and makes up a part of their domestic constitutional orders. In this way, a part of the federal constitution lives at the heart of the Member States' constitutions. An important consequence of this state transformation is that the Member States no longer have full control over their own citizens and borders. Being Union citizens, the citizens of the Member States, subject to some conditions and limitations, will have rights of free movement and the right to be treated on equal terms with the citizens of host Member States (*Chapters 1:III* and *2:III:A*).

For the Member States, the authority generating nexus between people and government that characterizes state sovereignty as a relational concept is relativized.[28]

[24] Christopher J Bickerton, *European Integration: From Nation-States to Member States* (OUP 2012) 21.
[25] ibid.
[26] Beaud (n 4) 215, my translation.
[27] ibid 207ff.
[28] Martin Loughlin and Stephen Tierney, 'The Shibboleth of Sovereignty' (2018) 81 Modern Law Review 989, 1014.

The Member State governments understand their authority and the activity of governing not merely in relation to their own peoples but also in relation to the Union and the other Member States. A central aspect of this transformation is that the relationship between state and society is relativized because it becomes one relationship amongst others that are constitutive of statehood.[29] Member State governments, Bickerton writes, 'understand their power and identity as dependent upon their belonging to a wider group or community'.[30]

The concept of the 'Member State', following Bickerton, is not merely a legal title but a distinctive form of *status* or *statehood*.[31] 'Member-statehood' entails the voluntary consent of the Member States to constrain their exercise of public authority through the EU. It is a form of 'constrained statehood' where the exercise of public authority is limited through an 'external framework'.[32] Nevertheless, it would be a mistake to think of the constraints as purely 'external' to the Member States. In a federation, the legal order of the Union makes up a part of the Member States' own constitutions. Member-statehood always entails *constitutional internalization* of the constitutional order of the Union by the Member States. Notwithstanding that the constitutional orders of the Union and the Member States are autonomous they are also interrelated and interdependent.

The emergence and transformation of the constitutional settlements of the EU Member States is intimately linked to their membership in the EU and the constitutional order of the Union.[33] However, this process of constitutional internalization and transformation differs significantly between the Member States. The constitutional orders of all the Member States and the legal and political order of the Union are interdependent and interrelated, *but not in the same way*. Becoming and being a Member State is not experienced in the same way by each EU Member State. This has to do with the varieties of constitutionalism that characterize the EU Member States and hence the constitutional heterogeneity of the EU—or so it will be argued.[34] In what follows, I discuss three different experiences of constitutional internalization of EU member-statehood: the 'core' European states that founded the EEC, the 'continuous democracies' of the UK and Scandinavia, and the idea of the 'return to Europe' that influenced the reconstitution of post-communist Europe.

[29] Bickerton (n 24) 12. See also Michael A Wilkinson, *Authoritarian Liberalism and the Transformation of Modern Europe* (OUP forthcoming) ch 3.

[30] Bickerton (n 24) 12.

[31] ibid 51.

[32] ibid 61.

[33] John Erik Fossum and Agustín José Menéndez, *The Constitution's Gift: A Constitutional Theory for a Democratic European Union* (Rowman & Littlefield Publishers 2011).

[34] The constitutional heterogeneity of the EU Member States is discussed in more detail in Chapter 4:III:C. See also Bruce Ackerman, 'Three Paths to Constitutionalism—and the Crisis of the European Union' (2015) 45 British Journal of Political Science 705.

B. Constrained Democracy

For the founding Member States of the EEC, there is an inherent relationship between the internal constraints of the domestic constitutional orders and the external constraints of European integration. This is especially the case for post-WWII West Germany;[35] however, it applies to the other 'core' European states to a greater or lesser extent as well. The reason for that has to do with the shared project of reconstituting Europe after WWII. This project, as Michael Wilkinson argues, was shaped by a specific interpretation of the interwar period and WWII, focusing on the 'excesses' of democracy and popular sovereignty rather than the crisis of capitalism.[36] The post-WWII constitutional imagination was dominated by the view that unconstrained political power and mass politics were the direct causes leading to the legal and political collapse of the European states and rise of fascism, Nazism and communism. These 'political extremes' were all understood as manifestations of *totalitarianism*.[37] The fundamental distrust in popular sovereignty, including parliamentary sovereignty, resulted in the emergence of a new constitutional settlement after WWII centred on the idea of 'constrained' or 'militant' democracy.[38]

The crux of the argument for militant democracy was laid out by Karl Loewenstein in 1937. Fascism, according to Loewenstein, was not an ideology but a most effective governmental technique. For that reason, it should not be taken seriously as an alternative way of organizing social life but merely as a despicable means to accumulate power for power's sake.[39] The only way of conquering it was

[35] The commitment to become a 'European Germany' after WWII was so strong that a united Europe was preferred over a united Germany. The Federal Republic, Konrad Adenauer believed, could not remain neutral in the Cold War but had to commit itself to the 'free world' of the West, even if that precluded reunification with East Germany. The heart of Adenauer's policy was the idea of this *Westbindung* of the Federal Republic through European institutions. See Thomas Risse and Daniela Engelmann-Martin, 'Identity Politics and European Integration: The Case of Germany' in Anthony Pagden (ed), *The Idea of Europe: From Antiquity to the European Union* (CUP 2002); N Piers Ludlow, 'European Integration and the Cold War' in Melvyn P Leffler and Odd Arne Westad (eds), *The Cambridge History of the Cold War*, vol 2: Crises and Détente (CUP 2010) 183–85.

[36] Michael A Wilkinson, 'The Reconstitution of Post-War Europe: Liberal Excesses, Democratic Deficiencies' in Michael W Dowdle and Michael A Wilkinson (eds), *Constitutionalism beyond Liberalism* (CUP 2017). The idea of the 'excess' of democracy, or 'hyperdemocracy', is exemplified by José Ortega y Gasset, *The Revolt of the Masses* (George Allen & Unwin 1951).

[37] Hannah Arendt, *The Origins of Totalitarianism* (Harvest Books 1994); Carl J Friedrich (ed), *Totalitarianism* (Harvard University Press 1954). In the United States, constitutional thought was, at least in part, defined in opposition to totalitarianism, which was (or is) understood as comprising fascism as well as communism, see Richard Primus, 'A Brooding Omnipresence: Totalitarianism in Postwar Constitutional Thought' (1996) 106 The Yale Law Journal 423. See also Les K Adler and Thomas G Paterson, 'Red Fascism: The Merger of Nazi Germany and Soviet Russia in the American Image of Totalitarianism, 1930's–1950's' (1970) 75 The American Historical Review 1046.

[38] Jan-Werner Müller, *Contesting Democracy: Political Ideas in Twentieth-Century Europe* (Yale University Press 2011) 5; Jan-Werner Müller, 'Beyond Militant Democracy?' (2012) 73 New Left Review 41.

[39] Karl Loewenstein, 'Militant Democracy and Fundamental Rights, I' (1937) 31 The American Political Science Review 417.

to employ a governmental counter-technique, namely outlawing the enemies of democracy, such as through the ban of certain political parties. If liberal democracy was to protect itself from the lures of fascist emotionalism, Loewenstein reasoned, it must not be afraid to use drastic means: 'Democracy must become militant'.[40]

The principles of militant democracy became influential in post-WWII West Germany, including 'substantial democracy' in the constitution and empowering the Constitutional Court.[41] In this constitutional project a substantive order of values, with human dignity at its pinnacle, is prioritized over procedural aspects of democracy.[42] The fundamental idea of this form of constitutionalism is to weaken national parliaments and insulate certain aspects of social and political life, such as fundamental rights, from democratic control by way of a constitution protected by a strong constitutional court.[43] This constitutional project is concerned with constraining democracy by minimizing popular control of the state apparatus. Notwithstanding that the post-WWII constitutions imitate the revolutionary language of 'We, the people', the constituent power of the people was overwhelmingly perceived as a dangerous power that needed to be domesticated, importantly by bringing it within the scope of judicial review and by introducing 'eternity clauses' in order to preclude 'unconstitutional constitutional amendments'.[44] The post-WWII constitutional project is therefore fundamentally anti-revolutionary.[45]

The post-WWII constitutional regimes of the 'core' Member States and the project of European integration emerged together and should be understood as parts of the same broad political project. This project was advanced by the Christian Democratic parties that won terrain in all post-WWII Western European states that came to be the founders of the EEC.[46] Their success was brought about by the electoral alliance at the centre of the political spectrum between the middle class, labour, and the peasantry.[47] Distancing themselves from 'radical politics', the Christian Democratic parties presented themselves as the protectors of traditionalism and the dignity of the human person.[48] The post-WWII constitutional ethos

[40] ibid 423.

[41] Jan-Werner Müller, 'Militant Democracy' in András Sájo and Michel Rosenfeld (eds), *The Oxford Handbook of Comparative Constitutional Law* (OUP 2012).

[42] Alexander Somek, *The Cosmopolitan Constitution* (OUP 2014) ch 2 has described this as 'constitutionalism 2.0'.

[43] Müller, *Contesting Democracy* (n 38) 148; Müller, 'Beyond Militant Democracy?' (n 38) 43.

[44] Yaniv Roznai, *Unconstitutional Constitutional Amendments: The Limits of Amendment Powers* (OUP 2017); Christoph Möllers, '"We Are (Afraid of) the People": Constituent Power in German Constitutionalism' in Martin Loughlin and Neil Walker (eds), *The Paradox of Constitutionalism: Constituent Power and Constitutional Form* (OUP 2008).

[45] Hannah Arendt, *On Revolution* (Penguin 2006) 135; Wilkinson (n 36).

[46] Wolfram Kaiser, *Christian Democracy and the Origins of European Union* (CUP 2007) 163–90; Stathis N Kalyvas, *The Rise of Christian Democracy in Europe* (Cornell University Press 1996).

[47] Kaiser (n 46) 223; Milward (n 23).

[48] Carlo Invernizzi Accetti, *What Is Christian Democracy? Politics, Religion and Ideology* (CUP 2019) 53–79; Patrick Pasture, 'Catholic and Christian Democratic Views on Europe Before and After World War II: Continuities and Discontinuities' in Piotr H Kosicki and Sławomir Łukasiewicz (eds), *Christian*

they advanced was not merely institutionalized in constitutional courts but also through the transfer of power to other independent institutions and administrative agencies subject to judicial oversight.[49]

This project, however, was not merely pursued 'domestically' but equally via the project of uniting Europe after WWII. A central way of constraining national democracy was via European integration, which was 'part and parcel of the new "constitutionalist ethos", with its inbuilt distrust of popular sovereignty and the delegation of tasks to agencies that remained under the close supervision of national governments'.[50] For the Christian Democratic Founders of the EEC—Alcide De Gasperi, Konrad Adenauer, and Robert Schumann—national sovereignty was feared and had to be constrained. For that reason, the founding Member States of the EEC 'consciously delegated powers to unelected domestic institutions and to supranational bodies, in order to "lock in" liberal-democratic arrangements and prevent any backsliding towards authoritarianism'.[51]

European integration, as we saw in Chapter 2, was understood to be an integral part of stabilizing and reconstituting Europe after WWII. Crucially, it allowed the Member States to stabilize themselves through a common Union by providing the conditions for 'economic security' through the creation of a common market.[52] European integration was central to the creation of a new Europe that aspired to go beyond the 'dangers of the nation-state' and the balance power. The core task for the new order was to control and defeat the 'dark side' of democracy. The project of uniting Europe in a federation was understood as the key to precluding the rise of totalitarianism in Europe not only by the Christian Democrats but also by the Americans.[53]

Democracy Across the Iron Curtain: Europe Redefined (Palgrave Macmillan 2018) 34ff; Tony Judt, *Postwar: A History of Europe since 1945* (Vintage Books 2005) ch VIII.

[49] Müller, *Contesting Democracy* (n 38); Pierre Rosanvallon, *Democratic Legitimacy: Impartiality, Reflexivity, Proximity* (Arthur Goldhammer tr, Princeton University Press 2011).

[50] Müller, 'Beyond Militant Democracy?' (n 38) 43. See also Marco Duranti's account of the origins of the European Convention on Human Rights in his *The Conservative Human Rights Revolution: European Identity, Transnational Politics, and the Origins of the European Convention* (OUP 2017).

[51] Müller, 'Beyond Militant Democracy?' (n 38) 43. See also Andrew Moravcsik, 'The Origins of Human Rights Regimes: Democratic Delegation in Postwar Europe' (2000) 54 International Organization 217, 226ff.

[52] This was understood not merely as the conditions for internal pacification of Western Europe but also as the means to winning the 'battle of reconstruction' against the Soviet Union, see Milward (n 23) 173–74. For a further discussion, see Chapter 2:II:B.

[53] 'Through the opposition between freedom and totalitarianism … the entire political action of the United States in Europe was rationalized in a vision of the world in which federalism was opposed to totalitarianism like pluralism to despotism, and (democratic) decentralization to (bureaucratic) centralism, but also West Germany to both East Germany and Nazi Germany, and finally, the new Federal Europe to both the defeated Nazi Europe and to the still threatening Soviet Europe', see Antonin Cohen, 'Constitutionalism Without Constitution: Transnational Elites Between Political Mobilization and Legal Expertise in the Making of a Constitution for Europe (1940s–1960s)' (2007) 32 Law & Social Inquiry 109, 125.

For the 'Founding Fathers of Europe', the European rescue was furthermore part of the spiritual foundation of the post-WWII era that should protect the new order from the internal threat of 'political extremism' on either the right (fascism) or the left (communism).[54] Together with the Christian values, 'Europeanism' became the viable myth for the post-WWII Christian democratic parties that came to found the EEC.[55] Following Italian Prime Minister Alcide de Gasperi, a European federation became the Sorelian myth of the post-WWII era.[56] Whereas Sorel believed the class struggle of the proletariat could be fuelled by the myth of the general strike,[57] the post-WWII Christian Democrats came to understand Europe as the myth that would allow for the rescue of the European states from their—primarily internal—enemies.

The post-WWII political project, to which European integration belongs, is post-fascist or anti-fascist, and at least to some extent, anti-communist.[58] European integration became a means of preserving the post-WWII constitutional identity of liberal democracy via non-elected 'independent' institutions. For that reason, the constitutional internalization of the demands of European integration is largely compatible with the Christian Democratic constitutional project that influenced the founding Member States of the EEC.

The project of European integration is a central aspect of the post-WWII constitutional model developed in Western Europe. It is therefore not surprising that the limitation of national sovereign rights to achieve European and international peace is written into several constitutions of the 'core' European states.[59] The constitution of the EEC is a foundational moment made with 'implicit reference to

[54] Risse and Engelmann-Martin (n 35).

[55] See, eg, Konrad Adenauer, *World Indivisible—With Liberty and Justice for All* (George Allen & Unwin Ltd 1956) 5–15. For a discussion of the significance of Europeanism for Italian post-WWII public intellectuals, hereunder the Christian Democrats, see Mario Telò, 'Italy and the Idea of Europe' in Kalypso Nicolaïdes and Justine Lacroix (eds), *European Stories: Intellectual Debates on Europe in National Contexts* (OUP 2010).

[56] Milward (n 23) 333.

[57] Georges Sorel, *Reflections on Violence* (CUP 2004) 20–24.

[58] In the Federal Republic of Germany not only the neo-Nazi Reich Party but also the Communist Party of Germany were understood as dangers to the new constitutional settlement and hence banned after WWII (respectively in 1952 and 1956), see Peter Niesen, 'Banning the Former Ruling Party' (2012) 19 Constellations 540, 542. Konrad Adenauer (n 55) 25 expressed a greater fear of communism than the return of fascism: 'Communism remains a danger to which the Federal Government is ever alive, for its well-camouflaged front organizations, supported by extremely effective propaganda and by financial subsidies from Soviet Russia, can undertake dangerous subversive activity. Extremism of the right is at present not dangerous. Its development is being carefully checked. The Federal Government, as its measures against the Communist Party and the extreme rightist Socialist Reich Party prove, is determined to employ the full rigour of the law against all those whose acts are opposed to the Constitution.'

[59] Poul F Kjær and Niklas Olsen, 'Conclusion and Perspectives: The Reconstitution of Europe' in Poul F Kjær and Niklas Olsen (eds), *Critical Theories of Crisis in Europe: From Weimar to the Euro* (Rowman & Littlefield International 2016). For a discussion of the special case of the Netherlands, see Bruno De Witte and Monica Claes, 'Report on the Netherlands' in Anne-Marie Slaughter, Joseph HH Weiler, and Alec Stone Sweet (eds), *The European Court and National Courts—Doctrine and Jurisprudence: Legal Change in its Social Context* (Hart 1998) 189ff.

the six national constitutions of the founding member states'.[60] In the Preamble to the French Constitution of 1946, it is declared that 'subject to reciprocity, France consents to limitations of sovereignty necessary for the realisation and the defence of peace'. The Italian Constitution of 1948 contains a similar statement: 'Italy may consent, on equal terms with other States, to limitations of sovereignty necessary to establish an order ensuring peace and justice among nations'. The clearest example is the German Basic Law, which proclaims that 'the German people, in the exercise of their constituent power' constitute the Federal Republic on the basis of their 'determination to promote world peace as an equal partner in a united Europe'.[61] For that reason, a united Europe lies at the heart of the constitutional project of post-WWII West Germany. In the words of the German Constitutional Court: 'The Basic Law calls for European integration'.[62]

With the birth of the project of European integration, the constitutions of the Original Six started to live a 'double constitutional life'.[63] Together with their role as national constitutions, they took on a 'new role as part of the collective supranational constitution'.[64] Because of the affinity between the core European states and the project of European integration, it was possible to achieve a relative 'constitutional synthesis' between the European legal order and the domestic constitutional settlements.[65] At a fundamental level, they belong to the same political and constitutional project of 'constraining' democracy.

C. Constitutional Modernization

The constitutional internalization of EU membership has presented the UK and the Scandinavian Member States (Denmark and Sweden[66]) with a qualitatively distinct challenge from that of the founding Member States of the EEC. Neither Denmark and Sweden nor the UK has the collapse of the interwar period and WWII as the defining watershed for their constitutional orders and none of these

[60] Fossum and Menéndez (n 33) 18–19. See also Bruno De Witte, 'The EU as an International Legal Experiment' in Joseph HH Weiler and Gráinne De Búrca (eds), *The Worlds of European Constitutionalism* (CUP 2012).

[61] The Preamble of the 1949 German Basic Law opens with the following statement: 'Conscious of their responsibility before God and man, Inspired by the determination to promote world peace as an equal partner in a united Europe, the German people, in the exercise of their constituent power, have adopted this Basic Law'.

[62] BVerfG, Judgment of the Second Senate of 30 June 2009—2 BvE 2/08 (*Lisbon Ruling*), para 225.

[63] Fossum and Menéndez (n 33) 9–10.

[64] ibid.

[65] ibid 45ff.

[66] The third Scandinavian country, Norway, is an outlier. Norway is not a member of the EU (but a member of the European Economic Area) and was the first European country to recognize judicial review, see Marlene Wind, 'When Parliament Comes First—The Danish Concept of Democracy Meets the European Union' (2009) 27 Nordic Journal of Human Rights 272, 281; Andreas Føllesdal, 'Rawls in the Nordic Countries' (2002) 183 European Journal of Political Theory 183.

states think of themselves as 'constrained democracies'. In their constitutional self-understanding, these states are 'continuous democracies', predating the post-WWII world. Instead of being founded on the fear of sovereignty, these Member States are proud of their parliamentary traditions and are all characterized by judicial self-restraint and a relative lack of judicial review.[67]

With its uncodified constitution characterized by the relatively unrestrained authority of Crown in Parliament, the UK is perhaps the emblematic example.[68] The UK Constitution has evolved historically in incremental steps, allowing it to develop a modern constitutional order without a modern revolution. The incrementalism of British constitutional history means that WWII is not a particularly significant moment in the British constitutional self-understanding or, if so, it is only to illustrate and reinforce the power of parliamentary democracy. The same applies to the Scandinavian Member States:

> While the horrors of World War II led many Europeans to realise the necessity of constraining and checking the legislative branch to prevent the commission of future atrocities in the name of the 'nation', the Nordic peoples emerged with their national patriotism relatively unscathed. If anything, their experience underscored the illegitimacy of foreign interference with the popular will.[69]

The two Scandinavian Member States share important constitutional features with the UK. As is the case for the UK, the primacy of Parliament is the bedrock of the constitutional orders of Denmark and Sweden.[70] For that reason, the idea of judicial review of Acts of Parliament is viewed with suspicion as a political exercise of power by the judiciary.[71] The judiciary in Denmark and Sweden has therefore been cautious of exercising judicial review. The Danish Supreme Court, for example, has only once declared an Act of Parliament unconstitutional[72] and the Danish

[67] Jens Elo Rytter and Marlene Wind, 'In Need of Juristocracy—The Silence of Denmark in the Development of European Legal Norms Symposium: Nordic Juristocracy' (2011) 9 International Journal of Constitutional Law 470; Martin Scheinin, 'Constitutionalism and Approaches to Rights in the Nordic Countries' in Joakim Nergelius (ed), *Constitutionalism: New Challenges—European Law from a Nordic Perspective* (Martinus Nijhoff Publishers 2008) 137; Mikael Rask Madsen, Henrik Palmer Olsen, and Urška Šadl, 'Competing Supremacies and Clashing Institutional Rationalities: The Danish Supreme Court's Decision in the Ajos Case and the National Limits of Judicial Cooperation' (2017) 23 European Law Journal 140.

[68] Vernon Bogdanor, *The New British Constitution* (Hart 2009) 9–13.

[69] Andreas Føllesdal and Marlene Wind, 'Nordic Reluctance towards Judicial Review under Siege' (2009) 27 Nordic Journal of Human Rights 131, 137.

[70] Marlene Wind, 'The Nordics, the EU and the Reluctance Towards Supranational Judicial Review' (2010) 48 Journal of Common Market Studies 1039.

[71] As was recently reaffirmed by the Danish Supreme Court in the controversial *Ajos case*. Danish Supreme Court, Judgment of 6 December 2016, Case 15/2014 *Dansk Industri (DI) acting for Ajos A/S v The estate left by A*.

[72] The Danish Supreme Court, Judgment of 19 February 1999, Case 295/1998—*Den Selvejende Institution Friskolen i Veddinge Bakker mod Undervisningsministeriet* [*The Self-owning Institution, the Free School in Veddinge Bakker v the Ministry of Education*] (*Tvind case*).

Constitution is silent on the question of whether judicial review is allowed.[73] Sweden presents a similar case.[74]

This kind of constitutional system is largely incompatible with the demands of EU law, which relies on domestic courts to set aside national legislation that infringes EU law. The demands of member-statehood have therefore necessitated a relatively drastic constitutional transformation of these three states, paving the way for a system of judicial review of domestic law (to ensure conformity with EU law),[75] despite the effort, one might add, of some Scandinavian courts to avoid it, by not making use of the preliminary reference procedure.[76] The introduction of judicial review has led to significant critique from media and politicians, on the basis that it conflicts with democracy understood as the relatively unbound power and authority of Parliament.[77] In other words, the continuous democracies understand the constraints of member-statehood as *externally imposed*. Nevertheless, EU membership has in fact fundamentally transformed the domestic constitutional regimes of majoritarian democracy, parliamentary sovereignty and judicial self-restraint characterizing these three states.

The most drastic constitutional change has arguably taken place in the UK. For the British, the external constraints of European law could never be easily internalized as an act of self-binding of the people because the idea of popular sovereignty—let alone constrained democracy—is foreign to the British constitution. That being said, after acceding to the EU, Britain was required, by virtue of EU law, to govern itself as a 'constrained democracy' and respect the supremacy and direct effect of European law. Through EU membership, the British Constitution has undergone a process of 'modernization' that has enabled judicial review to ensure the conformity of British law with EU law, the adoption of fundamental rights and a distinction between constitutional statutes and ordinary legislation previously foreign

[73] Ran Hirschl, 'The Nordic Counternarrative: Democracy, Human Development, and Judicial Review Symposium: Nordic Juristocracy' (2011) 9 International Journal of Constitutional Law 449, 450–51.

[74] Joakim Nergelius, 'Judicial Review in Swedish Law—A Critical Analysis' (2009) 27 Nordisk Tidsskrift for Menneskerettigheter 142.

[75] In relation to the transformation of the Swedish constitution, Joakim Nergelius, 'The Nordic Countries and Constitutional Theory of the 21st Century' in Joakim Nergelius (ed), *Constitutionalism: New Challenges—European Law from a Nordic Perspective* (Martinus Nijhoff Publishers 2008) 150 remarks: 'I think it is fair to say that the "sub-ordination," more or less, of Swedish law to European law represents the most important constitutional change in modern Swedish constitutional history'. For a discussion of the transformation of the Danish Constitution, see Henning Koch, 'Dansk Forfatningsret i Transnational Belysning [Danish Constitutional Law from a Transnational Perspective]' (1999) 81 Juristen 213, 217–18. For a discussion of the transformation of the British Constitution, see Bogdanor (n 68); Vernon Bogdanor, *Beyond Brexit: Britain's Unprotected Constitution* (IB Tauris 2019).

[76] Rytter and Wind (n 67); Nergelius (n 74) 152.

[77] In the UK, *The Daily Mail* notoriously pronounced the judges in the *Miller* case 'enemies of the people', see James Slack, 'Enemies of the people: Fury over "out of touch" judges who have "declared war on democracy" by defying 17.4m Brexit voters and who could trigger constitutional crisis' *The Daily Mail* (London, 4 November 2016).

to the British Constitution, and introduced the idea that popular sovereignty can express itself via referenda.[78]

The transformation of the British Constitution, however, should not be understood exclusively as an incorporation of the demands of the European order. The British Constitution has, at least since the end of WWII, been understood as being in need of a fundamental reform. The need for reform, importantly, springs from an erosion of the underlying social and political foundations that sustained the old constitutional settlement.[79] Without the revolutionary conditions present to affect a fundamental constitutional change, the constitutional modernization of Britain has taken place via EU membership. EU membership has allowed the UK to undergo a constitutional modernization that has broadly brought it in line with continental constitutional regimes.

In a structurally similar manner to Milward's argument of the European rescue of the nation-state, Martin Loughlin maintains that EU membership has provided the conditions that have allowed the UK constitutional regime to modernize and thereby rescue it from its 'institutional and conceptual sclerosis'.[80] Importantly, EU membership has provided the conditions for a peace settlement in Northern Ireland by providing the conditions for its unique cross-border arrangement and helped develop its constitutional system of devolution of powers to its constituent nations.[81]

That Britain's membership in the EU has facilitated a fundamental political change to the UK Constitution went unnoticed for a long time. As argued by the UK Supreme Court in *Miller*, until the 1990s 'it is fair to say that the legal consequences of the United Kingdom's accession to the EEC were not fully appreciated by many lawyers'.[82] Beyond the legal profession, however, the constitutional significance of EU membership has only truly dawned on Britain in recent years as a consequence of the tremendous difficulties associated with trying to leave the EU (the question of the future of Northern Ireland is a significant example). An important reason for this late reckoning among the general public is, perhaps, that the constitutional transformation undergone by the continuous democracies has largely not been achieved by popular deliberation or through formal constitutional amendments: 'The debate since the 1970s has been conducted primarily amongst the elite', Vernon Bogdanor writes. 'The people have, on the whole, been little interested, and perhaps even unaware of the wide-ranging nature of the constitutional changes that have been introduced'.[83]

78 Bogdanor (n 68) 7, 27–33, 43–49; Martin Loughlin, 'The British Constitution: Thoughts on the Cause of the Present Discontents' (2018) 16 New Zealand Journal of Public and International Law.

79 Loughlin (n 78) 8; Loughlin and Tierney (n 28) 1005–06.

80 Loughlin (n 78) 5–7.

81 ibid 6, 13. See also Loughlin and Tierney (n 28) 1011.

82 *R (Miller) v Secretary of State for Exiting the European Union* [2017] UKSC 5, para 60.

83 Bogdanor (n 68) 6; Loughlin (n 78) 6.

For that reason, the UK has been able to hold on to the fiction that 'the shibboleth of parliamentary sovereignty'[84] is still alive and well. Or, rather, the idea is that Brexit will allow the UK to 'take back control' and restore parliamentary sovereignty. The constraints on the sovereignty of Parliament, following this line of argument, are purely external, the shackles of a foreign power. However, the constraints are created equally by the erosion of the underlying social and political foundations of the 'old' constitution together with the new constitutional settlement that has emerged during the UK's time as a Member State. As Loughlin puts it: 'Those who think that the main threat to parliamentary sovereignty comes from the principle of the supremacy of EU law and that after exit the doctrine's status will be restored are surely mistaken'.[85]

Membership in a federation always entails constitutional internalizations and transformation. Having undergone a fundamental political change via its membership of the EU, the implication of Brexit, therefore, is not merely that the UK leaves the Union, but also that the UK will undergo a new and radical constitutional transformation in the process of disentangling itself from the EU. Brexit has profound political consequences for the UK, beyond its future relationship to 'Europe', touching upon the relationship between the people(s) and its (or their) representatives, in general, and the relationship between government, Parliament, and the courts; devolution; and the peace process of Northern Ireland, in particular.[86] The EU, in the words of the European Union Select Committee of the House of Lords, 'has been, in effect, part of the glue holding the United Kingdom together since 1997'.[87] Brexit, in other words, is dissolving the adhesive that held together the constitutional settlement of the UK, hereunder devolution and the unique position of Northern Ireland. In this way, Brexit entails a constitutional crisis—or a constitutional moment—for the UK.

D. The 'Return to Europe'

After the fall of the Soviet Union, Central and East Central Europe underwent a radical social, political, economic, and constitutional transformation (*Chapters 4:II:C* and *4:III:B*). The adoption of new liberal democratic constitutions was a central part of this process of state transformation.[88] In a similar manner to

[84] Loughlin (n 78) 6.
[85] ibid 9.
[86] Bogdanor (n 75); Loughlin (n 78).
[87] HL 9, 2017–18, *Brexit: Devolution*, p 12 as cited by Bogdanor (n 75) 268.
[88] Anneli Albi, *EU Enlargement and the Constitutions of Central and Eastern Europe* (CUP 2005); Paul Blokker, *New Democracies in Crisis? A Comparative Constitutional Study of the Czech Republic, Hungary, Poland, Romania and Slovakia* (Routledge 2014); Wojciech Sadurski, *Rights Before Courts: A Study of Constitutional Courts in Postcommunist States of Central and Eastern Europe* (Springer 2014); Herman Schwartz, *The Struggle for Constitutional Justice in Post-Communist Europe* (University of Chicago Press

the post-fascist constitutions adopted after WWII, the new post-communist constitutions removed all references to the previous regime to mark a symbolic break with the past. Nevertheless, the constitutional imagination that emerged differs from the political and constitutional project of the post-WWII era. Communism was not understood as the internal collapse of the legal and political order—as Nazism and fascism came to be understood—but rather as something imposed by a foreign imperial power, the Soviet Union, against the will of the people. The founding myth of these post-communist states is a tale of *victimhood*, or in Milan Kundera's words, the 'abduction' of the East.[89] Communism and the communists were perceived as a 'them' and not 'us'. For that reason, the fear of the people is not the founding myth of the post-communist constitutions as it is for the 'constrained democracies'. Rather, the post-communist constitutions are expressions of a joyful return of political freedom understood in terms of national self-determination. Post-communist constitutionalism celebrates what the constrained democracies aspired to overcome, namely the nation-state and national sovereignty.[90]

The new constitutional regimes in Central and Eastern Europe attempted to (re) create the political autonomy of the state by simultaneously stressing international independence and internal self-determination as the inalienable rights of the nation.[91] The Central and Eastern European states were not keen on allowing for the possibility of the creation of a new form of imperialism by legal means and for that reason they were *fundamentally closed* to the outside world. The constitutions of Central and Eastern Europe, as a rule, did not therefore allow for the transfer of sovereign powers to European or international organizations and institutions. In order to join the EU, the Central and Eastern European countries had to amend their constitutions.[92]

Nevertheless, the process of state transformation that took place in Central and Eastern Central Europe was intimately linked to the process of becoming Member States in the EU in the first place. Membership in the EU was one of the key events to shape the emergence of the new constitutional settlements in Central and

2000); Radoslav Procházka, *Mission Accomplished: On Founding Constitutional Adjudication in Central Europe* (Central European University Press 2002).

[89] Milan Kundera, 'Un Occident kidnappé: ou la tragédie de l'Europe centrale' (1983) 27 Le Débat 3. See also Tony Judt, 'The Past Is Another Country: Myth and Memory in Post-War Europe' in Jan-Werner Müller (ed), *Memory and Power in Post-War Europe: Studies in the Presence of the Past* (CUP 2002).

[90] The post-communist constitutions, Albi (n 88) 24–25 remarks 'are distinctly more protective of sovereignty than most constitutions in Western Europe'. See also Cesary Mik, 'State Sovereignty and European Integration: Public International Law, EU Law and Constitutional Law in a Polish Context' in Neil Walker (ed), *Sovereignty in Transition* (Hart Publishing 2003) 395–96; Blokker (n 88) 52.

[91] Anneli Albi, 'Postmodern Versus Retrospective Sovereignty: Two Different Discourses in the EU and Candidate Countries?' in Neil Walker (ed), *Sovereignty in Transition* (Hart Publishing 2003).

[92] Estonia's constitution was not formally amended but 'supplemented' by an independent constitutional act, see Albi (n 88) 19, 111.

Eastern Europe.[93] The idea of 'returning to Europe' by becoming Member States in the EU was conceived of in mythical terms as the fulfilment of the true destiny of the Member States. The ideas of a 'reunification of Europe' or a 'return to Europe' provided a strong historical myth that was capable of making a bond between the future and the past by constituting the present in the image of 'homecoming'.[94] As the prominent Polish political activist and intellectual Adam Michnik put it: 'For now two roads lie open before my country and our newly freed neighbours . . . one road leads to nationalism and isolationism, the other to a return to our "native Europe."'[95] Similarly, in a speech to the European Parliament in 2009, Václav Havel stated: 'I tend to say somewhat poetically that Europe is the "homeland of our homelands."'[96]

The idea of a shared kinship and destiny of the Member States lies at the root of federalism. Etymologically, there is a direct link between the idea of *foedus* (pact, alliance) and *fides* (fidelity, faith).[97] These two aspects of federalism are united in the idea of the covenant used by the American Founding Fathers. The original biblical sense of covenant is the pact between God and man. A similar political-theological root can be found in the concept *Bund*, which was originally used by Luther to describe the alliance between the people and God. For the Anglican dissidents, some of the first immigrants to the United States, the covenant was also used to describe the contractual founding of the protestant church.[98] Here, the faithful play a decisive role in creating the community to which they already belong. When the Americans wanted to give themselves political institutions they turned to the community they knew best: the religious community.[99] The religious community can break the cycle of the constituent and constituted power[100] by virtue of being destined to create that to which it already belongs. In this way, it is capable of mediating between the past and the future by introducing a cyclical element to the federal contract. Similarly, the *federation is created by the states that are destined to belong to it*.

The idea of the 'ever-closer union of the peoples of Europe' has an element of political theology because it mimics the idea of the founding of the protestant

93 Wojciech Sadurski, *Constitutionalism and the Enlargement of Europe* (OUP 2012) xii, 148ff; Jacques Rupnik and Jan Zielonka, 'Introduction: The State of Democracy 20 Years on: Domestic and External Factors' (2013) 27 East European Politics and Societies and Cultures 11.

94 Marise Cremona, 'Introduction', *The Enlargements of the European Union* (OUP 2003) 2; Milada Anna Vachudová, *Europe Undivided: Democracy, Leverage, and Integration after Communism* (OUP 2005) 83ff.

95 Adam Michnik, *Letters from Prison and Other Essays* (University of California Press 1985) 150.

96 European Parliament Press Release: 'Václav Havel and Jerzy Buzek on the 20th anniversary of political change' (European Parliament Plenary Session, 11 November 2009).

97 Beaud (n 4) 112; Solomon Rufus Davis, *The Federal Principle: A Journey through Time in Quest of a Meaning* (University of California Press 1978) 3; Riker (n 20) 10.

98 Beaud (n 4) 113.

99 Donald S Lutz, 'From Covenant to Constitution in American Political Thought' (1980) 10 Publius 101.

100 Arendt (n 45) 175–76.

church mentioned above: the European peoples (*the faithful*) play an active role in forming the EU (*the church*) to which they already belong as peoples of Europe (*the religious community*). The process of state transformation entailed in coming together in a common union is in this way conceived as the fulfilment of destiny. For the Founding Fathers of European integration, 'Europe' was the Sorellian myth for the post-WWII era that was meant to unite the Member States and to fill the void left behind by totalitarianism.[101] Any prospective EU Member State therefore has to be a 'European state', describing not merely a region but a 'way of life' centred on common values.[102] The significance of this accession criteria lies in the mythical quality of 'Europe': *'European states' can accede to the European Union because they already belong to 'Europe'*. 'Returning to Europe' signifies the reunion of a family, the reestablishment of the 'natural order' of things, righting a wrong.

The revolutions in Central and Eastern Europe, following this logic, have been conceptualized as 'rectifying revolutions'.[103] The fall of communism, the story goes, brought the Central and Eastern European states back on the path they would have been on had they not been under Soviet rule. 'Revolution' is, as pointed out by Hannah Arendt, another concept capable of mediating between the past and the future by bringing something back to its original place in an act of 'restoration'.[104] The political myth of 'the reunification of Europe' allowed the states to imagine a return to the pre-communist era and take the path they would otherwise have taken—their true path—the path of the West: 'For many Czechs, Hungarians and Poles, this development was merely a *restoration* of the region's historical and cultural unity with the West'.[105] As depicted in the 1990 Czechoslovakian Civic Forum election poster (Figure 3.1), returning to Europe was imagined as crawling out of the abyss. The Eastern European peoples had literally fallen off the map.

III. Teleology and Specialization

A. Union Authority

The process of state transformation means that the Member States of a federation are not fully independent sovereign states. Nevertheless, sovereignty is not

[101] Milward (n 23) 333; Sorel (n 57) 20–24.

[102] Article 2 of the Consolidated version of the Treaty on European Union [2016] OJ C202/13 (hereafter TEU) reads: 'The Union is founded on the values of respect for human dignity, freedom, democracy, equality, the rule of law and respect for human rights, including the rights of persons belonging to minorities. These values are common to the Member States in a society in which pluralism, non-discrimination, tolerance, justice, solidarity and equality between women and men prevail'. This is discussed in more detail in Chapter 4:III:B.

[103] Jürgen Habermas, 'What Does Socialism Mean Today? The Rectifying Revolution and the Need for New Thinking on the Left' (1990) I/183 New Left Review 3.

[104] Arendt (n 45) 32ff.

[105] Jirí Přibáň, *Legal Symbolism: On Law, Time and European Identity* (Ashgate 2007) 94.

Figure 3.1 *Back to Europe!*, unknown artist, 600 × 850 mm, offset print. Image reproduced with the permission of the City of Prague Museum. The Museum's accompanying text to the poster reads:
'The "Back to Europe!" poster calls for a return from the totalitarian abyss back to the European society of free democratic nations. The demand for democracy, which had been emphasized so much at the rallies and demonstrations in November 1989, was also understood to mean a return to the western cultural traditions of the pre-war Czechoslovakia of TG Masaryk. Our country's post-November foreign policy was clearly aimed at strengthening European ties. The Czech Republic joined the European Union on 1 May 2004'.

'transferred' to the federation either. The Member States are not subordinated to a new federal 'super-state'.[106] They are neither dependencies nor administrative regions of the union and the foundations of Union authority are different from that of the state. The public powers of the Union are born out of the Member States coming together in a common union to obtain the common ends or goals of the federation. Union authority is therefore 'functionally' derived from the collective purposes of the Union. To understand the foundations of Union authority we have to think in terms of the *purposes* for which it was created. The aims of a federation are what limit and justify its exercise of public powers. The public powers of the federation are directed towards, and limited in relation to, the aim specific to the federation, that is, the federal *telos* (*Chapter 2:I*). Union government is therefore always *teleological*.

The constitutional significance of the teleological orientation of the federation consists in the political intent of the federal founding and it is part of the institutional and juridical architecture of the federation as a constitutional order. The states unite to obtain certain aims and they provide the institutional structure presiding over the Union with the powers to obtain those aims. For that reason, the foundation of Union authority is the constitutional aims for which the states united. There is a direct constitutional link between the *competences* and the *aims* of a federation.[107]

But does the teleological orientation of the federation make it qualitatively distinct from the state? If the state is defined by the *means* specific to it, namely the monopoly of the legitimate use of physical force,[108] this is clearly the case. The federation is characterized by a duality of public powers over the same territory and the same population. The Union can therefore be defined by its *lack of a monopoly* of the use of public power, which is another way of saying that the Union is not a new super-state. Nevertheless, the federation is more akin to the classical definition of the state that accentuates its *ends*. In its early history, the state cannot be understood as independent from its telos. In this view, the state is born out of a social contract between individuals to ensure, above all else, their mutual safety. That being said, the federation differs somewhat from this teleological definition of the state for the simple reason that the federation is not free to set its own aims or purposes.[109] In contrast to the state, the federation is not 'omni-competent'.[110] For example, the German Confederation of 1815 'in contrast to a genuine state did not possess a universality of state-ends [Staateszwecks]', Ernst Rudolf Huber writes.[111]

106 Kenneth C Wheare, *What Federal Government Is* (MacMillan 1941) 23.

107 Beaud (n 4) 274; Ernst Rudolf Huber, *Deutsche Verfassungsgeschichte seit 1789*, vol 1: Reform und Restauration 1789 bis 1830 (Verlag W Kohlhammer 1957) 597.

108 Max Weber, 'Politics as a Vocation' in Hans Heinrich Gerth and Charles Wright Mills (eds), *Max Weber: Essays in Sociology* (OUP 1946).

109 Beaud (n 4) 317.

110 ibid 348.

111 Huber (n 107) 594, my translation.

Rather it was 'limited to certain individual ends [Einzelszweck] that the federal treaty enumerated, whereby it at the same time limited the federal competences ("enumeratio, ergo limitatio")'.[112]

With regard to the EU, the public powers of the Union are born out of the constraint, not annihilation, of the Member States and the national legal orders.[113] For that reason, EU institutions have competences to act only within limited fields and it is within those fields alone that EU law enjoys supremacy over Member State law.[114] The supremacy or primacy of EU law is therefore neither absolute nor unconditional.[115] The Member States have limited their powers in order to preserve themselves politically in a common union, and therefore government by Union institutions is always directed towards this constitutional aim.

In the EU, the link between competences and the aims or objectives of the Union is made in Article 1 TEU:

> By this Treaty, the High Contracting Parties establish among themselves a European Union, hereinafter called the Union on which the Member States *confer competences to attain objectives* they have in common.[116]

In contrast to a state, it is impossible to understand the public powers of the EU independently of the Treaty aims that, at the same time, are their foundation and limitation: 'The Union shall pursue its objectives by appropriate means commensurate with the competences which are conferred upon it in the Treaties'.[117] The idea that Union authority is derived from its ends or purpose is at the heart of both Hans-Peter Ipsen's classical theory of European integration as *Zweckverbände funktioneller Integration* (a 'purpose union for functional integration')[118] and Turkuler Isiksel's more recent work on Europe's 'functional constitution'.[119] That this teleological orientation is a fundamentally *federal* characteristic, however, is not recognized by either of these scholars.[120]

[112] ibid 594.

[113] See Case C-33/67 *Dietrich Kurrer v Council of the European Communities* [1968] ECR 127, 135 stating that the Union is 'composed of States, each of which retains its own national legal order'.

[114] Robert Schütze, *European Constitutional Law* (CUP 2015) 207.

[115] Matej Avbelj, 'The Legal Viability of European Integration in the Absence of Constitutional Hierarchy' in Daniel Augenstein (ed), *'Integration through Law' Revisited: The Making of the European Polity* (Routledge 2012) 39–41.

[116] Article 1 TEU, emphasis added.

[117] Article 3(6) TEU.

[118] Hans Peter Ipsen, *Europäisches Gemeinschaftsrecht* (Mohr 1972) 196–200; Peter L Lindseth, *Power and Legitimacy Reconciling Europe and the Nation-State* (OUP 2011) 36.

[119] Turkuler Isiksel, *Europe's Functional Constitution: A Theory of Constitutionalism beyond the State* (OUP 2016).

[120] Isiksel relies on the statist conception of a federation as the federal state and argues that the EU is not a federation because its constitutional system is limited in its scope (ibid 80).

B. Union Institutions

The constitution of a federation always entails the creation of a permanent institutional apparatus, but it can consist, as a minimum, of a single institution: the federal diet (assembly, council or senate) composed of representatives of all the Member States.[121] Whereas the federation is characterized by a division of powers between the Union and the Member States, the Union institution(s) are not necessarily characterized by a separation of powers into legislative, executive, and judicial branches.[122] The federal diet can be the sole federal institution exercising a wide array of legislative, executive, and judicial powers. Nevertheless, the federal diet has to be collegial and, as such, the federal institution always entails a political balance between its Member States: it is meant to prevent the 'tyranny by the large states over the small'.[123]

The federal diet is a genuine expression of federal principles because its operational logic is neither purely interstate nor purely intrastate. As such, it differs from both a diplomatic conference and a state parliament.[124] On the one hand, the federal diet is distinct from an interstate diplomatic conference because its decisions will be immediately binding on the Member States, without further ratification.[125] On the other hand, the federal diet differs from a national government because the Member States' representatives are derived from another government; they are not elected for office but appointed by the Member State governments, parliaments, or other designated institutions.[126] The federal diet is in that sense an intergovernmental assembly. The Member States are generally equally represented irrespective of the size of their populations, reflecting the political equality of the Member States. The federal diet is therefore not based on the modern conception of political equality of citizens expressed in the idea of 'one person, one vote'. The federation is first and foremost a union of *states*.

Nevertheless, federations of democratic or republican states tend to represent not merely the states but also their peoples.[127] This double representation is ideal—typically expressed in the bicameralism of Congress in the United States, with the

[121] Beaud (n 4) 351.

[122] ibid 352.

[123] William H Riker, *Federalism: Origin, Operation, Significance* (Little, Brown and Company 1964) 88.

[124] Beaud (n 4) 353.

[125] Schmitt, *Constitutional Theory* (n 10) 401.

[126] That was the case for, for example, the Old Swiss Confederation (1291–1798) and the German Confederation (in the period 1815–1848). See Murray Forsyth, *Union of States: The Theory and Practice of Confederations* (Leicester University Press 1981) 24, 47; Emmanuel N Roussakis, *Friedrich List, the Zollverein, and the Uniting of Europe* (College of Europe 1968) 19–20. Before the ratification in 1913 of the 17th Amendment to the Constitution of the United States, US senators were elected by state legislatures rather than the people of the states.

[127] Murray Forsyth, 'Towards a New Concept of Confederation', *The Modern Concept of Confederation* (Venice Commission 1994).

House of Representatives as the 'popular chamber' and the Senate as the 'state chamber'. In the popular chamber, the size of the population of the individual states will, as a rule, be considered. Bicameralism, however, is not a necessary character trait of a federation.[128] The EU has incorporated double representation to some degree, with the European Parliament as the popular chamber representing the European citizens, and the Council of the EU as the state chamber representing the Member States' governments.[129] The Member States are, furthermore, represented by their heads of states/governments in the European Council, and the Eurozone Member States are (informally) represented by their finance ministers in the Eurogroup.

The most peculiar aspect of the EU's institutional apparatus from the perspective of the theory of the federation is the powerful role played by three 'independent' or 'counter-majoritarian' institutions: the ECJ, the ECB, and the Commission.[130] That being said, in the antebellum United States, counter-majoritarian institutions also played an important role. The ECJ, as is well known, has a predecessor in the US Supreme Court.[131] The ECB is often compared to the Federal Reserve (established in 1913); however, the attempts to establish a central bank in the United States goes back to the founding.[132] The Commission is arguably the most unique institution, but the Constitution of the United States of 1787 also constituted a non-partisan executive office that was not elected directly by the people: the Presidency. In the early republic, the Presidency was not a plebiscitary office that carried with it a mandate from the people—as we tend to think of the office today.[133] On the contrary, the Electoral College was designed by the Founding Fathers in order to avoid the rise of a 'demagogue'. It 'aimed to encourage the selection of the man with the most distinguished past service to the Republic. *Republican virtue, not populist demagogy*, was to be the principal qualification'.[134] In the early republic, the

[128] Beaud (n 4) 359.

[129] Both the European Parliament and the Council, however, are based on a compromise between the 'federal' principle of Member State equality and the 'democratic' principle of 'one person, one vote'. The European Parliament is thus based on a digressive proportional system. The Council is based on a system of weighted votes, as a constitutional default it makes decisions on qualified majority voting requiring a triple majority, namely, a majority of weighted votes, cast by a majority of the Member State that together represents a majority of the Union population, see Schütze (n 114) 156–57, 180–81.

[130] With minor exceptions, the legislative initiative is the constitutional prerogative of the European Commission (ibid 164–65). See also Giandomenico Majone, 'Federation, Confederation, and Mixed Government: A EU–US Comparison' in Anand Menon and Martin A Schain (eds), *Comparative Federalism: The European Union and the United States in Comparative Perspective* (OUP 2006).

[131] Michel Rosenfeld, 'Comparing Constitutional Review by the European Court of Justice and the U.S. Supreme Court' (2006) 4 International Journal of Constitutional Law 618.

[132] Waltraud Schelkle, *The Political Economy of Monetary Solidarity: Understanding the Euro Experiment* (OUP 2017) 91ff; Kathleen R McNamara, 'Making Money: Political Development, the Greenback, and the Euro' [2004] Working Paper PEIF-15.

[133] Ackerman (n 3) 67ff. For an account of the transformation of the Presidency in the twentieth century, see Bruce Ackerman, *The Decline and Fall of the American Republic* (Belknap Press of Harvard University Press 2010).

[134] Ackerman (n 3) 68, emphasis added.

presidential veto was not a means for the presidents to further their 'programmatic ambitions'.[135] Rather, it was used as a mechanism of constitutional defence.[136]

C. European Guardians

The foundations of the authority of the Commission, the ECJ, and the ECB can be understood based on the principles of federal government, namely, teleology and specialization. The independents are constitutionally limited teleological institutions and their independence is intimately tied to the federal telos. This means that they have neither the authority to set their own aims nor are they endowed with a set of prerogative powers. Rather, their independence consists in the duty to pursue a constitutionally specified aim without outside influence. The source of the independents' authority is not *representation* but *delegation* or *commission*: they are entrusted with the authority to do a certain task by the constitution. Their authority relies on a constitutional mandate to ensure the federal *telos*. They are 'European guardians'.

The constitutional mandate of the independents has two distinct meanings. First, it is *conservative:* the independents are there to uphold the constitutional contract between the Member States. Together with the ECJ, which ensures 'that in the interpretation and application of the Treaties the law is observed',[137] the Commission is generally understood as the 'guardian of the Treaties'.[138] The European guardians, like domestic constitutional courts, are not political institutions with arbitrary prerogative powers. On the contrary, they were created as a counter-model to parliamentary democracy.[139] The delegation of powers to independent institutions is part of the post-WWII settlement aiming at the limitation of political power of parliaments in order to secure long-term governmental stability.[140] The authority of the independents is grounded in their exteriority to 'democratic passions' and 'national egoism'.[141]

Being a guardian of the constitution, however, is not merely a conservative task looking towards the past. It is also a transformative or *creative* task. In the act of uniting, the Member States express their foundational intention of being 'resolved

[135] ibid 68.
[136] ibid 68–69.
[137] Article 19(1) TEU.
[138] The idea of the Commission as the (co-)guardian of the Treaties, though not explicitly stated, is generally based on Article 258 TFEU: 'If the Commission considers that a Member State has failed to fulfil an obligation under the Treaties, it shall deliver a reasoned opinion on the matter after giving the State concerned the opportunity to submit its observations. If the State concerned does not comply with the opinion within the period laid down by the Commission, the latter may bring the matter before the Court of Justice of the European Union.'
[139] Antoine Vauchez, *Démocratiser l'Europe* (Éditions du Seuil 2014) 34.
[140] Lindseth (n 118) 79.
[141] Vauchez (n 139) 34–35.

to continue the process of *creating* an ever-closer union among the peoples of Europe'.[142] The institutional framework of the EU, following the Treaties, 'shall aim to promote its values, advance its objectives, serve its interests, those of its citizens and those of the Member States, and ensure the consistency, effectiveness and continuity of its policies and actions'.[143] The independents are, therefore, also commissioned to look towards the future. The Member States have united for aspirational reasons in order to create a not-yet-there. The overall aims of the Union are of that nature: 'to promote peace, its values and the well-being of its peoples'.[144] In addition to their conservative mandate, the independents have a constitutional mandate to promote the objectives of the Union for the benefit of which the Member States decided to unite in the first place.

An important way of balancing the creative and conservative forces of the independents' constitutional mandate is by employing the 'idea of Europe' as a political myth, or what Joseph Weiler has characterized as Europe's 'political messianism'.[145] In this way, the European institutions assist the 'chosen' peoples of Europe in fulfilling their destiny and reaching the 'promised land' of 'peace and prosperity'. The authority of the independents relies on this European 'political messianism'. The independents do not ground their authority in the 'general will' of the peoples of Europe, Antoine Vauchez argues, but rather in 'the existence of "Europe" as an "idea", "spirit", "consciousness" or specific "project"'.[146] The independents are 'guardians' of the European project.

This 'European form of government', Vauchez argues, manifests itself in a 'judicial tradition' and in a 'bureaucratic tradition'.[147] The judicial tradition is apparent in the early case law of the ECJ. The ECJ is a constitutional guardian without any legislative power. Nevertheless, it can interpret the Treaties in a teleological manner based on their aims.[148] The case law can thus be construed not as new or original law but, rather, as a clarification of the Treaties in light of its telos, the reason for which the Member States united in the first place. In this way, the Court can mediate between the creative and conservative forces of its constitutional mandate.

The bureaucratic tradition invented is the 'Monnet method' of integration through 'de facto solidarity' and the 'spill-overs' to other fields of integration.[149] The teleological meaning of the bureaucratic tradition is best captured in the principle of implied powers.[150] The public powers of the Union are always limited *in*

[142] Preamble TEU, emphasis added.
[143] Article 13(1) TEU.
[144] Article 3 TEU.
[145] Joseph HH Weiler, 'Europe in Crisis—On "Political Messianism", "Legitimacy" and the "Rule of Law"' [2012] Singapore Journal of Legal Studies 248, 258.
[146] Vauchez (n 139) 42, my translation.
[147] ibid 42–43.
[148] Schütze (n 114) 207.
[149] Vauchez (n 139) 43.
[150] See also Case C-22/70 *Commission of the European Communities v Council of the European Communities* [1971] ECR 263.

relation to the aims of the federation, and therefore, the Member States must arguably have provided the federation with the means *necessary* to achieve those aims. The idea that the executive branch of government is intrinsically linked to the notions of rationalism, technicality, and necessity, however, is not unique to the EU. This connection lies at the origins of the modern state and the birth of government based on socio-practical experience.[151] As such, the Commission and the ECB introduce an element of reason of state[152] into the Union. As the next two chapters will show, reason of state constitutes a threat to the internal balance between the Union and the Member States because general aims can justify unlimited means.

[151] Carl Schmitt, *Dictatorship: From the Origin of the Modern Concept of Sovereignty to the Proletarian Class Struggle* (Polity Press 2014) 8–10; Michel Foucault, *Security, Territory, Population: Lectures at the Collège de France, 1977–1978* (Michel Senellart and Arnold Ira Davidson eds, Palgrave Macmillan 2007).

[152] For Schmitt's discussion of reason of state, see *Dictatorship* (n 151) ch 1. See also Foucault (n 151) lectures 9–12; Thomas Poole, *Reason of State: Law, Prerogative and Empire* (CUP 2015).

4
Balance

How can the federation strike an internal balance between its dual political existence and its dual governmental structure? This chapter is concerned with understanding the main problem that characterizes the federation as a political form: the problem of the federal balance. This chapter maintains that the federation as a political form is characterized by a fundamental internal contradiction expressed in the dual nature of the federal constitutional aim: the creation of an ever closer union between the peoples of the Member States *and* the protection of the autonomy and diversity of the Member States.

A federation is a political union constituted by its Member States because for one reason or another they have found it difficult to maintain their political existence. The raison d'être of all federations is therefore to perpetuate the political existence of their Member States. However, this is not the sole aim of the federation. By coming together in a federation, the Member States aim to constitute a *new political existence*, the Union. A federal constitution is therefore committed to create and protect the political existence of the Union as a whole. Whereas a state, if understood in terms of ends and not means, has a unified (if not unitary) *telos*—the security and wellbeing of its people—the federation has a *double telos* which is planted in it with the founding: the will to preserve the states as autonomous and the will to live together in a common union. The double federal aim means that the Union is committed simultaneously to unity and diversity, transformation and conservation, the past and the future.

In order to persist as a political form, the federation needs to strike a balance between these contradictory forces. This chapter is concerned with the *precariousness* of this balance. In recent years, this has manifested itself in the EU with the rise of authoritarian constitutionalism in Poland and Hungary seemingly breaching the foundational values of the Union. This chapter is concerned with understanding whether, how, and to what extent a federal union of states can maintain the federal balance if one of its Member States adopts a constitution that is hostile to the Union's constitution. Does the EU have the authority to intervene in the constitutional developments of its Member States in order to 'save' a Member State, and the Union at large, from the 'dangers of democratic choice'? How can the EU live up to its motto of being 'United in Diversity'?

The Constitutional Theory of the Federation and the European Union. Signe Rehling Larsen, Oxford University Press (2021).
 DOI: 10.1093/oso/9780198859260.003.0005

I. The Problem of the Federal Balance

A. The Double Telos

The double telos of the federation originates in the peculiar sentiment from which all federal constitutions are born: the wish to live together, without being one; and the wish to remain autonomous, without being fully separate from one another. The precondition for the establishment of a federation is in the words of Albert Venn Dicey:

> [T]he existence of a very peculiar sentiment among the inhabitants of the countries which it is proposed to unite. They must desire union, and must not desire unity. If there be no desire to unite, there is clearly no basis for federalism … If, on the other hand there be a desire for unity, the wish will naturally find its satisfaction, not under a federal, but under a unitary constitution … [T]he sense of common interest, or common national feeling, may be too strong to allow of that combination of union and separation which is the foundation of federalism.[1]

In the context of the EU, this 'peculiar sentiment' is perfectly captured in the constitutional aim of the Union: 'the ever closer union among the peoples of Europe'. The EU is born out of an aspiration for *an ever closer union* among the peoples of Europe, a clear expression of a desire for *union*. At the same time, this union can never become a *unity*. The constitutional aim insists that it is a union among *the peoples of Europe*. The constitutional aim of the EU is in other words a desire for union but not unity, paraphrasing Dicey. A similar interpretation of the political aim of the EU has been advanced by Joseph Weiler:

> No matter how close the Union, it is to remain a union among distinct peoples, distinct political identities, distinct political communities … The rejection by Europe of that One Nation ideal or destiny is, as indicated above, usually understood as intended to preserve the rich diversity, cultural and other, of the distinct European peoples as well as to respect their political self-determination.[2]

In Weiler's interpretation, the idea of 'the ever closer union of the peoples of Europe' comes to symbolize what he understands to be the 'unique brand of European constitutional federalism', the normative hallmark of which is 'constitutional tolerance'.[3] That is, the prevalence of Member State obedience to European law despite

[1] Albert V Dicey, *Introduction to the Study of the Law of the Constitution* (Liberty Fund 1982) 75–76.

[2] Joseph HH Weiler, 'Federalism without Constitutionalism: Europe's Sonderweg' in Kalypso Nicolaïdes and Robert Howse (eds), *The Federal Vision: Legitimacy and Levels of Governance in the United States and the European Union* (OUP 2001) 67.

[3] ibid 61–70.

the absence of a sovereign act of the people of Europe as its source of authority.[4] Contrary to what Weiler argues, however, the double telos of the EU expressed in its constitutional aim is a clear manifestation of the 'peculiar sentiment' that is at the origins of *all federations*, not just the EU. For that reason, *neither* the aim of 'an ever closer union of the peoples of Europe' *nor* the absence of a sovereign people as the source of constitutional authority is unique.[5]

In contrast to what is often argued, the United States at the time of the Constitutional Convention were not a modern nation.[6] 'Most citizens of the United States in 1790', Samuel Morison writes 'if asked their country or nation, would not have answered American but Carolinian, Virginian, Pennsylvanian, New Yorker or New Englander'.[7] Following Eric Hobsbawm:

> Early political discourse in the USA preferred to speak of 'the people', 'the union', 'the confederation', 'our common land', 'the public', 'public welfare' or 'the community' in order to avoid the centralizing and unitary implications of the term 'nation' against the rights of the federated states.[8]

The characteristics that in Weiler's view make the EU unique are shared with other federal unions of states. This is not recognized by Weiler because he relies on the flawed statist dichotomy between a federal state (*Bundesstaat*) and a confederation of states (*Staatenbund*) (*Chapter 1:I:B*).

[4] ibid 68.

[5] On the contrary, they are core constitutional principles of all federations. As Dicey (n 1) 76 puts it: 'a federal government will hardly be formed unless many of the inhabitants of the separate States feel stronger allegiance to their own State than to the federal state represented by the common government. This was certainly the case in America towards the end of the eighteenth century, and in Switzerland at the middle of the nineteenth century, in 1787 a Virginia citizen of Massachusetts felt a far stronger attachment to Virginia or to Massachusetts than to the body of the confederated States. In 1848 the citizens of Lucerne felt far keener loyalty to their Canton than to the confederacy, and the same thing, no doubt, held true in a less degree of the men of Berne or of Zurich. The sentiment therefore which creates a federal state is the prevalence throughout the citizens of more or less allied countries of two feelings which are to a certain extent inconsistent—the desire for national unity and the determination to maintain the independence of each man's separate State. The aim of federalism is to give effect as far as possible to both these sentiments'. For a further discussion, see Chapters 1:II and 3:I.

[6] Today, 'the United States' is no longer a plural noun but rather a singular noun in English: 'The United States *is* or *was*'. That the United States originally were described as a plurality, however, is clear from how they are described in the 1787 Constitution, see, eg, Article III, section 3: 'Treason against the United States, shall consist only in levying war against *them*' (emphasis added). In several other European languages, however, 'the United States' is still a plural noun (French, German, Italian, Portuguese). See Robert Schütze, *From Dual to Cooperative Federalism: The Changing Structure of European Law* (OUP 2013) 29 n 56.

[7] Samuel Eliot Morison, *The Oxford History of the United States, 1783–1917*, vol 1 (OUP 1927) 10. See also Merrill Jensen, *The Articles of Confederation: An Interpretation of the Social-Constitutional History of the American Revolution, 1774–1781* (The University of Wisconsin Press 1970) 163: 'The "nationalism" of the individual state is factor too often overlooked. It was the loyalty to one's country that moved men, whether radical or conservative, and one's country was the state in which one lived, not the thirteen more or less united states along the Atlantic Coast'.

[8] Eric Hobsbawm, *Nations and Nationalism since 1780: Programme, Myth, Reality* (CUP 1990) 18.

Notwithstanding that it has been more pronounced in the case of the EU than in other young federations,[9] the phenomenon of 'constitutional tolerance' is not unique to the EU either. Constitutional tolerance, as will be argued in this chapter, is a manifestation of how the federation governs itself when the internal tensions and contradictions pertaining to the federation as a political form can be managed. As we shall see, it is only under certain circumstances that the federation can manage internal constitutional conflicts and maintain 'constitutional tolerance'. 'Constitutional tolerance' is not an unconditional gift of federalism. The reason for this has to do with the internal contradiction or tension pertaining to the federal aim:

> Federalism is always an arrangement pointed in two contradictory directions or aimed at securing *two contradictory ends*. One end is always found in the reason why the member units do not simply consolidate themselves into one large unitary country; the other end is always found in the reason why the member units do not choose to remain simply small wholly autonomous countries ... [A]ny given federal structure is always the institutional expression of *the contradiction or tension* between the particular reasons the member units have for remaining small and autonomous but not wholly, and large and consolidated but not quite.[10]

Following Martin Diamond, the 'peculiar federal sentiment' discussed above means that the double telos of the federation is *inherently contradictory*. On the one hand, the states come together in a new common Union because they want to preserve their own political identity and autonomy; they come together in order to remain who they are.[11] The federation is for that reason always *conservative* in nature, directed towards the *past* and committed to preserving the *diversity* of its Member States.[12] This is the 'particularistic aim' of the federation in the sense that it is particular to the individual Member States of the Union, and it introduces a *centrifugal force* into the federation.[13]

On the other hand, the federation is constituted because the Member States have rejected the status quo and desire to come together into an 'ever closer union' with their future fellow Member States. The federation is for this reason always *creative* in nature, directed towards the *future* and committed to constitute and perpetuate the *unity* of its Member States. This is the 'common aim' of the federation because

[9] Leslie Goldstein, *Constituting Federal Sovereignty: The European Union in Comparative Context* (Johns Hopkins University Press 2001).

[10] Martin Diamond, 'The Ends of Federalism' (1973) 3 Publius 129, 130, emphasis added.

[11] 'In other words, in spite of the federation or rather still because of it, they want to stay themselves, that is, remain autonomous political entities', see Olivier Beaud, *Théorie de la fédération* (Presses universitaires de France 2007) 279, my translation.

[12] Christopher Hughes, *Confederacies: An Inaugural Lecture Delivered in the University of Leicester 8 November 1962* (Leicester University Press 1963) 4.

[13] Beaud (n 11) 279.

all the founding states converge around it, and it introduces a *centripetal force* into the federation.[14] The federation as a political form is therefore characterized by two political forces that haul it in opposite directions: the creation and protection of the common political Union and the conservation of the political existence and autonomy of its Member States. These contradictory political forces pertaining to the double telos are at the heart of all federations precisely because the federation is a *new political existence* ('common aim') constituted in order to perpetuate the *political existence of its Member States* ('particularistic aim').

The double telos of the federation will therefore always threaten to pull the federation apart: 'Paradoxically, the capacity of a federal system to reflect diversity constitutes a built-in weakness since it allows for conflicts to emerge and be politicized'.[15] The federation as a political form is characterized by a fundamental contradiction that it constantly needs to balance in order to preserve itself. This is what Schmitt refers to when he writes: '*The federation exists only in this existential connection and in this balance*'.[16] If this balance is not struck, the federation as a political form will tend to either fuse the Member States into a fully fledged federal state or dissolve into its composite states, or new 'sub-unions' or alliances, composed of some of the Member States. There will be a full realization of either the particularistic aim or the common aim of the federation. The logic of sovereignty will prevail either in the form of one sovereign state or several.

The federation is therefore always conditioned on an *incomplete realization* of the two core aims of the federation.[17] The aspiration of the Member States of remaining fully autonomous must be curbed because membership in a federal union imposes limits on the sovereignty of the Member States. Membership of a federation always entails the transformation from a relatively independent state to a 'Member State' (*Chapters 1:III* and *3:II*). Yet, the aspiration of an 'ever closer union' must be curbed because the powers of the Union are inherently limited. The federation does not enjoy the 'omni-competence' of a state. Its powers are always governed by the principles of specialization and teleology (*Chapter 3:III*).

If a constitutional conflict erupts between the Union and one or more of its Member States, there is ultimately no legal answer to the question of *what* constitution(s) should prevail and *who* settles that question. Or rather, there are

[14] ibid. See also Alain-G Gagnon, 'Canadian Federalism: A Working Balance' in Murray Forsyth (ed), *Federalism and Nationalism* (Leicester University Press 1989).

[15] Alain-G Gagnon, 'The Political Uses of Federalism' in Michael Burgess and Alain-G Gagnon (eds), *Comparative Federalism and Federation: Competing Traditions and Future Directions* (Harvest Wheatsheaf 1993) 18.

[16] Carl Schmitt, *Constitutional Theory* (Jeffrey Seitzer ed, Duke University Press 2008) 388, emphasis added.

[17] Beaud (n 11) 280.

two strong, viable claims based in the public law of the Union and the constitutions of the Member States respectively as ultimate sources of authority (*Chapters 1:IV* and *5:I*). This chapter is concerned with understanding the conditions, both legal and extra-legal, for the persistence of a federal balance.

B. The Political Balance

The main problem for the Founding Fathers of the United States, Hannah Arendt writes, was 'how to establish a union out of thirteen "sovereign", duly constituted republics; their task was the foundation of a "confederate republic" '.[18] The task of the Constitution, she continued, was not constitutionalism in the sense of securing a negative sphere of freedom from government but the 'erection of a system of powers that would check and balance in such a way that the power neither of the union nor its parts, the duly constituted states, would decrease or destroy one another'.[19] The core of the problem of the founders, as it is for all federations, was how to balance the political existence of the Union with the political existence of the Member States: 'Both kinds of legal-political existences must continue to survive side by side, otherwise the federation can no longer exist. The mark of the federation is therefore a precarious condition of equilibrium, a *state of uncertainty*'.[20] The only way for the federal balance between unity and diversity to persist is to ensure a political balance between the Union and its Member States.

A federal union of states is always characterized by a division of competences, or a division of powers, between the Union and its Member States. The study of the legal foundations of federal authority might therefore suggest that the danger of upsetting the balance between the constitutional orders of the Union and those of its Member States is overstated because this can be solved by 'constitutional engineering'. The federal balance can be protected by 'sound laws' setting up a clear-cut division of labour between the Union and its Member States. The powers of the Union are, after all, 'enumerated' and hence limited.[21] The division of competences between the Union and the Member States is an important aspect of federal public law, and it dominates much of the literature on federalism. Nevertheless,

[18] Hannah Arendt, *On Revolution* (Penguin 2006) 143.
[19] ibid.
[20] Christoph Schönberger, 'Die Europäische Union als Bund: Zugleich ein Beitrag zur Verabschiedung des Staatenbund-Bundesstaat-Schemas' (2004) 129 Archiv des öffentlichen Rechts 81, 105, my translation.
[21] In the EU, this is spelled out by the principle of conferral, see Article 5 of the Consolidated version of the Treaty on European Union [2016] OJ C202/13 (hereafter TEU).

in itself, a division of competences cannot protect the federal balance. As William Riker puts it: 'The division and sharing of administrative responsibilities, which is often said to be at the heart of federal arrangements, has little or nothing to do with maintaining the [federal] bargain'.[22]

The study of federations as well as the EU suggests that there tends to be a gap between the formal division of competences and the real allocation of powers between the Union and the Member States.[23] A legalistic study of a federal constitution, in other words, might not tell us much about the real balance of power between the Union and the Member States. The reason for that has to do with the origins of federal unions of states and the teleological orientation of federal authority. Federal unions of states are constituted because the Member States are incapable of securing one or more of their substantial aims: security and welfare, military defence, and economic prosperity (*Chapter 2*). The powers of the Union are constituted and limited in relation to these aims (the principles of specialization and teleology, see *Chapter 3:III*). In the context of the EU, the powers of the Union have from the very beginning been limited on a 'functional basis' in relation to the broad aims and objectives of the Treaties, importantly, the creation of the internal market. The competences of the EU have their foundation and limitation in these aims: 'As a result, the way in which the objectives of the Treaty were construed dictated the reality of the allocation of powers between the Community and its Member States'.[24] The objectives of the Treaty 'dictate' the allocation of powers. The governmental structure of the Union, thus conceived, will have the governmental authority *necessary* to obtain the aim for which it was constituted. In the Treaties, this is expressed in Article 6(4) of the TEU: 'The Union shall provide itself with the means necessary to attain its objectives and carry through its policies'.[25] This is the doctrine of 'implied powers',[26] adequately summarized in a statement by ECJ Judge Pescatore: 'the vision of objectives must be accompanied by a corresponding reality of powers'.[27]

[22] William H Riker, *Federalism: Origin, Operation, Significance* (Little, Brown and Company 1964) 135.

[23] '[I]mportant discrepancies exist between the formal allocation of powers provided in the Treaties and the actual legal practice', see Loïc Azoulai, 'Introduction: The Question of Competence' in Loïc Azoulai (ed), *The Question of Competence in the European Union* (OUP 2014) 3.

[24] ibid 6.

[25] Article 6(4) TEU.

[26] In the context of the EU, the paradigmatic case is Case C-22/70 *Commission of the European Communities v Council of the European Communities* [1971] ECR 263 (*ERTA*). For a discussion, see, eg, Azoulai (n 23) 4ff; JHH Weiler, 'The Transformation of Europe' (1991) 100 The Yale Law Journal 2403, 2415–17; Piet Eeckhout, *EU External Relations Law* (OUP 2011) ch 3.

[27] Pierre Pescatore, *The Law of Integration: Emergence of a New Phenomenon in International Relations, Based on the Experience of the European Communities* (Sijthoof 1974) 41–42.

This form of teleological government is not unique to the EU. The possibility for an expansion of the governmental powers of the Union is an inherent feature of the structure of federal government.[28] The limitation of the powers of the Union in relation to the 'common aim' means that the limited character of Union government (the principle of conferral or enumerated power) tends to be undermined by its teleological orientation. If it is deemed necessary, the Union can authorize an expansion of federal authority in order to realize the federal aims. The teleological orientation of Union government means that constitutional balance of the federation cannot be checked merely by the enumeration of powers: 'He who wills the end must also will the means'.[29]

If a real political conflict emerges between the Union and its Member States, legal limitations of power are of little value. As remarked by Loïc Azoulai: 'Confronted with real value conflicts and substantial solidarity issues, legal rules of conflict resolution like the pre-emption rule, the primacy rule, or the rules of competence laid down by the Treaties are of little use'.[30] This does not mean that legal limitations of power are unimportant. The argument is rather that, ultimately, they will not be able to protect the balance between the Union and its Member States. The early history of the United States attests to this. The question that dominated the political life in the antebellum United States was how to keep the Republic together under the 'splintering pressures' or the diverging interests of the different States. The American political establishment 'recognized that no constitutional or legalistic device could save the republic, unless the underlying real forces could be kept in equilibrium'.[31] Only power checks power, in the celebrated words of Montesquieu.[32] 'That is', Hannah Arendt added, 'without destroying it, without putting impotence in the place of power'. 'Laws', she continued, are 'always in danger of being abolished by the power of the many, and in a conflict between law and power it is seldom the law which will emerge as victor'.[33]

[28] For a history of the expansion of the powers of the federal government in the United States from the founding until today, see Gary Gerstle, *Liberty and Coercion: The Paradox of American Government from the Founding to the Present* (University Press 2018). For the expansion of federal powers in the US under the 'Commerce Clause' and a comparison with the construction of the EU internal market, see Robert Schütze, 'Limits to the Union's "Internal Market" Competence(s)' in Loïc Azoulai (ed), *The Question of Competence in the European Union* (OUP 2014).

[29] Ernst Rudolf Huber, *Deutsche Verfassungsgeschichte seit 1789*, vol 1: Reform und Restauration 1789 bis 1830 (Verlag W Kohlhammer 1957) 597, my translation.

[30] Azoulai (n 23) 15.

[31] John Fischer, 'Prerequisites of Balance' in Arthur W MacMahon (ed), *Federalism: Mature and Emergent* (Doubleday & Company 1955) 63.

[32] 'So that one cannot abuse power, power must check power by the arrangement of things', Montesquieu, *The Spirit of the Laws* (Anne M Cohler, Basia C Miller and Harold Stone eds, CUP 1989) bk XI, ch 4.

[33] Arendt (n 18) 142.

That a formal division of power was insufficient to stabilize federal government was acknowledged by Alexis de Tocqueville in *Democracy in America*. In a federation, de Tocqueville writes, a system is created that always confronts two sovereignties with each other. The legislators can make the interaction of 'these two sovereignties as simple and equal as possible and is to enclose both of them into their own carefully defined spheres of action. But he cannot meld them together into one single entity or prevent their bumping into each other at some point'.[34] Since the legislators, he continues, cannot pre-empt conflicts between the two sovereignties of any federal system, 'their efforts to divert confederated peoples from war must be supplemented with special arrangements for promoting peace'.[35] For that reason, de Tocqueville concludes 'the federal agreement cannot last long unless, in the peoples to which it applies, certain conditions of union guarantee a measure of comfort in their common life as well as smoothing out the task of government'. [36] In all federal systems, de Tocqueville argues, a system of 'sound laws' is incapable of preventing a clash between the powers of the Union and those of the states: 'Thus *the federal system not only needs sound laws to achieve success but also favourable circumstances*'.[37] Law is ultimately incapable of diverting the confederate peoples from war. Federations that only adhere to the federal 'letter of the law' like Mexico (in the 1830s) will fail, he continues, because they will be incapable of transferring the necessary 'spirit which gave it life'.[38] The federal balance necessitates not only sound laws but also a federal 'spirit' and some circumstances favourable to it. But what are they?

II. The Conditions for the Federal Balance

A. The Principle of Homogeneity

The political balance between the Union and its Member States can be maintained as long as there is *a general convergence of the wills* of all the Member States. As long as the will of one, on a fundamental level, is the same as the will of all, an existential conflict between the Union and its Member States can be repressed and the federal balance can be maintained. In this case, there is no fundamental conflict between the 'common aim' and the 'particularistic aim' of the federation. If there is a convergence of the wills of the Member States, there is little ground for an existential

34 Alexis de Tocqueville, *Democracy in America* (Penguin 2003) 192–93 [first published 1835].
35 ibid 196.
36 ibid.
37 ibid emphasis added.
38 ibid 194.

conflict between them and hence the question of sovereignty can be ignored. As long as there is a convergence of wills, who ultimately decides can remain an idle theoretical question. But under what conditions will there be a general convergence of the wills of the Member States?

Following the theory of the federation, the primary requirement for the convergence of the wills of the Member States is the persistence of a *substantial homogeneity across the Member States*. Every federation, Schmitt writes, rests on 'an essential presupposition, namely the *homogeneity of all the Member States*, that is, on a substantial similarity that lays the foundation for the conformity of the concrete mode of being [*seinsmäßige Übereinstimmung*] of the Member States and ensures that the extreme case of conflict does not occur within the federation'.[39] In other words, the condition for the coexistence of unity and diversity in the federation is that its Member States do not differ too much from one another on a fundamental level; that they converge with regard to their 'mode of being'. The federal constitution, Montesquieu wrote, 'should be composed of states of the same nature'.[40] While the 'common interest' or 'common national feeling' can be too strong for a proper foundation for federalism, so is the case that, on a fundamental level, the Member States need to be substantially similar for the federal balance to be maintained. There is, in other words, *a stark limitation to the degree of plurality that can exist in a federation*. In the context of the EU, this has been most clearly expressed by Jan-Werner Müller: 'the EU has always been about *pluralism within common political parameters*'.[41]

With regard to its tolerance of plurality, the federation lies in between the two other forms of political modernity: the empire and the state.[42] When compared with the political form of the state, both the empire and the federation are characterized by a high tolerance of diversity. The empire rules through domination and it does not need homogeneity to govern (and in many cases does not aspire to establish it).[43] The federation, in contrast, is founded on free contract and characterized by legal and political heterarchy. It therefore needs a certain degree of unity to preserve the order and stability of the Union as a whole. For that reason, the empire can tolerate more diversity than the federation. There is a general consensus regarding the necessity of a relative homogeneity between

[39] Carl Schmitt, *Verfassungslehre* (10th edn, Duncker & Humblot 2010) 376, my translation.

[40] Montesquieu (n 32) bk IX, ch 2.

[41] Jan-Werner Müller, 'Protecting the Rule of Law (and Democracy!) In the EU: The Idea of a Copenhagen Commission' in Carlos Closa and Dimitry Kochenov (eds), *Reinforcing Rule of Law Oversight in the European Union* (CUP 2016) 221, emphasis in original.

[42] Olivier Beaud, 'Federation and Empire: About a Conceptual Distinction of Political Forms' in Amnon Lev (ed), *The Federal Idea: Public Law between Governance and Political Life* (Hart Publishing 2016).

[43] ibid.

the Member States of a federation. Nevertheless, its substance remains contested. What is it that needs to be shared by the Member States in order for the federal balance to be preserved?

B. Federalism and Nationalism

Returning to *Democracy in America,* the answer given by de Tocqueville is, first, *shared material interests.*[44] States tend to federate on the basis of *necessity* because they are incapable of providing for the defence or welfare of their peoples and hence incapable of maintaining themselves politically. But in itself, this is not enough to preserve the federal balance. 'To ensure the long life of a confederation', de Tocqueville writes, 'a uniformity of civilization is no less necessary than a uniformity of needs in the diverse peoples forming it'.[45] On that basis, de Tocqueville maintained that the government of Switzerland was not 'truly federal' because of what he perceived as being a strong civilizational heterogeneity between the cantons: 'The difference between the canton of Vaud and that of Uri resembles the difference between the nineteenth and fifteenth centuries'.[46] De Tocqueville was, for a similar reason, critical of the prospects of Canada, which he understood to be 'divided into two hostile nations'.[47] The good fortune of the United States in contrast to Switzerland and Canada, in de Tocqueville's eyes, was therefore that,

> From the state of Maine to that of Georgia is a distance of some one thousand miles. However, there is less difference between the civilization of Maine and that of Georgia than between that of Normandy and that of Brittany. Consequently, Maine and Georgia, at the distant ends of a vast empire, have by nature more real opportunities to forge a confederation than Normandy and Brittany, separated only by a stream.[48]

A similar answer had been given by John Jay in Federalist 2:

> Providence has been pleased to give this one connected country, to one united people; a people descended from the same ancestors, speaking the same language,

[44] De Tocqueville (n 34) 196. See also Robert R Bowie, 'The Process of Federating Europe' in Arthur W MacMahon (ed), *Federalism: Mature and Emergent* (Doubleday & Company 1955) 493.
[45] De Tocqueville (n 34) 196–97.
[46] ibid 197.
[47] ibid 199.
[48] ibid 197.

> professing the same religion, attached to the same principles of government, very similar in their manners and customs.[49]

Under Jay's (and de Tocqueville's) idea of a community granted by 'providence', however, hides a very different historical reality. There are good reasons to be sceptical of essentialist arguments that present homogeneity as something 'natural' or 'pre-given'.

Leaving aside problematic notions of common 'ancestors' for the 'American people',[50] like the other Founding Fathers, Jay ignored the populations of non-European decent inhabiting the United States: the Native Americans and the enslaved black population. These populations were, by the founders, not considered to belong to 'We, the people'.

With the infamous three-fifths compromise,[51] the 1787 Constitution of the United States constructed the slave population explicitly as inferior human beings to the 'American people'. In concrete terms, for the representation and taxation purposes of the States, each slave counted for three-fifths of a white person. This was reinforced in the 1856 *Dred Scott* case where the Supreme Court answered in the negative the following question:

> [C]an a negro whose ancestors were imported into this country and sold as slaves become a member of the political community formed and brought into existence by the Constitution of the United States, and as such become entitled to all the rights, and privileges, and immunities, guarantied by that instrument to the citizen[?][52]

Nor were the Native American tribes considered to be part of the 'American people'. However, in contrast to the enslaved population, they were considered to be distinct

[49] *The Federalist Papers* (Lawrence Goldman ed, OUP 2008) 14–17.

[50] Looking back on the revolutionary war of 1776, John Adams saw the event as somewhat miraculous since before it, 'The colonies had grown up under constitutions of government so different, there was so great a variety of religions, they were composed of so many different nations, their customs, manners, and habits had so little resemblance, and their intercourse had been so rare, and their knowledge of each other so imperfect, that to unite them in the same principles in theory and the same system of action, was certainly a very difficult enterprise. The complete accomplishment of it, in so short a time and by such simple means, was perhaps a singular example in the history of Mankind. Thirteen clocks were made to strike together. A perfection of mechanism, which no artist had ever before effected'. See letter from John Adams to Hezekiah Niles on 13 February 1818 in John Adams, *The Works of John Adams, Second President of the United States: With a Life of the Author, Notes and Illustrations* (Charles Francis Adams ed, Little, Brown and Company 1856) <https://oll.libertyfund.org/titles/2127>.

[51] 'Representatives and direct Taxes shall be apportioned among the several States which may be included within this Union, according to their respective Numbers, which shall be determined by adding to the whole Number of free Persons, including those bound to Service for a Term of Years, and excluding Indians not taxed, *three fifths of all other Persons*' (The Constitution of the United States, Article I, Section 2, emphasis added).

[52] US Supreme Court, *Dred Scott v Sandford*, 60 U.S. 393 (1856)

political communities, independent nations, but not of equal status. In the 1831 case of the Supreme Court of the United States, *Cherokee Nation v Georgia*,[53] Native Americans were excluded from federal jurisdiction by the Supreme Court on the grounds that they were a 'domestic dependent nation' standing in a relationship to the United States resembling that of a 'ward to his guardian'.[54] The Cherokees, the Supreme Court ruled, were neither citizens of the United States nor were they entitled to be treated as a true foreign nation or state. In *Worcester v Georgia*, however, the Supreme Court maintained that the Cherokees *were* a 'sovereign nation'.[55] Nevertheless, throughout most of the history of the United States, the Native Americans were not treated as equals but rather as 'shadow nations'[56] and on numerous occasions they were forcibly removed from their territory.[57]

That the United States was constituted by white settlers only was, in other words, not down to the 'providence' of a pre-given existence of a homogenous population (in terms of culture, civilization, language, or ethnicity) on the territory of the United States but the *construction of political identity along racist lines*. This is a deeply *political project* of inclusion and exclusion. The constitution of a political community is always both *of* and *by* the community as a collective self.[58] The question of who belongs to 'the people' is a deeply political one. The homogeneity that, following Jay and de Tocqueville, constitutes the 'good fortune' of the United States, in other words, is down to a *political decision on who 'the people' is*. The emergent American nationalism of the late eighteenth and (early) nineteenth century was, in this way, relying on racism as an ideology.

The case of the United States is a neat illustration of the fact that rather than relying on a homogenous common nationality granted by 'providence', the constitution of a federation entails the *political construction of a new people*, a federal nation. That is, the federation is not constituted by the federal nation; it is the other

[53] US Supreme Court, *Cherokee Nation v Georgia*, 30 U.S. 1 (1831), Section 2.

[54] ibid.

[55] US Supreme Court, *Worcester v Georgia*, 31 U.S. 515 (1832). For a legal and political history of the status granted to Native Americans and the doctrine of 'tribal sovereignty', see Robert N Clinton, 'There Is No Federal Supremacy Clause for Indian Tribes Symposium on Cultural Sovereignty' (2002) 34 Arizona State Law Journal 113.

[56] Bruce Duthu, *Shadow Nations: Tribal Sovereignty and the Limits of Legal Pluralism* (OUP 2013). See also Stuart Banner, *How the Indians Lost Their Land: Law and Power on the Frontier* (Harvard University Press 2009) 7: 'To be sure, American law has always treated tribes as sovereigns in their own right, in the sense that tribes have always exercised powers of self-governance, powers that have fluctuated in their extent over time. But that treatment has never been inconsistent with the broader assertion of white sovereignty over Indians. White Americans routinely distinguished, for example, between "American" Indians, "British" Indians, "French" Indians, and so on, based on which nation claimed sovereignty over the territory where the Indians lived, even while Indian tribes were sovereign within their own domains'.

[57] A stark example is the so-called Trail of Tears: the forced removal of Native American Tribes from their ancestral home after the passage of the Indian Removal Act in 1830. For an historical account, see Theda Perdue and Michael D Green, *The Cherokee Nation and the Trail of Tears* (Penguin Books 2008).

[58] For a discussion of the reflexive identity of 'the people', see Hans Lindahl, 'Constituent Power and Reflexive Identity: Towards an Ontology of Collective Selfhood' in Martin Loughlin and Neil Walker (eds), *The Paradox of Constitutionalism: Constituent Power and Constitutional Form* (OUP 2008).

way around.[59] This is the strongest possible expression of the 'common aim' of the federation: 'The deepest meaning of the federal mission is to *transform the entirety of the different regions into a political community* ... all the while safeguarding the initial allegiance of the individual members with respect to the member-state[s]'.[60]

All federations are characterized by a double construction of political identity.[61] These are the 'common aim' and the 'particular aim' of the federation. The double construction of political identity is clearly visible in federal citizenship law that always consists of dual citizenship: the citizenship of the original Member States and the construction of a new common federal citizenship that, at least in young and emergent federations, is derived from Member State citizenship. Federal citizenship establishes a common *Indigenat* (*Chapter 1:III:A*): a common status that forbids the Member States to treat citizens of other Member States as 'aliens'; that is, the right to be treated equally with the 'natives' in the other Member States. As a minimum, the common status of the *Indigenat* is the content of the embryonic 'federal nationality' that is constructed by the constitution of a federation. Because of the structure of federal citizenship law, a federation is always characterized by 'dual nationality'.[62]

The question is what influence cultural heterogeneity has on this double construction of political identity? In Forsyth's view, in 'a heterogeneous federal system there will be an additional, natural, built-in limit on the nation-building capacity of the centre'.[63] Notwithstanding the probable influence of a cultural, ethnic, and linguistic heterogeneity between the Member States for the construction of a common federal political identity, its significance can easily be overstated. After all, few if any states could rely on a pre-given homogeneity for their nation-building: 'in ethnic, linguistic, or any other terms', Hobsbawm writes 'most states of any size were not homogenous and, could not simply be equated with nations'.[64] A 'nation' is not a product of 'nature'

[59] For a similar argument, see Jacques Derrida, 'Declaration of Independence' in Jacques Derrida, *Negotiations: Interventions and Interviews, 1971–2001* (Elizabeth Rottenberg tr/ed, Stanford University Press 2002). Before the representatives signed the American Declaration of Independence, 'the good people,' Derrida (ibid 49) writes does '*not* exist as an entity, the entity does not exist *before* this declaration, not *as such*. If it gives birth to itself, as free and independent subject, as possible signer, this can hold only in the act of the signature. The signature invents the signer'.

[60] Olivier Beaud, 'The Question of Nationality within a Federation: A Neglected Issue in Nationality Law' in Randall Hansen and Patrick Weil (eds), *Dual Nationality, Social Rights and Federal Citizenship in the U.S. and Europe: The Reinvention of Citizenship* (Berghahn Books 2002) 319, emphasis added.

[61] Murray Forsyth, 'The Relevance of Classical Approaches' in Joachim Jens Hesse, Vincent Wright, and Wright Hesse (eds), *Federalizing Europe? The Costs, Benefits, and Preconditions of Federal Political Systems* (OUP 1996) 35.

[62] '[A] federation features only one true form of nationality: dual nationality. By dual nationality we mean not the classic state-based notion, according to which an individual would be at the same time a national of two different countries ... but the coexistence of two nationalities that do not necessarily depend on the existence of two separate countries', Beaud (n 60) 317. For a further discussion of federal citizenship, see Chapters 1:III and 2:III:B.

[63] Forsyth (n 61) 33.

[64] Hobsbawm (n 8) 17. Later in the book (ibid 33), Hobsbawm adds: 'In any case, nobody ever denied the actual multinationality or multilinguality or multiethnicity of the older and most unquestionable nation-states, eg Britain, France and Spain'. For Hobsbawm's critique of linguistic or ethnic homogeneity as a necessary pregiven condition for the construction of nationhood, see ibid 51–67. See also Charles Tilly, *Coercion, Capital, and European States, AD 990–1990* (Blackwell 1990) 3.

and it is less dependent on 'pre-given similarity' than its ideological and political capacity to construct and enforce one: 'Nations as a natural, God-given way of classifying men ... as an inherent political destiny is a myth; nationalism, which sometimes takes pre-existing cultures and turns them into nations, sometimes invents them, and often obliterates pre-existing cultures; *that* is a reality'.[65] The political homogeneity on which a federation relies, as is the case with all political identity, is not something natural but an ideological product of history. It is not something that springs into life spontaneously. On the contrary, it is, for the most part, constructed 'from above'.[66] Nations are a product of nationalism, not the other way around.[67]

Although it is definitely the case that federalism, both in the case of federal unions and federal states,[68] is only capable of dealing with a certain degree of sub-union nationalism, this is not down to the existence of multiple heterogeneous populations but to the existence of strong *political ideologies* of Member State nationalisms. A multinational federation is preconditioned on the mutual recognition of the legitimate claim of a share of public power of all the sub-union nationalities and the development, at least to some degree, of a common federal nationality or political identity: 'When people of different nationalities are unwilling to accept these consequences, federal union cannot be made to fit their case'.[69] Federalism and extreme nationalism, be it manifest in 'nation-building at the centre and province-building at the periphery',[70] are incompatible with one another.

During the nineteenth century, a number of ethnically and linguistically heterogeneous federations and federal polities emerged, most importantly the Restored Swiss Confederation of 1815 constituted, for the first time, on the basis of the political equality of the Germanophone and Francophone Cantons.[71] The Swiss example provides proof that the 'civilization thesis' put forward by de Tocqueville is overstated. Another example is the Canadian Confederation that, however, from the perspective of this book, will have to be treated with caution because it was united under the British Crown by the Constitution Act of 1867 and not as an autonomous federation on the basis of a federal compact.[72] In the twentieth century, federalism via devolution, and hence not the political form of the federation described in this book, has been used as a way of managing strong manifestations of diversity in previously unitary states.[73] With its current twenty-four official

[65] Ernest Gellner, *Nations and Nationalism* (OUP 1983) 48–49. See also Timothy Snyder, *The Reconstruction of Nations: Poland, Ukraine, Lithuania, Belarus, 1569–1999* (Yale University Press 2003).

[66] Hobsbawm (n 8) 10.

[67] ibid.

[68] The secession of Pakistan from India is a good example, see Kenneth C Wheare, 'Federalism and the Making of Nations' in Arthur W MacMahon (ed), *Federalism: Mature and Emergent* (Doubleday & Company 1955) 30–31.

[69] ibid 30.

[70] Forsyth (n 61) 33. See also Wheare (n 68) 35.

[71] Murray Forsyth, 'Introduction' in Murray Forsyth (ed), *Federalism and Nationalism* (Leicester University Press 1989) 3; Beaud (n 42) 71.

[72] See, however, Beaud (n 11) 126.

[73] Forsyth (n 71) 4–5.

languages, the EU surpasses all previous federal unions with regard to linguistic and cultural heterogeneity and the content of its substantive homogeneity is clearly not that of a common pre-given linguistic, ethnic, or cultural homogeneity. The homogeneity of the EU is not constructed along the lines of 'ethno-nationalism'.

C. Friend and Enemy

In his writings on the constitutional theory of the federation, Schmitt argued in line with his political existentialism that the content of the substantive homogeneity was unimportant: 'There can be a national, religious, cultural, social, class, or another type of homogeneity'.[74] What mattered, in Schmitt's view, was that the *intensity of the connection* was sufficiently strong to maintain a concrete existential agreement between the Member States ensuring that that no extreme case of conflict emerged within the federation.[75] The political, in Schmitt's view, ultimately boils down to the friend–enemy distinction: a discrimination between 'us' and 'them'. Following Forsyth, in a federation a firm line is always drawn between insiders and outsiders to the community:

> At the minimum – in a union whose content is economic [an 'economic federation'] – it means a body in which systematic preference is given by insiders to insiders within an enclosed economic space. The maximum, it means a body capable of conducting war – the most intense form of the friend-enemy relation.[76]

The substantive homogeneity existing between the Member States is manifest in the justification of the new common status of 'member-statehood' that, for example, does not allow the Member States to treat the citizens of other Member States as 'aliens'. The content of the substantive homogeneity of a concrete federation, therefore, will be what is perceived to be most politically salient for the Member States. It will be something close to their political or constitutional identity. The substantive homogeneity of any given federation is therefore unique.

Schmitt considered 'national similarity' to be the dominant content around which the friend–enemy distinction was drawn. An important exception in his eyes, however, was the ideology of the Soviet Union (that, it should be noted, was federation in name only). The opening statement from the preamble of the 1924 Soviet Constitution, the Constitution of the Federation of Soviet Socialist Republics, attests to this:

> Since the foundation of the Soviet Republics, the states of the world have been divided into two camps: the camp of capitalism and the camp of socialism. There, in the

[74] Schmitt (n 16) 392.
[75] ibid.
[76] Forsyth (n 61) 37.

> camp of capitalism: national hate and inequality, colonial slavery and chauvinism, national oppression and massacres, brutalities and imperialistic wars. Here, in the camp of socialism: reciprocal confidence and peace, national liberty and equality, the pacific co-existence and fraternal collaboration of peoples ... It is only in the camp of the Soviets, only under the conditions of the dictatorship of the proletariat that has grouped around itself the majority of the people, that it has been possible to eliminate the oppressions of nationalities, to create an atmosphere of mutual confidence and to establish the basis of a free collaborations of peoples.[77]

The substantial homogeneity set out by the 1924 Constitution between the different peoples of the Soviet Union is that *they all belong to the proletariat*. Nationalism is on the basis of the 1924 constitution understood as being incapable of solving the problem of peaceful 'collaboration of peoples'. It belongs to the world of capitalism and imperialism. The Constitution of the Russian Socialist Federated Soviet Republic of 1918 is even more explicit in that citizenship is determined neither on the basis of blood nor soil but *exclusively on class*. Any foreigner living in the Soviet Republic and who belongs to the 'toiling class' is granted political rights and can obtain citizenship 'without complicated formality' (Article 20). The Soviet Republic recognizes 'the equal right of all citizens, irrespective of their racial or national connection' and further forbids any discrimination on the basis hereof (Article 22). Capitalism is the enemy in relation to whom the political identity of the Soviet Union is constructed.

This discrimination between friend and enemy is often very present in emergent federations because they are, for the most part, *defensive* in origin. In order to maintain the political autonomy of the Member States, however, a federation is never exclusively concerned with defence in a material sense. With the modern revolutions, the constitution of federations is part of the creation and solidification of a legal and political order. As constitutional projects, federations are also concerned with the protection of a certain 'way of life' and their common political identity—their political homogeneity—tends to be constructed around that constitutional project. A *common constitutional project* made manifest in a common form of government can therefore be one of the most important ways of *securing a political homogeneity* between the Member States of a federation: 'A Federation has better chances of surviving when the Member States have the same form of government'.[78]

This observation was already made by Montesquieu, who argued that 'a confederate government ought to be composed of states of the same nature, especially of the republican kind'.[79] Montesquieu favoured republicanism over monarchy

[77] The 1924 Constitution of the USSR, the Constitution of the Union of Socialist Soviet Republics reprinted in Rex A Wade, *Documents of Soviet History Volume 3: Lenin's Heirs 1923–1925* (Academic International Press 1995) 147–56.

[78] Beaud (n 42) 70.

[79] Montesquieu (n 32) bk IX, ch 2.

because he considered the spirit of the latter to be warlike and prone to enlargement by domination whereas the spirit of republicanism was that of peace and moderation.[80] For that reason, Montesquieu considered the Holy Roman Empire, a political union of monarchies and free cities, to be inferior to that of the United Provinces of the Netherlands and Switzerland.[81] But history supports neither Montesquieu's thesis of the incompatibility of the federation as a political form with the monarchical form of government of its Member States nor his thesis of the inherently peaceful nature of republican federations. The monarchical German Confederation as well as the republican federations of Switzerland and the United States had civil wars in the nineteenth century.

This does not mean that Montesquieu was wrong about the importance of homogeneity with regard to the governmental form of the Member States: 'opposing types of state principles and political outlook cannot exist together in a federalist construct'.[82] At least from the modern revolutions onwards, homogeneity with regard to the constitutional identity of the Member States provides one of the most important substantial contents for the political homogeneity of federal unions.

D. Homogeneity in the European Union

The early period of European integration is also characterized by the protection of a certain political 'way of life', not merely from the concrete territorial threat of the USSR, but also from the political ideologies of *fascism* and *communism*. These ideologies are understood as Western Europe's 'other': an internal and external threat that European integration was perceived as being key in checking. The constitutional project of the EU as an 'elite construction' belongs to the post-WWII 'constitutional ethos' of 'constrained democracy' (*Chapter 3:II:B*). An important tenet of the construction of a common political homogeneity in the EU, as was the case for the modern revolutionary federations, is around this shared constitutional project.

Formally, the EU is a 'mixed federation' of republics and constitutional monarchies. This does not mean that the EU is without a constitutional identity, but rather that it does not belong to the modern revolutionary type. The EU is neither born out of a modern republican revolution against monarchy nor a monarchical counter-revolution to republicanism. It guarantees neither the republican nor the monarchical form of government of its Member States. The question of 'constitutional monarchy' or 'republic' is not politically significant for the Union and does not in any way divide the Member States politically. It is therefore a mistake to

[80] ibid.
[81] ibid.
[82] Schmitt (n 16) 392.

think about constitutional identity in the EU on the basis of the classical forms of government (democracy, aristocracy, monarchy) or those of the modern revolutions (constitutional monarchy and republicanism).

From a formal perspective, the constitutional identity of the Union is expressed in Article 2 TEU, which has its origins in the post-WWII projects of 'constrained democracy' and 'value order constitutionalism'. Article 2 TEU states:

> The Union is founded on the values of respect for human dignity, freedom, democracy, equality, the rule of law and respect for human rights, including the rights of persons belonging to minorities. *These values are common to the Member States* in a society in which pluralism, non-discrimination, tolerance, justice, solidarity and equality between women and men prevail.[83]

That democracy, following Article 2 TEU, is understood as a substantive 'value' to be respected as part of a broader value order, and *not as a form of government* comparable to, for example, monarchy, highlights that the constitutional identity of the EU would be incomprehensible from the perspective of the modern republican revolutionary tradition. The constitution of the EU is understood as a substantive order of values.[84]

The presupposition of Article 2 TEU is that there is a relatively *homogenous constitutional identity* across the Union ('these values are common to the Member States'). Article 2 surmises that the Member States share a similar understanding of the constitution as a value order and that this value order is identical to, or at least compatible with, that of the EU. This is the very foundation of the mutual trust and mutual recognition between the Member States. As argued by the ECJ in *Associação Sindical Dos Juízes Portugueses*, the 'mutual trust between the Member States and, in particular, their courts and tribunals is based on the fundamental premise that Member States share a set of common values on which the European Union is founded, as stated in Article 2 TEU'.[85] If the constitutional identities of the Member States are not compatible with Article 2 TEU, there is an open constitutional conflict at the heart of the EU. This would spell the end of, or at least constitute a fundamental threat to, 'constitutional tolerance' and 'constitutional pluralism'. As we shall see, this may very well be the case because of the constitutional heterogeneity of the Member States that have acceded to the Union.

The most significant reason for the introduction of political heterogeneity in the case of the EU is its enlargements. The mostly Christian Democratic political elites of the founding Member States were relatively united around the same anti-fascist, and to some extent anti-communist, political and constitutional

[83] Article 2 TEU, emphasis added.

[84] For a discussion of the idea of the constitution as an order of values, see Martin Loughlin, 'The Silences of Constitutions' (2018) 16 International Journal of Constitutional Law 922.

[85] Case C-64/16 *Associação Sindical Dos Juízes Portugueses* [2018] ECLI:EU:C:2018:117, para 30. See also Case C-216/18 *PPU Minister For Justice And Equality* [2018] ECLI:EU:C:2018:586, para 35.

project of 'constrained democracy', with European integration as a focal point (*Chapter 3:II*).[86] This project that has shaped the constitutional identity of the EU, however, is not shared to the same degree by all the Member States that later acceded to the EU. The enlargement of the EU has therefore introduced a strong element of political heterogeneity. Notwithstanding that the EU prescribes a certain constitutional identity, it is not a given that *all* its Member States belong to this constitutional type, or at least experience the same intensity of relationship to it.

An argument in favour of the compatibility of the value order of the Union and the constitutional identities of the Member States can be advanced with regard to the states of the Mediterranean enlargements (Spain, Portugal, and Greece). These states adopted constitutional settlements that fit the notion of constitutionalism as a 'value order' because of their direct experience of fascism, dictatorship, or authoritarianism. They belong to the world of 'constrained democracy' or what Alexander Somek calls 'Constitutionalism 2.0' because of their experience of the breakdown of the liberal constitutional order.[87] For these states, membership of the EU has been understood as an important protection against the return of political extremism, specifically of fascism or authoritarianism. This sentiment was aptly expressed by the European Commission in 1978 in the context of the Mediterranean enlargements:

> When Greece, Portugal and Spain, newly emerging as democratic States after a long period of dictatorship, asked to be admitted to the Community, they were making a commitment which is primarily a political one. Their choice is double significant, both reflecting the concerns of these three new democracies for *their own consolidation and protection against the return of dictatorship* and constituting an act of faith in a united Europe, which demonstrates that the ideas inspiring the creation of the Community have lost none of their vigour or relevance.[88]

For these states, member-statehood of the EU has been an important way of realizing their own understanding of constitutional autonomy by protecting themselves, via membership in the EU, from the return of the main enemy of the liberal constitution: *fascist dictatorship*. For both the founding Member States and the Mediterranean enlargement Member States, the project of European unification was understood as a possibility for the realization of a new domestic constitutionalism by constraining the possibilities of democratic choice.[89] In a very concrete

[86] Gaullism proved, however, to be the very significant exception to this general pattern and led, as we saw in Chapter 2, to the collapse of the project of a European military federation in the 1950s.

[87] Alexander Somek, *The Cosmopolitan Constitution* (OUP 2014) ch 2.

[88] European Commission, 'General Considerations on the Problems of Enlargement'. Communication sent by the Commission to the Council on 20 April 1978 (COM (78) 120 final. Bulletin of the European Communities, Supplement 1/78) 6 emphasis added.

[89] The transition from authoritarianism to liberal democracy after the Franco regime was closely linked to the accession to the EEC, see Cristina Blanco Sío-López, 'Reconditioning the "Return to Europe": The Influence of Spanish Accession in Shaping the EU's Eastern Enlargement Process' [2018] The Crisis of EU Enlargement - LSE IDEAS Special Report 26; Cristina Blanco Sío-López, 'Transitional

sense, it is a part of their own domestic constitutional settlements.[90] There is accordingly a strong affinity between the identity of the European project and the constitutional project of those Member States. For that reason, the Commission continues, 'The three countries have entrusted the Community with a political responsibility which it cannot refuse, except at the price of denying the principles in which it is itself grounded'.[91]

This shared understanding of constitutionalism, however, is much less prevalent in both the 'continuous democracies' of Scandinavia and the UK and the 'new democracies' in the Central and Eastern European states of the eastern enlargements. These Member States tend to have a much stronger 'sovereigntist' understanding of their constitutions. In the constitutional self-understanding of the 'continuous democracies', the constitution is a 'framework for regulating political conflicts'[92] and not a substantive order of values. The constitutional imagination of these states belongs in many ways to the pre-WWII world. Their constitutional orders are not based on a fear of internal collapse into fascism and for that reason the idea of granting a substantive value order the status of 'super-legality' has not become part of their constitutional imagination. Rather, democracy is still envisioned, as it was in the pre-WWII constitutional imagination, as a *parliamentary government*.

The idea of 'constrained democracy', however, did not have a strong resonance for the acceding Central and Eastern European states either. In some ways this is surprising, taking into account their own experience of authoritarian rule and the central role of EU membership to their constitutional reform process.[93] A process that, as had been the case of the Mediterranean states, was understood as an important part of national renewal and the achievement of the countries' 'true destiny', allowing their 'return to Europe' (*Chapter 3:II:D*). Nevertheless, there is an

Margins to Re-Join the West Spain's Dual Strategy of Democratisation and Europeanisation' in Laurien Crump and Susanna Erlandsson (eds), *Margins for Manoeuvre in Cold War Europe The Influence of Smaller Powers* (Routledge 2019). In connection to Greece's application of membership in the EEC, the Greek Prime Minister, Constantinos Karamalis, said: 'Greece belongs to Europe and desires to belong to Europe ... Greece does not desire full membership solely on economic grounds, the reasons are mainly political and refer to the consolidation of democracy and the future of the nation', see Eirini Karamouzi, 'A Strategy for Greece: Democratization and European Integration, 1974–1975' [2015] Cahiers de la Méditerranée 11, 11.

[90] Jürgen Habermas, 'Why Europe Needs a Constitution' (2001) 11 New Left Review 21, therefore, speaks for these states when he writes: 'What forms the common core of a European identity is the character of the painful learning process it has gone through, as much as its results. It is the lasting memory of nationalist excess and moral abyss that lends to our present commitments the quality of a peculiar achievement. This historical background should ease the transition to a post-national democracy based on the mutual recognition of the differences between strong and proud national cultures'.

[91] European Commission, 'General Considerations on the Problems of Enlargement' (n 88) emphasis added.

[92] Loughlin (n 84) 928. For a discussion of the constitutional imagination of the 'evolutionary democracies', see Chapter 3:II:C.

[93] Jirí Přibáň, *Legal Symbolism: On Law, Time and European Identity* (Ashgate 2007); Wojciech Sadurski, *Constitutionalism and the Enlargement of Europe* (OUP 2012).

important difference between the constitutional imagination of the post-fascist and the post-communist states. In contrast to the post-fascist constitutions, the post-communist constitutions were not understood as born out of the internal legal and political collapse of the state but out of the collapse of the Soviet Union. The 'enemy of the constitution' for the Central and Eastern European states was represented by an *external imperial foe* (the *Soviet Union* and *communism* as an ideology), not as an 'enemy within'.

Many, if not most, of the Central and Eastern European countries gave themselves constitutions with a strong accentuation of national sovereignty after the fall of the Soviet Union.[94] For these countries, in contrast to the post-fascist countries, sovereignty and nationalism were not perceived as being threats to democracy but, on the contrary, vehicles for it. The necessary limitation of sovereignty entailed in EU membership, therefore, was not always met with great enthusiasm. At times it was even understood as a new form of foreign dominance ('We have just got rid of Moscow's domination and are about to subject ourselves to domination by Brussels' was the slogan of some anti-EU political movements[95]). This may partly explain why the constitutions of these countries, despite the use of Europe as a myth, are less 'open to European law'. In the Polish Constitutional Tribunal's accession ruling, the Court flatly rejected the notion of supranationality entirely; 'the Tribunal's reasoning was based on fears of losing sovereignty, or not retaining enough of it'.[96]

The accession to the EU was therefore for the Central and Eastern European states characterized by the paradox that accession was understood as a key factor in the consolidation of their newly won democratic freedoms, yet their constitutional regimes relied on a strong emphasis on nationalism and sovereignty incompatible with the constitutional order of the Union they were acceding to: 'the EU is thus perceived both as a source of the *promotion* of democracy and as a *threat* to democracy'.[97]

E. The Government of Homogeneity and Heterogeneity

Enlargement of a federation is a clear (but not the only) example of why the initial shared material interests and sense of a common enemy is insufficient for the

[94] Sadurski (n 93) 71–74. See also András Sájo, 'Becoming "Europeans": The Impact of EU "Constitutionalism" on Post-Communist Pre-Modernity' in Wojciech Sadurski, Martin Krygier, and Adam Czarnota (eds), *Spreading Democracy and Rule of Law? The Impact of EU Enlargement on Rule of Law, Democracy and Constitutionalism in Post-Communist Legal Orders* (Springer 2006) 178–79.

[95] Sadurski (n 93) 67. See also Tony Judt, 'The Past Is Another Country: Myth and Memory in Post-War Europe' in Jan-Werner Müller (ed), *Memory and Power in Post-War Europe: Studies in the Presence of the Past* (CUP 2002) 177.

[96] Sadurski (n 93) 121.

[97] ibid 103.

long-term stability and survival of a federal union. A political homogeneity consisting in a common threat and common material interests changes with the political winds and fortunes of its Member States and is therefore highly *volatile*. In contrast to districts or provinces of a state, the Member States of a federation retain their political autonomy and hence their right to decide on their own fate. This means that they constantly have the potential to develop in opposite directions and give themselves constitutions that are incompatible with the political homogeneity of the federation. If the federation is to maintain its internal balance, it will need to find a more stable and permanent solution to deal with the political, social, and constitutional changes of its Member States beyond the fortuitous existence of a common enemy and shared interests in providing a political homogeneity.

The federation therefore needs to foster and protect the content of the substantial homogeneity of its Member States if the federation is to survive. The content of the political homogeneity of the Member States of any given federation is ultimately an extra-legal question, but the *government* of the homogeneity of the Member States is a question of federal public law. The Union employs a variety of laws and measures in order to protect what it understands to be the politically salient substantial homogeneity of its Member States.

The rest of this chapter examines two of the most important tools for the government of political homogeneity and heterogeneity in the federation: the government of the states acceding to a federation (section III) and provisions relating to the government of the constitutional identity or form of government of the Member States (section IV). These governmental tools are important because the federation manages its internal constitutional contradictions by securing the unity of its Member States with regard to their fundamental substantial homogeneity. That being said, this exercise of public powers presents a new conundrum for the federation that will be discussed throughout the rest of the book: how does the federation ensure a continuous political homogeneity of its Member States without destroying their political autonomy? The government of federal homogeneity and heterogeneity, in other words, risks reproducing the problem it was indirectly meant to solve, the problem of the federal balance, by eroding the political autonomy of its Member States.

III. Admission of New Member States

A. The Government of Accession

An important way for a federation to protect the federal balance is to make sure that no state with a 'different nature' from the existing Member States (in the eyes of the Union) is allowed to accede to the federation. One way of protecting the federal balance is simply not to allow for any new Member States. Switzerland is often portrayed as an example of such a 'closed' or 'restricted' federation that has been extremely cautious with regard to the admission of new Member States, even those understood to be of a 'similar nature'. After the collapse of the Austro-Hungarian Empire with WWI, Vorarlberg attempted to leave Austria for Switzerland. Despite the people of Voralberg voting 80 per cent in favour of acceding to Switzerland in the 1919 referendum, and despite public support in Switzerland for their membership, the government of Switzerland let the Allies decide the question in the Treaty of Saint-Germain-en-Laye (which they did in favour of Austria).[98] Because of its commitment to neutrality and its internal balance between the Germanophone and Francophone communities, the Swiss government withheld any opinion in order not to jeopardize either their internal balance or their relationship with Austria, which could have endangered their continued neutrality: 'The Swiss federation, a small state surrounded by powerful neighbours, found it therefore wiser to refuse to admit any new State to safeguard its external security and its internal cultural balance'.[99]

Federations are not necessarily expansive in nature. In contrast to the United States, both Switzerland (pre-1848) and the German Confederation have been relatively restricted federations. Nevertheless, they have both had to deal with the problem of admitting new Member States. Switzerland has not admitted any new Member States since the full and equal inclusion of the francophone cantons (Neuchâtel, Geneva, and Valais) in 1815. From its foundation in 1291, however, it has grown from its original three (Uri, Schwytz, and Unterwalden) to twenty-two cantons.[100] The German Confederation was also a relatively closed federation. This is manifest in one of its founding treaties, which states that the federation is 'restricted to the states currently participating' and only allows for the admission of new Member States 'when the entirety of the Confederal membership finds such to be compatible with existing circumstances and appropriate to the advantage of the whole'.[101] Nevertheless, in 1820 it allowed for the inclusion of five new Member States.

[98] George Cavallar, 'Eye-Deep in Hell: Heinrich Lammasch, the Confederation of Neutral States, and Austrian Neutrality, 1899–1920' in Rebecka Lettevall, Geert Somsen, and Sven Widmalm (eds), *Neutrality in Twentieth-Century Europe Intersections of Science, Culture, and Politics after the First World War* (Routledge 2012).

[99] Carl J Friedrich, 'Admission of New States, Territorial Adjustment, and Secession' in Carl J Friedrich and Robert R Bowie (eds), *Studies in Federalism* (Boston and Toronto, Little, Brown and Company 1954) 761. The 1820 Missouri compromise in the United States is another example where the admission of new states had the potential to upset the internal federal balance. This political compromise involved the federal balance in the United States between slave states and non-slave states in relation to the expansion of the United States. Missouri (slave state) was only allowed to accede to the Union if Maine (non-slave state) was allowed to accede as well. For a history of the Missouri compromise, see Robert Pierce Forbes, *The Missouri Compromise and Its Aftermath: Slavery & the Meaning of America* (University of North Carolina Press 2007).

[100] Beaud (n 11) 234–35.

[101] Final Act of the Congress of Vienna (*Wiener Schlussakte*) (15 May 1820), Article 6 <http://germanhistorydocs.ghi-dc.org/pdf/eng/1_C_NS4_Vienna%20Final%20Act.pdf> accessed 27 October 2017.

The European Economic Community (EEC)/EU was from the very beginning conceived of as an *expansive* union that was meant to 'unite Europe'; not merely the Original Six. In the Preamble to the Treaty of Rome, the founding Member States are 'calling upon the other peoples of Europe who share their ideal to join in their efforts'. In a 2002 speech on the enlargements of the Union, the then President of the European Commission, Romano Prodi, reaffirmed this view:

> we have restored the historical unity of the peoples of Europe. Our common destiny is once again to build a common future. A future built on shared fundamental values: those of peace, democracy, the rule of law, human rights and the protection of minorities ... [the] enlargement is not just about economics. It is important primarily for political and ethical reasons. Enlargement is the fulfilment of the European project. This project has given us half a century of peace and prosperity, and it should be extended to the whole continent.[102]

Together with the EU—which, true to its original aim, has more than quadrupled over the years—the United States is the most expansive federation. Nevertheless, only two of the states that acceded to the Union, Vermont (1791) and Texas (1845), were independent states at the time of accession. The majority of the states admitted gained their statehood through the United States' expansion into the western territories. The westward expansion of the United States was governed by a number of laws (importantly the Land Ordinances of 1784 and 1785 and the Northwest Ordinances of 1787 and 1789), stipulating the conditions under which the western territories would be included into the United States 'on equal footing' with the original thirteen states.[103]

These territories were ceded to the United States from some of its Member States, occupied by American settlers or acquired from other colonial empires or Indian Tribes, with more or less force. What they had in common was that they were not yet states.[104] An important part of the aforementioned laws is therefore

[102] Speech by Romano Prodi, President of the European Commission: 'Enlargement—the final lap' (European Parliament Brussels, 9 October 2002).

[103] For a history of the territorial expansion of the United States, see Adam D Burns, *American Imperialism: The Territorial Expansion of the United States, 1783–2013* (University Press 2017). See also Gerstle (n 28) ch 1. For a constitutional analysis of the American history of territorial expansion, see Gary Lawson and Guy Seidman, *The Constitution of Empire: Territorial Expansion and American Legal History* (Yale University Press 2004). For an introduction to the Northwest Ordinance, see Peter S Onuf, *Statehood and Union: A History of the Northwest Ordinance* (Indiana University Press 1987).

[104] This does not mean that the western territories of the United States were 'virgin land'. First and foremost, there were the Native Americans who were removed from their lands to make way for the settlers, with more or less extortion (Banner (n 56) 4). But even where that was not the case, the state-building did not commence *ex nihilo* but had to deal with an already unruly situation and territorial disputes, see Burns (n 103) chs 1–2; George Van Cleve, *We Have Not a Government: The Articles of Confederation and the Road to the Constitution* (University of Chicago Press 2017) ch 5. The idea of 'virgin land', however, became an important myth for American state-building and the construction of cultural identity; see Henry Nash Smith, *Virgin Land the American West as Symbol and Myth* (Harvard University Press 1970).

concerned with state-building measures, such as procedures for the basic spatial organization of the territories that would make them governable.[105] This entailed the geographical division of land into states and townships, a standardized system for the acquisition of settler land, documentation of natural resources, and the share of Congress in these resources, such as precious metals.[106] Moreover, on entering into the Union, the new Member States were to be liable for parts of the debt of the United States.[107] The question of governability was crucial on a political level because the westward expansion was controversial at the time ('many easterners feared that it would lead to the depopulation and impoverishment of their states and to the weakening of the union'[108]). A federation always entails the mutualization of risk and it therefore needs to make sure that acceding Member States are governable. The Land Ordinances and the Northwest Ordinances are moreover concerned with the *form* of government of the new states. Importantly, the new states needed to give themselves constitutional forms of governments, specifically, a republican form of government. The westward expansion of the United States, in this way, entailed a process of state-building.

The EU, being situated in the middle of the Old World, is presented with a qualitatively different problem than that of the United States. The United States was faced with the problem that the territories were not yet states, whereas the EU is faced with the problem of how to make sure that the state apparatuses, constitutional regimes, and societal models *already present* in the acceding states, whether fragile or consolidated, new or old, do not become a threat to the Union as a whole. Being situated in the Old World, the potential Member States of the EU have all had long histories and political, cultural, and societal norms of their own. This is clearly shown in the fact that six of the Member States that have acceded to the EU—the UK, Ireland, Austria, Finland, and the Scandinavian states—were consolidated states with stable constitutional regimes of their own at the time of accession.

Notwithstanding the long histories and very diverse societies of the rest of the states that have joined the EU, they have an interesting commonality with the expansion of the United States into the western territories. For all these states, accession to the EU has been tied to a political, societal, and constitutional 'rebirth of the state' after the collapse of either an authoritarian/fascist regime (Greece, Spain, and Portugal) or the collapse of communism that led to independence for some states (Poland, Hungary, Bulgaria, and Romania) and statehood for others (the Baltic states, Czech Republic, Slovakia, and Slovenia). In all these cases, the

[105] See James C Scott, *Seeing like a State: How Certain Schemes to Improve the Human Condition Have Failed* (Yale University Press 1998) 49–51. See also Burns (n 103) 12ff.

[106] The 'Land Ordinance of 1784', see the Library of Congress's Collection of 'Documents from the Continental Congress and the Constitutional Convention, 1774 to 1789'.

[107] 'An Ordinance for the Government of the Territory of the United States North-West of the River Ohio, the Northwest Ordinance was passed on July 13, 1787' (the 'Northwest Ordinance 1787'); the Land Ordinance of 1784 (n 105).

[108] Onuf (n 103) xv.

states had to be radically rebuilt politically, culturally, socially, and economically. Because of the long histories of these states and regions, the EU has nonetheless been confronted with the need to govern an unprecedented amount of plurality. As has been noted by Bruce Ackerman, a distinctive feature of the EU differentiating it from 'other great federations—most notably the United States' is that the Member States of the EU have approached the EU along different constitutional paths.[109] The *constitutional* diversity of the EU is much more pronounced than in any previous federation.

The EU has attempted to protect its constitutional homogeneity when admitting new Member States through the establishment of a set of provisions that the acceding states should adhere to if they are to be admitted: accession criteria. The accession criteria, as we saw in the case of the westward expansion of the United States, allow for extensive government of the acceding states. They allow the Union to pre-emptively 'engineer' new Member States that are substantially homogeneous with its existing Member States with regard to what it perceives to be most politically salient.

In contrast to what Jan Zielonka has argued in the context of the eastern enlargements, accession processes are *not imperial* because the new Member States accede on the basis of their own initiative, on free contract, and the acceding states are promised to become politically equal partners (*Chapter 1:II:B*).[110] To be sure, this does not mean that accession conditionality is not a means for the federation to extend its power and authority and gain influence over the acceding states. On the contrary, the accession process is a very effective foreign-policy instrument of the Union that allows it to influence the domestic and foreign policy of the applicant state.[111] As the accession of the post-communist states to the EU bears witness to, accession conditionality can be equally as intrusive for the political and constitutional structures of the acceding states as for states under imperial dominance. For the period of the accession, the acceding state is *de facto* if not *de jure* a kind of dependency of the Union, albeit on a voluntary basis and with the promise of political equality post-accession.

Notwithstanding that Zielonka's analysis of the EU as empire from a public law perspective is incorrect, he is nonetheless right with regard to the power and authority of the Union over the acceding states. The eastern enlargements were without a doubt a means for the Union to exercise political as well as economic control over its eastern neighbours after the fall of communism.[112] That being

[109] Bruce Ackerman, 'Three Paths to Constitutionalism—and the Crisis of the European Union' (2015) 45 British Journal of Political Science 705, 712.

[110] Jan Zielonka, *Europe as Empire: The Nature of the Enlarged European Union* (OUP 2006) 44–59.

[111] Karen E Smith, 'The Evolution and Application of EU Membership Conditionality' in Marise Cremona (ed), *The Enlargement of the European Union* (OUP 2003) 108; Milada Anna Vachudová, *Europe Undivided: Democracy, Leverage, and Integration after Communism* (OUP 2005).

[112] Zielonka (n 110) 44–45.

said, in contrast to imperialism, federalism allows for the creation of a concrete economic order established not on land-grabbing but on mutual promises and pledges. Despite the intrusiveness of accession conditionality, an accession process to a federation is a voluntary expansion of the federal union and market.

B. The Copenhagen Criteria

The EU accession criteria are of great interest because they are a manifestation of what the EU perceives to be the most important, substantial character traits pertaining to its Member States. They are in this way an important source for understanding the EU's 'constitutional identity'. In concrete terms, there will of course always be discrepancies between the criteria for the acceding states and the 'reality' of the old Member States. The accession criteria are therefore, in precise terms, a source for understanding the *ideology* of a federation. In the context of the United States, it was thus an important debate whether the newly admitted states were to allow for slavery or not.[113] It is not only about what the Union *is* but just as importantly what it understands itself destined to *become*.

Accession to the EU is governed by Article 49 TEU, which tells us that 'Any European State which respects the values referred to in Article 2 and is committed to promoting them may apply to become a member of the Union'. The criterion of being a 'European state' is not legally specified. Since there are no clear geographical, historical or cultural borders to Europe, it is a *political question* for the Union and its Member States to define, at their discretion, what they perceive as the borders of Europe and what constitutes a 'European State'.[114] Such criteria are therefore subject to geopolitical shifts and power relations between the Member States. After the fall of the Soviet Union, several countries belonging to the former Soviet Union or the Eastern bloc were thus permitted to 'return to Europe'. Turkey, on the other hand, has been unable to join despite submitting its formal application for membership three decades ago.

In order to be considered for membership in the Union, the 'European' state in question has to respect, and be committed to promote, the foundational values of the Union (as defined by Article 2 TEU). In the lead up to the eastern enlargement, the accession requirements were further developed and specified in the Copenhagen criteria, laid down by the European Council in Copenhagen in 1993:

> Membership requires that the candidate country has achieved stability of institutions guaranteeing democracy, the rule of law, human rights, respect for and

[113] Friedrich (n 99) 758.

[114] Dimitry Kochenov, *EU Enlargement and the Failure of Constitutionality: Pre-Accession Conditionality in the Fields of Democracy and the Rule of Law* (Kluwer Law International 2008) 15, 27ff.

> protection of minorities, the existence of a functioning market economy as well as the capacity to cope with competitive pressure and market forces within the Union. Membership presupposes the candidate's ability to take on the obligations of membership including adherence to the aims of political, economic and monetary union.[115]

The Copenhagen criteria can be broken down into three separate requirements. First, a 'functional' requirement regarding the candidate country's capacity to take on the obligations of Union membership. Another 'functional' requirement was added in Madrid in December 1995, regarding the candidate country's administrative and legislative capability to transpose and implement EU directives in a secure and sufficient manner. These requirements, stating that the Member State has to be capable of being a functional and law-observing member of the Union, aim to make the new Member States *governable* (like the Northwest and Land Ordinances of the United States). Paraphrasing James Scott, it makes the new Member States 'visible' to the Union; it makes them apprehensible in the eyes of an outsider.[116] This allows the EU institutions to evaluate and measure the exercise of governmental power by the new Member States. A federation is always based on a mutualization of risk and it can therefore not admit an ungovernable state into the Union.

The two other requirements are 'substantial requirements' regarding the implementation of a *concrete political and economic order*. The candidate country is required to maintain (and create) stable institutions capable of protecting the liberal-democratic political order: democracy, rule of law, human rights, and the protection of minorities. Moreover, the candidate country is required to implement and sustain a functioning market economy capable of coping with the competitive pressure and the market forces of the Union. One of the strongest criteria for a substantial homogeneity demanded and monitored by the Union for any state acceding to the Union is a requirement related to the Economic and Monetary Union (EMU). All states acceding to the EU commit themselves to adopt the euro as their legal tender. In order to do this, they will need to align their economies in accordance with the convergence criteria, which further insure a substantial homogeneity between the Member States of the Eurozone.[117] The convergence criteria require the Member States 'with a derogation'[118] to achieve a high degree of price stability, sustainable government finances, exchange-rate stability, and stability of long-term interest rates. The purpose of the convergence criteria is that the acceding Member States to the euro do not endanger its primary objective: price stability.[119]

[115] European Council in Copenhagen, 21–22 June 1993. Conclusion of the Presidency.

[116] Scott (n 105).

[117] Article 140 of the Consolidated version of the Treaty on the Functioning of the European Union [2016] OJ C202/47 (hereafter TFEU).

[118] Article 139(1) TFEU.

[119] Article 127 TFEU.

The Copenhagen criteria thus highlight the centrality of the protection by the Union of a constitutional homogeneity with regard to the 'economic constitutions' of its Member States. The economic order protected by the Union as part of the constitutional homogeneity of its Member States, however, is not identical over time. While the immediate post-WWII period of the 'trentes glorieuses' was characterized by different forms of 'embedded liberalism' aimed at market correction, protecting domestic welfare states and allowing for the development of different 'varieties of capitalism',[120] the collapse of the Soviet Union arguably signals a watershed in the development of Europe's economic constitutionalism. With the end of the Cold War, which signalled the global victory of American capitalism, European political economy and Europe itself began to acquire a new identity with the constitutionalization of the EMU—based on a 'substantive value order' influenced by ordoliberalism and neoliberalism—emphasizing, above all else, price stability.[121] Following this view, low inflation was not merely a desirable economic outcome but rather 'the essential pre-condition for general economic and political well-being. Without it the very fabric of the social structure was threatened'.[122]

However, if the constitutional identity protected by the EU is understood as including a specific economic order and a set of economic prescriptions, another problem of constitutional heterogeneity has to be raised, namely, that in the constitutional settlements of various Member States of the EU very different relationships between state and society and different economic models persist.[123] The most profound example is the difference between the economic and societal models for the countries of the eastern enlargements before and after the post-communist transition. The transformation of the former communist countries from centrally planned economies to market economies is one of the most radical state transformations imaginable.[124] As one scholar remarked:

[120] David Soskice and Peter Hall, *Varieties of Capitalism: The Institutional Foundations of Comparative Advantage* (OUP 2001).

[121] Wolfgang Streeck, *Buying Time: The Delayed Crisis of Democratic Capitalism* (Verso 2014); Étienne Balibar, 'The Rise and Fall of the European Union: Temporalities and Teleologies' (2014) 21 Constellations; Michael A Wilkinson, 'The Reconstitution of Post-War Europe: Liberal Excesses, Democratic Deficiencies' in Michael W Dowdle and Michael A Wilkinson (eds), *Constitutionalism beyond Liberalism* (CUP 2017).

[122] David McKay, *Federalism and European Union: A Political Economy Perspective* (OUP 1999) 101.

[123] Fritz W Scharpf, 'The Asymmetry of European Integration, or Why the EU Cannot Be a "Social Market Economy"' (2010) 8 Socio-Economic Review 211; Martin Höpner and Armin Schäfer, 'Integration Among Unequals: How the Heterogeneity of European Varieties of Capitalism Shapes the Social and Democratic Potential of the EU' (2012) 12 Max Planck Institute for the Study of Societies Working Paper.

[124] According to some scholars, the post-communist countries that have acceded to the EU are not the only Member States that have been required to substantially transform central aspects of their identity in order to conform to the economic constitution of the EU. Following Fritz Scharpf (ibid), the constitutionalization of the economy in the EU and the wide-ranging teleological interpretations of its main principles by the ECJ has led to an asymmetric dynamic of European integration because its liberalizing and deregulatory impact on the socio-economic regimes of the Member States is much stronger for the Continental and Scandinavian social market economies than the liberal market economies. See also, Fritz W Scharpf, 'Democratic Legitimacy Under Conditions of Regulatory Competition: Why

> The closest parallel to the disruption that the countries of formerly communist Europe are bringing on themselves is with natural or man-made disasters: floods, earthquakes, famines, or wars. But even those parallels understate the enormity of social dislocation that economic transition is bound to cause. It is an easier matter to repair physical damage, even if it is extensive, than to change the beliefs, the habits, and the skills of an entire population.[125]

The post-communist transition called for nothing less than an 'existential revolution': the introduction of a complete and comprehensive new societal 'way of life' and a complete 'liberation' from the past.[126] Notwithstanding that post-communist transition was not entirely tied to the process of accession to the Union, it was without a doubt one of the key events, if not *the* key event, to shape the new constitutional regimes that emerged post-1989.[127] The countries of Central and Eastern Europe provide the example where conformity with the Maastricht 'economic order', as laid out in the Copenhagen criteria, has entailed the most radical state transformation. In the words of Zielonka: 'before 1989 crossing the East-West divide was like entering a totally alien, if not hostile empire, with different laws, economy, education, ideology and culture'.[128]

The government of the accession to the EU has been a way for the EU to stay true to its founding mission of uniting Europe without allowing states of 'different nature' into the Union. By way of the accession criteria, especially the Copenhagen criteria used in the case of the eastern enlargements, the EU has 'engineered' the new Member States in what it perceives to be its own image. From a formal perspective, the radical state transformation associated with accession is not a danger to the autonomy and diversity of the acceding states because they undergo this transformation before they become Member States. The radical state transformation this has necessitated has been done pre-emptively, to ensure that the federal balance of the EU was not endangered by the admission of the new Member States.

Nevertheless, the problem is that the radical state transformation the Central and Eastern European states had to undergo to become Member States of the EU has not necessarily been genuinely internalized. The general scholarly view is that the post-communist Member States were adept at building democratic institutions

Europe Differs from the United States' in Kalypso Nicolaïdes and Robert Howse (eds), *The Federal Vision: Legitimacy and Levels of Governance in the United States and the European Union* (OUP 2001).

125 Michael Mandelbraum, 'Introduction' in Michael Mandelbaum and Shafiqul Islam (eds), *Making Markets: Economic Transformation in Eastern Europe and the Post-Soviet States* (Council on Foreign Relations Press 1993) 1–2.

126 Jan Komárek, 'Waiting for the Existential Revolution in Europe' (2014) 12 International Journal of Constitutional Law 190, 208.

127 Sadurski (n 93) xxi, 148ff; Jacques Rupnik and Jan Zielonka, 'Introduction: The State of Democracy 20 Years on: Domestic and External Factors' (2013) 27 East European Politics and Societies and Cultures 11.

128 Zielonka (n 110) 23.

but not necessarily democratic culture. They created a 'democracy without democrats'.[129] If it is not properly internalized, the demands of EU member-statehood are likely to be experienced as a 'foreign' or even 'imperial' force. In that case, there is no guarantee that the Member States will continue to adhere to the homogeneity imposed by the accession process. Accession criteria are meant to ensure that the states who *enter* into a federation are substantially similar to the existing Member States. It can, however, not ensure that *they stay the same.*

This leads us to a more general problem of the introduction of political heterogeneity into a federation: the problem of political and constitutional change. This problem, of course, applies to all the Member States of a federation, not merely to the danger of the 'new' Member States 'backsliding' into their 'old ways'. In a federation, the Member States remain politically and constitutionally autonomous and they are therefore politically free to decide on their own destiny and give themselves new constitutions. The question is this: what happens if a Member State gives itself a new constitution that is in conflict with the identity of the federation and therefore presents a threat to the federal balance? In what ways can the federation exercise constitutional defence?

IV. Constitutional Change and Constitutional Defence

A. The Federal Guarantee Clause

Radical political and constitutional changes in the constitutions of the Member States present the federation with a paradox. The federation cannot allow the Member States to develop politically and constitutionally in a way that is incompatible with the constitutional identity of the Union as a whole. This would endanger the substantial homogeneity between the Member States on which the federal balance and the very existence of the federation relies. But, the federation is created precisely in order to protect the political existence of its Member States. The political existence of a state is intimately linked to its political autonomy.[130] The political right of a community to decide on its own fate and give itself a new constitution is one of the most important expressions of the political autonomy of a

[129] Komárek (n 126) 195, citing Jiří Pehe, 'Demokracie bez demokratů: Úvahy o společnosti a politice' [Democracy without Democrats: Thoughtson Society and Politics] (2010). For a data collection on the citizens of the acceding states' support for different types of democratic communities see Zielonka (n 110) 41. See also Sájo (n 94) 175–78.

[130] Alexandre Kojève, 'Outline of a Doctrine Of French Policy' [2004] Policy Review 3, 20–21 expressed the link between political autonomy and political existence in the following way: 'the fundamental political category is that of independence or of autonomy ... Considered as a political entity, the State does nothing more than to bring about a will to autonomy; through it [the State] creates and maintains itself, for through it [the State] integrates and governs otherwise disparate particular wills by creating a "general will" out of them, which is nothing other than its own will to autonomy thus made explicit and effective'.

state. It is therefore highly controversial for the federation to interfere with the constitutional autonomy of its Member States.

Constitutional change in the Member States therefore presents the federation with a conundrum: it needs to limit the constitutional autonomy of its Member States without this limitation being understood as an intrusion into their constitutional autonomy. The problem of constitutional change is one of the most difficult expressions of the contradictory nature of the federal telos: how to balance unity and diversity when what is at stake is the very identity of the Member States.

One of the most important tools for the federation to manage constitutional change in its Member States is a 'federal guarantee clause', that is, a guarantee by federal law of the shared form of government/constitutional identity of its Member States. A federal guarantee clause has a *double purpose*: it is meant to create a new unitary order and extend the scope of federal power over the constitutional structure of the Member States; at the same time, it is meant to conserve the Member States' constitutional identities, their diversity, and distinct 'ways of life'.[131] The antebellum United States and the German Confederation are both good examples of the double role played by the federal guarantee of constitutional identity.

The United States, born out of the American Revolution, emerged in opposition to the absolute monarchy of the Old World. Desiring to protect their newly found republican freedom, the former colonies guaranteed a republican form of government, not merely via their own state constitutions, but also in the new federal Constitution of the United States:

> The United States shall guarantee to every State in this Union *a Republican Form of Government*, and shall protect each of them against Invasion; and on Application of the Legislature, or of the Executive (when the Legislature cannot be convened) against domestic Violence.[132]

By guaranteeing the republican form of government of the Member States, the Constitution of the United States is a clear expression of the preservation of the constitutional identities of its Member States. At the same time, this guarantee enabled the creation of a new federal constitutional unity and allowed for the possibility of the federal government intervening against 'unrepublican' constitutional amendments and uprisings in the Member States.[133] While preserving the constitutional identity of the States, the guarantee clause also extended the powers of the federal government over their constitutional development.

[131] William M Wiecek, *The Guarantee Clause of the US Constitution* (Cornell University Press 1972) 4.

[132] The Constitution of the United States, Article IV, Section 4, emphasis added.

[133] Wiecek (n 131) 1ff, 28, 33, 42, 67; Federalist 21 (Hamilton) (n 49) 101–05. See also Beaud (n 11) 369.

While the United States was meant to protect the spirit of the republican revolution from the monarchical order of the Old World, the German Confederation was created as an anti-revolutionary union of monarchies in order to suppress the liberal and nationalist revolutionary potential of the German states.[134] The German Confederation thus guaranteed the *monarchical form of government* in its Member States. On requests by individual princes, the federation performed numerous military federal interventions to quell liberal and nationalist uprisings in the individual Member States.[135] In this way, the relatively wide powers of the German Confederation to which the German princes submitted themselves were in a very concrete sense a means for constitutional self-preservation of the monarchical order for the individual Member States. At the same time, however, the federal guarantee of the monarchical form of government created the possibility for the federal level to intervene extensively in the internal affairs of the Member States in order to preserve the unity of the federation.[136]

The federal guarantee of the constitutional identity of the Member States is meant to protect the *constitutional orders of both the Union and its Member States*. It allows the federation to bridge the gap between the contradictory forces of the federation: the transformative forces directed towards the future and demanding unity, and the conservative forces directed towards the past and requiring diversity. A federal guarantee of the constitutional identity of the Member States is 'Janus-faced' because it allows for the articulation of transformation as a means of conservation, the creation of unity as the preservation of diversity, and the future as a return to or continuation of the past. The federal guarantee of constitutional identity can in this way allow for the articulation of the birth of a new unitary order and the transformation of the federating states as an expression of constitutional conservation and self-determination. It is in many ways an ingenious constitutional mechanism in that it allows for the possibility of balancing the contradictory forces of the federation. It is a means to square the circle. That being said, in order for it to work, at least two preconditions need to be met.

A federal guarantee clause of the Member States' shared form of government self-evidently requires that the Member States share the same form of government. They need to be relatively constitutionally homogeneous. The federal guarantee clause will grant the Union the authority to intervene in the internal constitutional affairs of the Member States. These interventions need to be authorized and preferably perceived as a 'help' on the part of the Member States for them to further their own constitutional projects and not as a threat to their autonomy. This only works if there is a relative homogeneity of the Member States' constitutional identities.

[134] Emmanuel N Roussakis, *Friedrich List, the Zollverein, and the Uniting of Europe* (College of Europe 1968) 20; Riker (n 22) 35–36; Huber (n 29) 595–96, 619–20.

[135] Ernst Rudolf Huber, 'Bundesexekution und Bundesintervention: Ein Beitrag zur Frage des Verfassungsschutzes im Deutschen Bund' (1953) 79 Archiv des öffentlichen Rechts 1.

[136] ibid; Beaud (n 11) 366–70. For a further discussion, see Chapter 5:I:B.

This entails not merely a 'formal' constitutional homogeneity, such as 'a republican form of government', but also a relatively homogeneous interpretation of the *meaning* of 'republicanism'.

The need for constitutional homogeneity is not surprising. The guarantee clause is, after all, meant to deal with the problem of constitutional change and it thus presupposes an already existing homogeneity. The second precondition is therefore more controversial. The possibility of constitutional change in the Member States needs to be limited *de jure* or only exercised to a limited degree *de facto* for the federal guarantee clause to work. The consequence of the guarantee of the constitutional identity of the Member States is a guarantee of the status quo of the constitutions of the Member States.[137] In other words, it gives the Member States *rigid constitutions.*

Constitutions, however, are always in flux. They are a process of becoming, and that is the case whether they are of an 'evolutionary' (UK), 'revolutionary' (USA), or 'elitist' (Germany) type.[138] Nevertheless, the constitutions of the Member States cannot be allowed to evolve so as to present a threat to the unity of the federal order. For example, the people of an individual State of the United States could not be allowed to give itself an 'unrepublican' constitution; neither could the German Confederation allow for the rise of republican/liberal constitutionalism in the individual *Länder.* What this means is that the federation is characterized by an inherent paradox, namely that in order to preserve the political existence of its Member States, it must impose restrictions on one of the most important expressions of the political existence of the state: its political right to decide on 'the type and form of its own political existence'.[139] For the sake of preserving the federal balance, the Member States should therefore preferably give themselves internally rigid constitutions that mirror that of the federation and thereby establish a constitutional 'double bind'.

The federal guarantee clause does not solve the problem of constitutional change in the Member States. Its primary purpose is the creation of a shared framework—a constitutional imaginary and, as we shall see in the next chapter, a governmental apparatus—through which the problem of constitutional change can be dealt with. In the context of the United States, it allowed constitutional changes and conflicts to be mediated through a political contestation over the meaning of 'republicanism'; a concept that changed radically over time from being primarily the antithesis to monarchy, nobility, and direct democracy at the time of the Founding to the idea of political equality and anti-slavery at the time of the Reconstruction. As the United States bears witness to, this framework can only deal peacefully with a certain degree of political and constitutional conflict. Ultimately, the debates over the

137 Wiecek (n 131) 78.
138 Ackerman (n 109).
139 Schmitt (n 16) 125.

compatibility of slavery with republicanism could not be settled through constitutional and political debates. In the end, the question was settled politically with the Civil War.

B. The Rise of Authoritarianism in the EU

How does the EU manage the problem of constitutional change in its Member States? This question is not of merely academic interest. There are currently two Member States where 'liberal democracy' and the foundational values of the Union set out in Article 2 TEU are under serious threat because of fundamental changes to their constitutional orders: Hungary and Poland.

Hungary's slide towards authoritarianism started with the election of the ultra right-wing party Fidesz led by Viktor Orbán to government in 2010. The political programme of Fidesz is often illustrated with reference to a speech Orbán gave in 2014 delivered to ethnic Hungarians in Romania where he declared that 'the new state that we are building is an illiberal state, a non-liberal state'.[140] Having the necessary two-thirds majority in Parliament, Fidesz has pushed through a number of constitutional and other fundamental reforms meant to consolidate their own power.[141] These fundamental reforms include an overhaul of the constitutional court ensuring that Fidesz-appointed judges are in the majority and a narrowing of the jurisdiction of the court; a new election law with legislative districts favourable to Fidesz; extension of voting rights to ethnic Hungarians in neighbouring countries who are deemed likely to vote for Fidesz; the creation of a new media authority run by Fidesz loyalists; and finally an amendment to the National Higher Education Act (nicknamed 'Lex CEU') that in practical terms has forced the Central European University (CEU) to leave Hungary and relocate in Vienna.[142] On 30 March 2020, in response to the coronavirus outbreak, Fidesz introduced an Enabling Act declaring a state of emergency that allows the government to rule by decree for an *unlimited period of time* ('until the end of the emergency').[143]

With the combined parliamentary and presidential victory of the Law and Justice Party (PiS) in 2015, a form of political authoritarianism has emerged in

[140] See 'Full text of Viktor Orbán's speech at Băile Tuşnad (Tusnádfürdő) of 26 July 2014' (*The Budapest Beacon*, 29 July 2014).

[141] Miklós Bánkuti, Gábor Halmai and Kim Lane Scheppele, 'Hungary's Illiberal Turn: Disabling the Constitution' (2012) 23 Journal of Democracy 138, 139.

[142] Gábor Halmai, 'Legally Sophisticated Authoritarians: the Hungarian Lex CEU' *Verfassungsblog* (31 March 2017); Gábor Attila Tóth, *Constitution for a Disunited Nation: On Hungary's 2011 Fundamental Law* (Central European University Press 2012); Editorial, 'Editorial Comments, Hungary's New Constitutional Order and "European Unity"' (2012) 49 Common Market Law Review 871; Armin von Bogdandy, *Constitutional Crisis in the European Constitutional Area: Theory, Law and Politics in Hungary and Romania* (Hart Publishing 2013).

[143] For a translation of the draft law that has been passed, see Eva S Balogh, 'Translation of Draft Law "On Protecting Against the Coronavirus"' (*Hungarian Spectrum*, 22 March 2020).

Poland that in many ways mirrors Hungarian developments. Like Fidesz, the PiS has taken over the control of the Constitutional Tribunal, engaged in blatant court packing, and fundamentally overhauled the general judiciary in a way, it is widely agreed, that brings the rule of law under fundamental threat if it has not been entirely eliminated in Poland.[144] The reform of the judiciary is the most discussed aspect of Polish authoritarianism, yet another important example is the amended counterterrorism laws, allowing the security services expansive powers over telecommunications and personal information. Moreover, both democratic and civil society institutions have been broadly dismantled and individual rights have come under attack.[145] Like Hungary under Orbán, Poland ruled by the PiS has clearly undergone constitutional changes, formal or informal,[146] that are incompatible with the constitutional identity of the EU as expressed in Article 2.

In contrast to the United States, the EU does not have one designated guarantee clause of a shared constitutional identity of its Member States. Article 2 TEU sets out the value order common to the Member States on which the Union understands itself to be founded. It is an expression of the 'common aim' of the federal telos. Nevertheless, Article 2 TEU does not guarantee this shared constitutional identity. The question of a guarantee of the constitutional identity of the Member States is dealt with in Articles 4(2) and 7 TEU. Article 4(2) reads:

> The Union shall respect the equality of Member States before the Treaties as well as their national identities, inherent in their fundamental structures, political and constitutional, inclusive of regional and local self-government. It shall respect their essential State functions, including ensuring the territorial integrity of the State, maintaining law and order and safeguarding national security. In particular, national security remains the sole responsibility of each Member State.

Article 2 is a manifestation of the 'common aim' of the Union, whereas Article 4(2) is a manifestation of the 'particularistic aim' of the Union. It is an expression of the Union's respect for the political and constitutional diversity and autonomy of its Member States.

In contrast to a federal guarantee clause, Articles 2 and 4(2) do not provide a cohesive constitutional mechanism for dealing with the problem of constitutional change in the Member States because the link between the 'particularistic aim' and

[144] For a detailed account, see Wojciech Sadurski, *Poland's Constitutional Breakdown* (OUP 2019).

[145] ibid 5–6.

[146] 'Many changes which are part of democratic backsliding occur *without a formal change* of institutions and procedures, so they are invisible to a purely legal account', Wojciech Sadurski, 'How Democracy Dies (in Poland): A Case Study of Anti-Constitutional Populist Backsliding' (2018) 18 Sydney Law School Research Paper 1, 5, italics in original. See also, Anna Śledzińska-Simon, 'Poland's Constitutional Tribunal under Siege' *Verfassungsblog* (4 December 2015); Gabór Halmai, 'The Making of "Illiberal Constitutionalism" with or without a New Constitution: The Case of Hungary and Poland' in David Landau and Hanna Lerner (eds) (Edward Elgar Publishing 2019).

the 'common aim' is not legally established. There is no direct legal identification of the value order on which the Union 'is founded' (Article 2) and the constitutional identities of the Member States that the Union is bound to 'respect' (Article 4(2)). *This identity is merely surmised* ('these values are common to the Member States'). There is no common overall denominator (however unspecific, eg, 'liberal democracy') that formally unifies Articles 2 and 4(2). It is therefore possible to justify a discrepancy between the constitutional identity prescribed by the Union (Article 2) and the constitutional identities of its Member States (Article 4(2)) on the basis of the framework of the Treaties.

Even in cases where such an overall denominator is present (eg 'a republican form of government' in the Constitution of the United States), there will always be a discrepancy between the identity clause in the federal constitution and the concrete manifestation of it in the constitutions of the Member States (tellingly it is not *the* republican form of government but *a* republican form of government). That being said, a common denominator allows for the contestation and negotiation of constitutional conflicts within the same constitutional framework and as a matter of federal law. The lack of a common denominator in the case of the EU, however vague, therefore limits the possibilities for managing constitutional conflicts as a matter of EU law.

Moreover, in contrast to the earlier discussed cases of the United States and the German Confederation, the EU does not *guarantee* the constitutional identity of its Member States. As argued, the guarantee clause is ingenious because it allows for the identification of the contradictory forces of the federation. It allows for the possibility of both the Member States and the Union internalizing each other's constitutional orders. Instead of guaranteeing the constitutional identity of its Member States, the Union, following Article 4(2) TEU, is bound to *respect* the identities of its Member States. The accentuation of the Union's need to 'respect' its Member States suggests that the Union is *more of a constitutional threat than a constitutional guardian*. Article 4(2) is a means for the Member States to protect themselves from the power of the Union.

In a similar manner, Article 7 is a means for the Union to protect itself from a *threat from the Member States*. It sets out the Union's primary powers of constitutional defence of the Union *against* its Member States. In contrast to a federal guarantee clause, it does not simultaneously protect the Union and its Member States. The scope of Article 7 is not limited to Union law, meaning that the EU may act in the event of any breach within all areas where the Member States act autonomously, because a breach of the fundamental values of the Union is likely to undermine the foundations of Union law. Article 7 TEU allows the Council to determine the existence of a persistent and serious breach, or clear risk of a serious breach, by a Member State of the foundational values of the Union expressed in Article 2 TEU. These are respectively known as the 'sanctioning arm' (Article 7(2)–(3)) and the 'preventive arm' (Article 7(1)). The two 'arms' of Article 7 can be triggered independently of one another, that is, the use of the 'sanctioning arm' does not require a previous use of the 'preventive arm'.

The 'preventive arm' has a lower threshold than the 'sanctioning arm'. Following Article 7(1), on a reasoned proposal by either one-third of the Member States, the European Parliament (EP), or the Commission, the Council, acting on a 4/5 majority after obtaining the consent of the EP, may determine that there is a clear risk of a serious breach by a Member State of the foundational values of the Union. The Council may further address recommendations to the Member State in question. In itself, this is an almost insurmountable threshold. The 'sanctioning arm', however, has an even higher threshold. As established by Article 7(2)–(3), the Council, acting unanimously (minus the Member State in question) on a proposal by either one-third of the Member States or the Commission and after obtaining the consent of the EP, may determine the existence of a serious and persistent breach of the values of Article 2 TEU.

If a persistent and serious breach by a Member State of the foundational values of the Union is established, the Council can authorize the suspension of certain Treaty rights including the political representation of the Member State in the Council.[147] These sanctions do not free the Member State in question from being bound by EU law.[148] The deprivation of political rights is quite radical: for the duration of the sanctions, it effectively reduces the Member State in question to a *dependency*. The Member State in question would be fully bound by Union law but deprived of political equality and influence. It effectively reverts to the legal and political status of an applicant state during the accession process. Nevertheless, the suspension of the political equality of the Member States is not necessarily effective. Even if applied, the Union could end up having a *de facto* authoritarian dependency instead of an authoritarian Member State. For that reason, there is an argument to be made that the Union needs to have stronger sanctions or the possibility of intervening directly in the internal affairs of the Member States in order to combat the rise of authoritarianism in a Member State. Article 7 does not provide this possibility. It allows the Union to 'insulate' itself from a recalcitrant Member State; 'it enables a kind of *moral quarantine*, not an actual intervention'.[149]

Until a few years ago, Article 7 had never been triggered and it was generally considered a 'nuclear option' deemed too controversial to be used. Nevertheless, in December 2017, the Commission, relying for the first time on Article 7(1) TEU and backed by the EP, called upon the Council to determine whether there is a clear risk of Poland breaching the foundational values of the Union.[150] This is in response to

[147] Article 7(3) TEU.

[148] Article 7(3) TEU.

[149] Jan-Werner Müller, 'Should the EU Protect Democracy and the Rule of Law inside Member States?' (2015) 21 European Law Journal 141, 144.

[150] European Commission, press release: 'Rule of Law: European Commission Acts to Defend Judicial Independence in Poland' (Brussels, 20 December 2017); European Commission: 'Reasoned Proposal in Accordance with Article 7(1) of the Treaty on European Union regarding the Rule of Law in

the complete overhaul of the Polish judiciary in recent years that has undermined judicial independence.[151] Moreover, in September 2018, the EP approved a request to initiate the Article 7(1) procedure against Hungary.[152] Between September and December 2019, the EU held two hearings with the Hungarian government, and, as is the case with Poland, it will be up to the Council to determine whether there is a clear risk of Hungary breaching the foundational values of the Union.[153]

Even if the clear risk is established, the probability that Poland or Hungary will be sanctioned through the Article 7 procedure is low. The threshold for the sanctioning arm of Article 7 is so high that it in practice it is very difficult if not impossible to rely on.[154] The requirement of unanimity in the Council for the establishment of a persistent and serious breach means that as long as the authoritarian state in question has just one ally, Article 7 cannot be used. Victor Orbán has pledged on several occasions to veto any EU attempts to sanction Poland.[155] In response to this situation, other scholars have suggested an *effet utile* interpretation of Article 7 that would allow the Council to bring a case against Poland and Hungary simultaneously and thereby deprive both of them of a vote.[156] Such an interpretation, however, has not yet been seriously considered by the EU.

How can the EU deal with the problem that as long as there is more than one 'bad egg', Article 7 cannot be triggered? Some scholars have suggested that the EU could attempt to prevent the authoritarian 'backsliding' through social pressure and shaming,[157] fundamental rights protection by national courts acting in the capacity of European courts,[158] systematic infringement procedures,[159] and

Poland—A Proposal for a Council Decision on the Determination of a Clear Risk of a Serious Breach by the Republic of Poland of the Rule of Law' (Brussels, 20 December 2017).

[151] For an overview of these reforms, see European Commission for Democracy through Law (Venice Commission): 'Poland: Opinion on the Draft Act Amending the Act on the National Council of the Judiciary, on the Draft Act Amending the act on the Supreme Court, Proposed by the President of Poland, and on the Act on the Organisation of Ordinary Courts' (Opinion No 904 /2017, CDL-AD (2017)031, Strasbourg 11 December 2017).

[152] EP, press release: 'Rule of law in Hungary: Parliament calls on the EU to act' (12 September 2018). Text adopted by the EP: 'The situation in Hungary', P8_TA(2018)0340.

[153] EP, briefing: 'Hungary and Poland: Parliament to assess progress of Article 7 proceedings' (Newsletter, 13–16 January 2020—Strasbourg plenary session).

[154] On top of this insurmountable threshold, EP party politics makes it even less likely for Article 7 to be triggered, see Ulrich Sedelmeier, 'Political Safeguards against Democratic Backsliding in the EU: The Limits of Material Sanctions and the Scope of Social Pressure' (2016) 24 Journal of European Public Policy 337, 339–41.

[155] Henry Foy, Jim Brunsden, and Andrew Byrne, 'Orban Promises to Veto Any EU Sanctions against Poland' *Financial Times* (8 January 2016).

[156] Laurent Pech and Kim Lane Scheppele, 'Illiberalism Within: Rule of Law Backsliding in the EU' (2017) 19 Cambridge Yearbook of European Legal Studies 3, 35.

[157] Ulrich Sedelmeier, 'Anchoring Democracy from Above? The European Union and Democratic Backsliding in Hungary and Romania' (2014) 52 Journal of Common Market Studies 105.

[158] Armin Von Bogdandy and others, 'Reverse Solange—Protecting the Essence of Fundamental Rights against EU Member States' (2012) 49 Common Market Law Review 489.

[159] Kim Lane Scheppele, 'Enforcing the Basic Principles of EU Law through Systemic Infringement Actions' in Carlos Closa and Dimitry Kochenov (eds), *Reinforcing Rule of Law Oversight in the European Union* (CUP 2016).

by recommendation via the Commission's 'rule of law framework'.[160] Many of the tools available to the EU institutions are, however, technical and therefore largely incapable of dealing with the general political challenge of the rise of authoritarianism. This is neatly illustrated by the fact that the Commission could deal with Orbán's court packing only as a matter of age discrimination[161] and that ultimately it was unable to reinstate the dismissed judges. Besides, the possibility of sanctions through these alternative routes is even weaker than Article 7 because there is no way of forcing the Member State to comply. As remarked by Jan-Werner Müller: 'as of now, the EU has no convincing toolkit to deal with the situation' in Poland and Hungary.[162]

For that reason, Müller has suggested a number of new sanctions: first, the establishment of a 'Copenhagen Commission' that should act as a political guardian of the Copenhagen criteria and be able to investigate Member States and, via the Commission, to apply sanctions in the form of cutting funding or imposing fines.[163] More radically, he also suggests that the Union should ultimately have the right to *expel a Member State* from the Union in order to save the constitutional integrity of the Union as a whole.[164] This would, however, be highly controversial because it goes against the spirit of Treaties by threatening the Union's political aim of 'ever closer union of the peoples of Europe'. It would endanger the very foundations of Union authority.

C. A Guardian of Liberal Democracy?

The constitutional defence of the EU as set out in Articles 2, 4(2) and 7 provides the Union with an insubstantial legal mandate to intervene directly in the internal constitutional developments of its Member States in order to prevent a 'constitutional capture'. At best, the EU can try to motivate the Member States not to stray from the path of liberal democracy via soft-law instruments and 'sensible discussions'[165] or to 'insulate' the recalcitrant Member States from the rest of the Union via the Article 7 procedure.[166] At present, the Treaties do not provide the Union with the

[160] Communication from the European Commission to the Council and the Parliament, 'A New EU Mechanism to Strengthen the Rule of Law' (COM(2014) 158 final/2, 10 March 2014). See Sadurski (n 144) 213ff.

[161] Case C-286/12 *Commission v Hungary* [2012] ECLI:EU:C:2012:687.

[162] Jan-Werner Müller, 'Safeguarding Democracy Inside the EU: Brussels and the Future of Liberal Order' (2013) 3 Transatlantic Academy 1, 4. See also Carlos Closa, Dimitry Kochenov, and Joseph HH Weiler, 'Reinforcing Rule of Law Oversight in the European Union' (2014) 25 EUI Working Papers Law 2.

[163] Müller (n 41) 25. See also Gábor Halmai, 'The Possibility and Desirability of Rule of Law Conditionality' (2019) 11 The Hague Journal on the Rule of Law 171; R Daniel Kelemen and Kim Lane Scheppele, 'How to Stop Funding Autocracy in the EU' *Verfassungsblog* (10 September 2018).

[164] Müller (n 162) 23; Müller (n 41) 212.

[165] Judith Mischke, 'Juncker Rejects Cutting EU Funds to Poland' *Politico* (1 September 2018).

[166] Müller (n 149); Müller (n 41) 212.

option of taking control of the governmental apparatus of a Member State in order to hinder 'constitutional capture'. As we shall see in the next chapter, this was largely the case in the German Confederation of 1815–66. Instead, the Treaties provide for two conflicting forms of constitutional defence: the defence of the Union *against* the Member States and the defence of the Member States *against* the Union.

That being said, the question is whether the EU has an extra-legal, that is, a *political* right to protect the Union and its Member States from 'democratic suicide'? After all, a 'Constitution is not a suicide pact'.[167] As will be discussed in more detail in Chapter 5, there is an argument to be made that the constitutional restrictions on the exercise of governmental powers must always be balanced, and ultimately set aside temporarily, in order to secure the survival of the political community. Notwithstanding the legal limitations, does the EU have the authority to act as a guardian of liberal democracy?[168]

Despite the comparatively limited possibilities provided by Articles 2, 4(2), and 7 TEU, for the EU to intervene in the internal constitutional developments of its Member States to 'save them from democratic suicide', there are strong, albeit controversial, political arguments in favour of the existence of the Union's right to do so. The strongest *political arguments* for the EU's right of intervention have been presented by Müller. The EU, Müller argues, has for most of its Member States been part of the formation and consolidation of the constitutional project of liberal democracy, albeit in different ways. For that reason, the EU is an extra layer of constitutional guarantee of liberal-democratic constitutionalism. Membership in the EU is a way for the Member States to 'lock in' liberal democracy. It is part and parcel of 'constrained democracy'.[169]

The rigid constitutionalism that member-statehood entails is a way for the Member States to guarantee an anti-authoritarian form of constitutionalism. 'Governments in turn sought to lock themselves into Europe to prevent "backsliding," ' Müller writes, 'it was like Ulysses binding himself to the mast in order to resist the siren songs of illiberal antidemocratic demagogues in the future'.[170] Membership in the EU was a way of 'anchoring democracy from above'.[171] Müller's argument is that a central reason for the constitution of the EU, like the United States and the German Confederation (though Müller does not make the connection), was the protection of a specific constitutional identity or 'way of life'. Following this argument, the *protection of liberal democracy is a central telos of the*

[167] *Terminiello v City of Chicago* 337 U.S. 1 (1949), 37. For a discussion, see Martin Loughlin, *The Idea of Public Law* (OUP 2003) 91–93.

[168] Jan-Werner Müller, 'The EU as a Militant Democracy, Or: Are There Limits to Constitutional Mutations Within EU Member States?' (2014) 165 Revista de Estudios Políticos 141. See also Ulrich Wagrandl, 'Transnational Militant Democracy' (2018) 7 Global Constitutionalism 143.

[169] Müller (n 162) 11.

[170] ibid 9.

[171] Sedelmeier (n 157). Another metaphor used is that of the EU as a 'democratic straightjacket', see Sadurski (n 144) 199.

EU. The Member States wanted to join the EU to protect themselves against the return of fascism. The EU, therefore, has not only a right but also a *duty to intervene* in the constitutional developments of its Member States in order to save them from 'democratic suicide'.

Nevertheless, there is a problem with this argument, namely that not all Member States of the EU belong to the constitutional type of constrained democracy.[172] The core Member States of the EU are, to a greater or lesser extent, constrained democracies, but this is, as we have seen, less so the case for the rest of the Member States. Seeing that EU membership was perceived as key to the consolidation of democracy for the Central and Eastern European countries, the continuous parliamentary democracies of the UK and Scandinavia are the only full exception to the project of constrained democracy. For these countries, the distrust of unrestrained popular sovereignty, including parliamentary sovereignty, is not part of their post-WWII DNA.[173] As argued earlier, despite the importance of the idea of 'the return to Europe', the countries of the eastern enlargements differ from the post-fascist countries because their constitutions are defined against an external imperial enemy and not internal democratic collapse. They are therefore to a lesser degree defined by a 'distrust' in sovereignty. For the Member States of the EU, it seems, there is no consensus on the question of whether 'democracy' means 'constrained democracy' and to what extent the EU is a legitimate guardian of European democracy.

The EU is not the first federation where the meaning of the constitutional identity of the Union as a whole has been highly politically contested. A good historical example is the debate over whether slavery was compatible with a republican form of government in the United States that began in the 1820s and which was settled only by the Civil War.[174] When the constitutional identity is highly politically contested, an intervention to save the Member States 'from themselves' is difficult to authorize and can lead to violent conflict or even civil war.

That being said, there is another political argument in favour of a Union right of intervention in order to prevent a Member State from committing 'democratic suicide' based on the principle of the *political interdependence* of the Member States. Like other federations, the EU is characterized by a high degree of *mutualization of risk*. The mutual trust between the Member States is therefore based on the premise that none of them present a danger to the Union as a whole. Because of the mutualization of risk, there are no 'internal affairs' of a Member State that do not have the potential to be of common concern for the Union at large.[175] 'Strictly

[172] Müller concedes to this to a certain degree, see Müller (n 149) 153.

[173] Müller (n 162) 10. See also Richard Tuck, 'Brexit: A Prize in Reach for the Left' *Policy Exchange* (17 July 2017).

[174] For the development of this debate and its relationship to Article IV, Section 4 of the Constitution of the United States (the 'guarantee clause') see Wiecek (n 131) chs 5–7.

[175] Beaud (n 11) 301.

speaking, there are no purely internal affairs in EU member states', Müller writes, 'all EU citizens are affected by developments in a particular member state'.[176]

In concrete terms, this means that the rise of authoritarian constitutionalism in one or more Member States has the potential to affect all the other Member States. An example given by Müller is that an authoritarian Member State, when acting through its representatives in the EU, will influence laws that are made for all the citizens of the Union.[177] The citizens of the authoritarian Member States are also citizens of the Union and the Union therefore has a political right to protect its citizens from any 'anti-constitutional behaviour' of its Member States. Following this line of argument, in order to save the citizens of the Union from authoritarian influence, the Union will therefore have to repress any form of authoritarian constitutionalism *in the name of the safety of the citizens of the European Union*. This political right, however, is highly controversial because both the Member States and the Union have a political right to act as the 'guardian of the constitution'. Moreover, as will become clear in Chapter 5, by relying on constitutional guardianship, the federation risks the destruction of the federal balance on which the federation relies.

The EU has, as yet, not been capable of intervening in any significant manner in the internal affairs of Poland or Hungary to combat the rise of authoritarian constitutionalism. The lack of cohesion between TEU Articles 2, 4(2), and 7, and the relatively limited possibility of sanctioning the 'backsliding' Member States are without a doubt important reasons for that. Nevertheless, the EU's inaction cannot be fully explained by these factors. As we shall see in Chapter 5, in response to the Eurozone crisis the EU has developed a strong executive apparatus that allows it to take more or less full control of the governmental apparatuses of 'deficit' Member States. Among other things, this has entailed a form of forced administration and demands for the constitutionalization of budgetary constraints in the Member States. These interventions, as we shall see, have been authorized in a similar manner structurally to the arguments in favour of an EU intervention in authoritarian Member States. This form of 'emergency government' conforms to the theory of executive constitutional defence in the federation. Chapter 5 demonstrates why this is a highly controversial and contradictory form of emergency government that threatens not only the autonomy of the Member States but ultimately also the very existence of the federation as a political form.

[176] Müller (n 162) 12.

[177] ibid. See also Carlos Closa, 'Reinforcing EU Monitoring of the Rule of Law: Normative Arguments, Institutional Proposals and the Procedural Limitations' in Carlos Closa and Dimitry Kochenov (eds), *Reinforcing Rule of Law Oversight in the European Union* (CUP 2016) 18.

5
Emergency Rule without a Sovereign

In the last decade, the question of whether the EU has the authority to intervene in the internal constitutional affairs of its Member States has not merely been raised in the context of the rise of 'illiberal democracy' (Chapter 4) but arguably to a greater extent in the context of the Eurozone crisis. A good example is the so-called golden rule that requires the Member States to introduce domestic constitutional guarantees for fiscal consolidation.[1] The intrusion by the EU into the constitutional affairs of its Member States during the Eurozone crisis, however, has not been limited to this. The government of the Eurozone crisis has been characterized by a radical extension in the governmental powers of the Union and 'micro-management' of deficit Member States to the degree that their political autonomy, *de facto* if not *de jure*, has been eroded. It is therefore generally maintained within academic debates that the government of the Eurozone has led to a change in the constitutional architecture, a constitutional transformation, a constitutional mutation or a distortion of the constitutional balance of the EU.[2] Extensive arguments pertaining to the implications for the constitutions of the Member States have been put forward regarding the erosion of the powers of Member State parliaments vis-à-vis the Member State executives and the infringement of constitutionally protected social rights.[3] The

[1] Maurice Adams, Federico Fabbrini, and Pierre Larouche, *The Constitutionalization of European Budgetary Constraints* (Hart Publishing 2016).

[2] Agustín José Menéndez, 'Editorial: A European Union in Constitutional Mutation?' (2014) 20 European Law Journal 127; Federico Fabbrini, 'States' Equality v States' Power: The Euro-Crisis, Inter-State Relations and the Paradox of Domination' (2015) 17 Cambridge Yearbook of European Legal Studies 3; Paul Craig, 'Economic Governance and the Euro Crisis: Constitutional Architecture and Constitutional Implications' in Maurice Adams, Federico Fabbrini, and Pierre Larouche (eds), *The Constitutionalization of European Budgetary Constraints* (Hart Publishing 2014); Christian Joerges, 'The European Economic Constitution and Its Transformation through the Financial Crisis' in Anna Södersten and Dennis Michael Patterson (eds), *A Companion to European Union Law and International Law* (John Wiley & Sons, Inc 2016); Kaarlo Tuori and Klaus Tuori, *The Eurozone Crisis : A Constitutional Analysis* (CUP 2014); Giuseppe Martinico, 'EU Crisis and Constitutional Mutations: A Review Article' (2014) 165 Revista de Estudios Politícos 247; Mark Dawson and Floris de Witte, 'Constitutional Balance in the EU after the Euro–Crisis' (2013) 76 The Modern Law Review 817; Koen Lenaerts, 'EMU and the European Union's Constitutional Framework' (2014) 39 European Law Review 753; Edoardo Chiti and Pedro Gustavo Teixeira, 'The Constitutional Implications of the European Responses to the Financial and Public Debt Crisis' (2013) 50 Common Market Law Review 683; Agustín José Menéndez, 'The Crisis of Law and the European Crises: From the Social and Democratic Rechtsstaat to the Consolidating State of (Pseudo-)Technocratic Governance' (2017) 44 Journal of Law and Society 56.

[3] Thomas Beukers, Bruno de Witte and Claire Kilpatrick, *Constitutional Change through Euro-Crisis Law* (CUP 2017); Bruno De Witte and Claire Kilpatrick (eds), *Social Rights in Times of Crisis in the Eurozone: The Role of Fundamental Rights' Challenges* (EUI Working Paper Series LAW 2014) (hereafter *Social Rights in Times of Crisis*). See also country specific reports published as part of the

The Constitutional Theory of the Federation and the European Union. Signe Rehling Larsen, Oxford University Press (2021).
 DOI: 10.1093/oso/9780198859260.003.0006

extraordinary measures used to govern the Eurozone crisis have been justified with reference to 'necessity' and an impending 'emergency'. It is therefore widely agreed that the government of the Eurozone crisis conforms to the idea of 'emergency politics', albeit not the classical statist model of the 'state of exception'.[4]

Notwithstanding the magnitude of the constitutional implications of the emergency government of the Eurozone, this chapter argues that—in one limited sense—the constitutional mutation thesis is overstated. The chapter maintains that the emergency government of the Eurozone can be understood as a manifestation of federal constitutional defence. What this means is that 'emergency Europe'[5] and the Europe of 'constitutional tolerance'[6] are both manifestations of how the federation as a form of political association governs itself, both in peaceful times and in times of profound crisis.

In other words, the constitutional balance or identity of the Union might have changed, whereas its constitutional character has not, at least not yet. This also provides an explanation for why the government of the Eurozone crisis can be a form of 'emergency rule without a sovereign'.[7] As this book argues, the federation is a discrete political form on a par with, though distinct from, the state and the empire. One of the main characteristics of the federation as a political form is the internal absence or repression of sovereignty. The federation also governs itself in a qualitatively different way than the state in times of crisis, or so it will be argued. This chapter demonstrates that 'emergency Europe' does not conform to the theory of the 'state of exception' because the EU is not a state but a federation.

Despite its controversial nature, emergency government or executive constitutional defence is crucial for the survival of all constitutional governments, including that of a federation. That being said, emergency government is particularly dangerous for the federation because it introduces a strong unitary element of reason of state that threatens the dual political nature of the federation. The government of an internal crisis can be what finally destroys the federal balance and takes the federation beyond its double political existence into the realm of statehood, either through the collapse of the Union or in the form of its transformation into a more unitary federal state. Notwithstanding that the government of the Eurozone crisis has arguably brought the Union closer to *both* the brink of collapse *and* statehood, neither of these scenarios has yet come to pass.

'Constitutional Change through Euro Crisis Law' project at the EUI <www.eurocrisislaw.eui.eu> accessed 26 January 2018.

4 Jonathan White, *Politics of Last Resort: Governing by Emergency in the European Union* (OUP 2019).

5 Jonathan White, 'Emergency Europe' (2015) 63 Political Studies 300.

6 Joseph HH Weiler, 'Prologue: Global and Pluralist Constitutionalism – Some Doubts' in Joseph HH Weiler and Gráinne De Búrca (eds), *The Worlds of European Constitutionalism* (CUP 2012).

7 White (n 5) 308.

The chapter is structured in three sections. First, a theory of constitutional defence and emergency politics in the federation as a political form is developed (section I). Special attention is given to the employment of different modes of constitutional defence and emergency politics in two historical federations: the antebellum United States and the nineteenth-century German Confederation (*Deutscher Bund*). Based on the theory developed, the chapter goes on to discuss, respectively, the emergency government of the Eurozone (section II) and its contestation by the Member States (section III).

I. Emergency Rule in the Federation

A. Mixed Emergency Rule

Being founded on a constitutional compact, federations have constitutional forms of government. This means that the exercise of governmental authority is subject to such limitations as institutional checks and in some cases protection of fundamental rights. The most important constitutional limitation in a federation is the constitutional balance between the Union and its Member States. Nonetheless, situations may arise (war, secession, subversion, insurrection, natural or socio-economic catastrophes or crises) where the survival of the federation necessitates measures incompatible with these constitutional limitations. In the words of Clinton Rossiter:

> Wars are not won by debating societies, rebellions are not suppressed by judicial injunctions, the reemployment of twelve million jobless citizens will not be effected through a scrupulous regard for the tenets of free enterprise, and hardships caused by the eruptions of nature cannot be mitigated by letting nature take its course.[8]

In such situations, the federal constitution must, in the same manner as the constitution of a state, *either* provide explicitly for the possibility of exercising emergency powers *or* the governmental structure of the Union must be provided with enough flexibility so that it can deal with the state of crisis through the exercise of similar extraordinary measures.[9] In either case, the difficulty consists in how the temporary relaxation of constitutional constraints can be ensured without incurring permanent harm to the constitutional norms and the constitutional balance of the

[8] Clinton Rossiter, *Constitutional Dictatorship: Crisis Government in the Modern Democracies* (Princeton University Press 1948) 6.

[9] Carl J Friedrich and Arthur E Sutherland, 'Defence of the Constitutional Order' in Carl J Friedrich and Robert R Bowie (eds), *Studies in Federalism* (Little, Brown and Company 1954) 676.

federation. The purpose of all constitutional emergency government—'constitutional dictatorship', that is, dictatorship in its concise meaning within constitutional theory—is neither more nor less than the re-establishment of the *status quo ante crisis*.[10] This is the general aporia of emergency politics that applies to the state and the federation alike.

Nevertheless, there are fundamental and qualitative differences between the mode of emergency government of the federation and the state.[11] In contrast to the state, the federation is a double political existence. This means that emergency politics can be exercised *by a variety of different constitutional actors* (Union actors and Member State actors) and wielded *on behalf of different existential units* (the Union and the Member States). The debate on who is the guardian of the constitution is therefore not reducible to the Schmitt/Kelsen debate on President versus constitutional court.[12] The federation allows for a contest not merely between different institutions but also between different political entities. It allows for rival claims to governmental authority by the Union and by the Member States that can lead to highly toxic conflicts.

Emergency politics in the federation is complex because the multiple constitutional orders of the federation stand in a relationship to one another of both *independence* and *interdependence* (*Chapter 3:I:B*). Since the constitutional orders of the Union and the Member States are *independent* from one another, the federation allows for two sets of emergency actors (Union and Member State actors) on behalf of two constitutional orders (Union and Member State constitutions). Yet, because the constitutional orders of the Union and the Member States are *interdependent*, there is no necessary correspondence between a crisis in a constitutional order and the actor claiming emergency authority to govern that particular crisis.

The interdependence has its roots in the fundamental *mutualization of risk* among the Member States.[13] By coming together in a common union, some of the most important concerns of the Member States (defence and/or welfare) become common concerns. A disequilibrium in one part of the Union can have repercussions in all the other parts of the Union. In a federation, there

[10] Rossiter (n 8) ch 1.

[11] There is a vast, and controversial, literature on emergency government in the state including Carl Schmitt, *Dictatorship: From the Origin of the Modern Concept of Sovereignty to the Proletarian Class Struggle* (Polity Press 2014); Carl Schmitt, *Political Theology: Four Chapters on the Concept of Sovereignty* (University of Chicago Press 2010); Giorgio Agamben, *State of Exception* (University of Chicago Press 2005); Ernst Fraenkel, *The Dual State: A Contribution to the Theory of Dictatorship* (OUP 1941); William E Scheuerman, 'The Economic State of Exception' 21 Cardozo Law Review 1869. A general review of this literature is outside the scope of this book. For a general introduction to the history and theory of emergency politics, see John Ferejohn and Pasquale Pasquino, 'The Law of the Exception: A Typology of Emergency Powers' (2004) 2 International Journal of Constitutional Law 210.

[12] See Lars Vinx (ed), *The Guardian of the Constitution: Hans Kelsen and Carl Schmitt on the Limits of Constitutional Law* (CUP 2015).

[13] Olivier Beaud, *Théorie de la fédération* (Presses universitaires de France 2007) 296.

are therefore no 'internal affairs' of the Member States that cannot *potentially* be understood as Union matters. Besides, by coming together in a common union, the Member States renounce their right to self-help and their relationship *inter se* is governed by the internal public law of the Union. This means that if one of the Member States breaches the fundamental law of the Union, the Member States no longer possess the rights of international law such as state retaliation or, ultimately, war. It is therefore necessary that the Union, by way of its own public law, can enforce and defend the constitution against constitutional threats or breaches by its Member States. All conflicts *between* the Member States and crises *within* the Member States are potentially matters of common security and stability for the Union as a whole and they have to be governed by Union law.

For that reason, emergency politics in the federation *cannot* be understood on the basis of the matrices: Member State crisis = Member State emergency rule; Union crisis = Union emergency rule. That is, when a Union institution exercises emergency politics, it is not necessarily with reference to a Union-wide state of exception, and seldom exclusively so. As we shall see, Union institutions will often justify the exercise of emergency powers with reference to both a crisis of one or more of the Member States and a crisis of the Union as a whole. Similarly, when a Member State exercises emergency politics, it is not necessarily purely with reference to a threat to its own constitutional order. The Member State may also claim to act as the guardian of the Union constitution. In other words, the fundamental interdependence of the constitutional orders of the federation means that the claims to emergency powers in the federation are not parallel but, rather, overlapping. Besides, the exercise of emergency politics in the federation will tend to involve both Union institutions and Member State institutions because of the interdependence of the governmental orders of the Union and the Member States. Federal emergency politics is a form of 'mixed emergency rule' more often than not involving multiple actors and multiple claims to emergency authority.

In this mixed form of emergency rule, the different actors can relate to each other in multiple ways. This is especially clear in that Union institutions tend to employ two different modes of emergency politics in relation to the Member States. The Union institutions can exercise emergency powers both *against* a Member State and *on behalf* of a Member State. First, they can act against a Member State that breaches or threatens the federal constitution. Second, they can act on behalf of a Member State that is incapable of dealing with an internal crisis or conflict. This latter form of intervention tends to be justified both with reference to the stability of the crisis-ridden Member State and the Union as a whole. The most coherent theory of these two qualitatively different forms of emergency politics has been developed on the basis of the praxis of the German Confederation to which we will now turn.

B. Federal Execution and Federal Intervention

In the German Confederation (*Deutscher Bund*)—established in 1815 after the collapse of the Holy Roman Empire and dissolved in 1866 after the Austro-Prussian War—two qualitatively distinct forms of executive constitutional defence were available to the federal diet (*Bundesversammlung/Bundestag*): the 'federal execution' (*Bundesexekution*) and the 'federal intervention' (*Bundesintervention*).[14] The federal execution authorized the use of executive measures *against* a non-complying Member State. The federal intervention authorized the use of executive measures on *behalf* of a Member State incapable of dealing with an internal crisis. The main legal basis for both the federal execution and the federal intervention was the second constitutional compact (*Verfassungsvertrag*) on which the German Confederation relied: The Final Act of the Congress of Vienna (*Wiener Schlussakte*) of 1820. The federal execution was governed by Articles 19 and 31–34, and the federal intervention by Articles 25–28 of the Final Act of the Congress of Vienna .[15]

These two forms of executive constitutional defence were frequently used during the lifespan of the German Confederation, notably to defend the 'monarchical form of government' of the Member States guaranteed by the German Confederation against the national-liberal political uprisings of the mid-nineteenth century.[16] In this way, executive constitutional defence was, in the German Confederation, intimately linked to the federal 'guarantee clause' (*Chapter 4:IV*). Federal emergency politics was used, such as against the revolutionaries of the *Frankfurter Wachensturm* of 1833, to authorize the federal occupation of Holstein during the Second Schleswig War of 1864, and in the attempt to stop Prussia seceding in 1866.[17] The most important theoretical study of federal constitutional defence in the German Confederation has been produced by the German constitutional historian and constitutional theorist, Ernst Rudolf Huber.[18]

According to Huber, federal execution and federal intervention have often, and for good reasons, been conflated.[19] The conflation happens because the concrete measures used in federal execution and federal intervention were often identical. The scope and intensity varied from case to case but ultimately military enforcement, temporary suspension of the targeted Member State's constitution in parts or

[14] Ernst Rudolf Huber, 'Bundesexekution und Bundesintervention: Ein Beitrag zur Frage des Verfassungsschutzes im Deutschen Bund' (1953) 79 Archiv des öffentlichen Rechts 1, 1–2.

[15] ibid 2.

[16] Ernst Rudolf Huber, *Deutsche Verfassungsgeschichte seit 1789*, vol 1: Reform und Restauration 1789 bis 1830 (Verlag W Kohlhammer 1957) 595–96, 619–20; Emmanuel N Roussakis, *Friedrich List, the Zollverein, and the Uniting of Europe* (College of Europe 1968) 20.

[17] Huber (n 14) 3.

[18] The works of Ernst Rudolf Huber are not widely studied, at least not within Anglo-American academia, but he is one of the most important theorists of the federation in the twentieth century. For an introduction to his writings, see Murray Forsyth, *Union of States: The Theory and Practice of Confederations* (Leicester University Press 1981) 155–59.

[19] Huber (n 14) 9.

in its entirety and 'forced administration' of a Member State could be authorized.[20] The 'federal commissioner' acting on behalf of the German Confederation could, in both a federal execution and a federal intervention, temporarily take over the whole governmental apparatus of the Member State concerned. Notwithstanding that they can be difficult to tell apart in practice, federal execution and federal intervention are distinct from one another in theory with regard to their mode of authorization.

The *federal execution* is the embodiment of the coercive executive measures or sanctions through which the Union can act *against* one of its Member States to persuade it to fulfil the constitutional obligations that it has neglected.[21] A federal execution is thus an executive act decided on and authorized by the Union in order to force a Member State, which in some way presents a threat to the constitution of the Union, to comply with the federal constitution. Federal execution is meant to secure the unity, order, and legal system of the Union against the reluctant or separatist state forces that can always be powerful in a federation. A federal execution is an act against the government of a Member State that has infringed the federal constitution and it is enforced against the will of the Member State in question. During the federal execution, the Member State that it concerns will be deprived of its political rights at the federal level.[22] The federal executioner who enforces the federal execution in the non-complying Member State can act as a 'commissarial dictator' in that Member State, temporarily taking over the full powers and authority of the Member State government.[23]

In contrast, the *federal intervention* is the embodiment of the coercive measures through which the Union is obligated to restore or maintain a Member State government, loyal to the federal constitution, if the internal security or order of the Member State or its constitution is under threat.[24] Historically, a federal intervention was used by the German princes to strengthen their power positions vis-à-vis national-liberal insurgencies by allowing the princes to rely not only on their own executive powers but also on those of all the other Member States. The federation will normally intervene on a formal request of the crisis-ridden Member State. However, if the Member State is incapable of requesting help because of internal instability, the federation is equally obligated to intervene *on behalf of* the Member State to preserve its internal order and stability.

In theory, therefore, the federal execution and the federal intervention are clearly distinct from one another. Nevertheless, the sharp distinction between the

[20] ibid 6–9; Huber (n 16) 636.

[21] Huber (n 16) 635; Huber (n 14) 6. The federal execution was included in all three German constitutions that succeeded the German Confederation. In Article 19 of the 1871 Imperial Constitution, in Article 48(1) of the ill-fated 1919 Weimar Constitution, and in Article 37 of the 1949 German Basic Law.

[22] Huber (n 16) 636.

[23] ibid 635–36.

[24] Huber (n 14) 4.

federal execution and the federal intervention is impossible to uphold because of the fundamental mutualization of risk in a federation. If the internal threat to the constitution of the Member State is understood as having effects beyond the boundaries of that state (which is arguably the case for most if not all serious crises of a Member State), the federation has a political, if not legal, right to intervene in the Member State concerned in the interest of the security and stability of the Union and its constitution as a whole.[25] Even in cases where the security interest of the Union is the dominating factor for a federal intervention, the Union is no less obligated to preserve the constitution of the Member State concerned as well. In this latter case, known as the '*unrequested* intervention', where the Member State has not requested the assistance or even explicitly requested the federation *not* to intervene, the Union may have to rely on the *fiction* that it saves the constitutional order of the Member State.[26]

If this proves untenable, that is, because of persistent resistance by the Member State concerned, it is possible to make a formal link between the federal execution and the federal intervention by making it a duty by federal law for the Member States to inform the federation of internal threats to their constitutional orders as was done in the German Confederation.[27] If the Member State chose to inform the Union of an internal instability and request assistance, the Union could act through a federal intervention; if the Member State chose not to inform the Union, the federation could intervene by way of a federal execution, maintaining that the Member State had neglected its constitutional duty to inform the Union of internal instabilities. In this way, the German Confederation established a *comprehensive apparatus of executive emergency powers* capable of intervening in practically all internal affairs of the Member States.

The executive emergency apparatus of the federal intervention and the federal execution has its foundation in federalism. It is created to resolve conflicts internal to the federation by way of federal public law. The raison d'être of this apparatus is that the Member States do not have to resort to the enforcement mechanisms of international law, such as state retaliation or war, that would be a threat to the public law of the Union. It is, in other words, an important way for the Union to protect the main principles of federalism. However, by intervening in the internal affairs of its Member States, executive emergency powers may destroy the foundational principles of federalism. *Federal executive constitutional defence is therefore inherently contradictory.*

The federal commissioner who acts either via a federal execution or a federal intervention will, if deemed necessary, have the authority to act as a constitutional dictator for the Member State concerned. During the federal intervention/

[25] ibid 5.
[26] ibid 10–11, 15–17.
[27] ibid 17.

execution, the federal commissioner becomes a kind of *protector* for the Member State and the Member State is degraded to a *de facto* dependency of the Union. Even if this is done following a request by the government of the Member State concerned, this action can be a threat to the principle of federalism because the government of the Member State, *de facto* if not *de jure*, might be without a choice. The government that has requested a federal intervention, following Huber's description, finds itself between the Scylla of the internal crisis it is incapable of solving and the Charybdis of the power and authority of the federal intervention.[28] If the Union decides to make an *unrequested* federal intervention in the internal affairs of its Member States, the situation is even more grievous for the principles of federalism. In this case, the Union oversteps the principle of the autonomy of the Member States, not only *de facto* but also *de jure*, by declaring a state of exception on its behalf. This action is authorized in the name of the security and stability of the Union as a whole. It is a form of 'union-wide state of exception' (*Bundes-Ausnahmezustand*)[29] in which the Union acts *as if* it was a state and the Member States were subordinate entities.

Together, the federal execution and the federal intervention make up a comprehensive apparatus of executive emergency government of the federation that potentially gives the Union the possibility of intervening in all the internal affairs of its Member States and declaring a state of exception both for the Union at large and for the individual Member States. Despite the fact that this governmental apparatus is derived from the principles of *federalism*—it is meant to ensure that the Member States do not resort to state retaliation or armed conflict—it has an extremely *unitary* or *statist* effect. Emergency government pushes the federation in the direction of statehood and for that reason it challenges the foundations of federal public law. The federal executive emergency government is constantly in danger of destroying the core principles of federalism: the constitutional balance between the Union and its Member States.

C. The Doctrine of States' Rights

The Founding Fathers of the US Constitution were acutely aware of the problems related to federal executive constitutional defence, especially the possibility of the employment of federal military force against a non-complying Member State. In the Virginia Plan, presented to the Federal Convention on 29 May 1787, a provision was included granting the new Congress the power 'to call forth the force of

[28] Huber (n 14) 10.
[29] ibid 12.

the Union against any member of the union failing to fulfil its duty'.[30] However, a few days after presenting the plan, Madison, who was its chief author, suffered a change of heart and recommended that the clause be postponed. According to the meeting minutes,

> Mr. Madison, observed that the more he reflected on the use of force, the more he doubted the practicability, the justice and the efficacy of it when applied to people collectively and not individually. – *A union of the States containing such an ingredient seemed to provide for its own destruction.* The use of force agst a State would look more like a declaration of war, than an infliction of punishment, and would probably be considered by the party attached as a dissolution of all previous compacts by which it might be bound. He hoped that such a system would be framed that might render this resource unnecessary.[31]

Instead of military coercion, Madison suggested what he termed a congressional negative on state laws, by which he meant a congressional veto on state legislation.[32] This solution was not accepted by the Convention. The question of military coercion of the states as a means of constitutional defence was hotly contested at the Convention but eventually the majority of the delegates 'preferred, and Madison and his associates ultimately accepted, the method of judicial review as that best suited to maintaining the supremacy of the constitution'.[33] Instead of executive constitutional defence, the Convention settled on judicial constitutional defence. The Constitution of the United States that came to be adopted, however, did also include the federal 'guarantee clause' and wide-ranging presidential powers, through which the federal government could ultimately exercise some degree of executive constitutional defence on behalf of and against the states.[34]

[30] Arthur N Holcombe, 'The Coercion of States in a Federal System' in Arthur W MacMahon (ed), *Federalism: Mature and Emergent* (Doubleday & Company 1955) 140. See also Max Farrand, *The Framing of the Constitution of the United States* (Yale University Press 1913) ch V: The Virginia Plan.

[31] United States Congress, House of Representatives, *Documents Illustrative of the Formation of the Union of the American States* (Charles Callan Tansill ed, Session 69th Congress, 1st Session Volume Serial Set Vol No 8573, Session Vol No12 1926) 131, emphasis added.

[32] Charles F Hobson, 'The Negative on State Laws: James Madison, the Constitution, and the Crisis of Republican Government' (1979) 36 The William and Mary Quarterly 215; Holcombe (n 30) 140.

[33] Holcombe (n 30) 141. For a critique of the argument that the Supreme Court under John Marshall established judicial review of federal legislation in *Marbury v Madison* 5 U.S. 137 (1803) without any authority or precedents to guide them and that the Founders never intended or authorized judicial review, see Charles A Beard, *The Supreme Court and the Constitution* (MacMillan 1916) ch 2, especially 33–34 and ch 6, 113–18. See also Saikrishna Prakash and John Yoo, 'The Origins of Judicial Review' (2003) 70 The University of Chicago Law Review 887, 891–92, 928ff, 939–40; Jack Rakove, 'The Origins of Judicial Review: A Plea for New Contexts' (1997) 49 Stanford Law Review 1031. The Supreme Court's authority to be the final arbiter of constitutional questions, however, remained contested until the Civil War, see, eg, Richard E Ellis, *The Union at Risk: Jacksonian Democracy, States' Rights and the Nullification Crisis* (OUP 1989) 185ff.

[34] The Constitution of the United States, Article IV. For the use of the US guarantee clause as a means to constitutional defence, see William M Wiecek, *The Guarantee Clause of the US Constitution* (Cornell University Press 1972). For the use of the guarantee clause during the Reconstruction, see specifically pp 166–210.

Nevertheless, federal constitutional defence, executive as well as judicial, is highly controversial. The history of all young federations attests to this.[35] From the perspective of the Member States, it is in no way self-evident that the Union has a right to act as the guardian of their constitutions or as the guardian of the federal constitution at the expense of their autonomy and right of self-determination. The Member States of a federation therefore often claim the right to act as the guardian of their own constitution *and* the Union constitution against constitutional breaches by the Union institutions by way of judicial, legislative as well as executive measures. Whereas the most comprehensive theory of executive constitutional defence by federal institutions has been put forward to understand the praxis of the German Confederation, the most comprehensive arguments for the Member States' right to act as the guardian of the constitution has been put forward in the context of the early history of the United States.[36]

There are several examples in early US constitutional history where a state decided to defend itself by a wide array of means, including executive measures, from what it perceived as *ultra vires* acts of the federal government or the US Supreme Court, such as the reaction of Ohio to *McCulloch v Maryland* (1819), the reaction of Georgia to *Cherokee Nation v Georgia* (1831), and *Worcester v Georgia* (1832).[37] These contestations of federal authority relied (rightly or wrongly) on the so-called doctrine of '98, namely the Kentucky and Virginia Resolutions of 1798 and 1799.[38] These resolutions were drafted by James Madison and Thomas Jefferson and they maintained that the ultimate authority to decide on the constitutionality of federal law lay with the states.[39] The controversial nature of the Supreme Court's authority to act as the guardian of the constitution is expressed in this way in the Kentucky Resolution: 'as in all other cases of compact among powers having no common judge, *each party has an equal right to judge for itself, as well of infractions as of the mode and measure of redress*'.[40]

Following the Southern States' interpretation of the 'doctrine of '98', the States had a right to declare void (nullify) federal law that they deemed to be unconstitutional.[41] In the United States Civil War, most Confederate States relied on an

[35] For a study of contestation of federal authority in young federations, see Leslie Goldstein, *Constituting Federal Sovereignty: The European Union in Comparative Context* (Johns Hopkins University Press 2001). Goldstein presents an impressive comparative study of constitutional contestation in the EU, the United Provinces of the Netherlands, the early American Republic, and the nineteenth-century Swiss federation.

[36] For a history of the origins and evolution of the states' rights argument in early American history, see Ellis (n 33).

[37] ibid 29ff; Goldstein (n 35) 21–31, 49–50.

[38] KR Constantine Gutzman, 'The Virginia and Kentucky Resolutions Reconsidered: "An Appeal to the Real Laws of Our Country"' (2000) 66 The Journal of Southern History 473; Adrienne Koch and Harry Ammon, 'The Virginia and Kentucky Resolutions: An Episode in Jefferson's and Madison's Defense of Civil Liberties' (1948) 5 The William and Mary Quarterly 145.

[39] Ellis (n 33) 9ff; Goldstein (n 35) 21.

[40] Resolutions adopted by the Kentucky General Assembly in *The Papers of Thomas Jefferson, Volume 30: 1 January 1798 to 31 January 1799* (Princeton University Press 2003) 550–56.

[41] Stanley M Elkins, *The Age of Federalism* (OUP 1993) 721–22.

interpretation of the 'doctrine of '98' and thus cited the 'dangerous infractions of the Constitution' by the Federal Government as one of the main reasons in their 'Declarations of Causes Justifying Secession'.[42] For example, the South Carolina 'Declaration' opens with the following statement:

> The people of the State of South Carolina, in Convention assembled, on the 26th day of April, A.D., 1852, declared that the frequent violations of the Constitution of the United States, by the Federal Government, and its encroachments upon the reserved rights of the States, fully justified this State in then withdrawing from the Federal Union.[43]

The argument that the Member States, and not the Union, are the guardians of the constitution was, in the history of the theory of the federation, first put forward in a comprehensive manner by the political theorist and seventh Vice President of the United States, John C Calhoun. Calhoun argued that the United States was a union of sovereign states constituted by a compact between them. Concluding his argument, Calhoun writes:

> Taken all together, it follows, from what has been stated, that the constitution was ordained and established *by* the several States, as *distinct, sovereign communities;* and that it was ordained and established by them for *themselves* – for their common welfare and safety, as *distinct and sovereign communities* ... the authority which ordained and established the constitution, was the joint and united authority of the States ratifying it; and that, among the effects of their ratification; it became a contract between them; and, *as a compact,* binding on them; – but only as such.[44]

Calhoun argued against the doctrine of divided sovereignty[45] that had been predominant in the early history of the United States and argued that sovereignty remained fully with the states-peoples of the Union; not with the people of the

[42] The 'Declarations of Causes Justifying Secession' <https://www.civilwar.org/learn/primary-sources/declaration-causes-seceding-states#South_Carolina> accessed 20 November 2017.

[43] ibid.

[44] John C Calhoun, 'A Discourse on the Constitution and Government of the United States' in Richard K Crallé (ed), *The Works of Calhoun Volume 1: A Disquisition on Government and a Discourse on the Constitution and Government of the United States* (Steam Power-Press 1851) 130–31 italics in original. See also ibid 111–16, 126–29.

[45] Calhoun's famous declaration against the notion of divided sovereignty reads: 'There is no difficulty in understanding how powers, appertaining to sovereignty, may be divided; and *the exercise* of one portion delegated to one set of agents, and another portion to another: or how sovereignty maybe be vested in one man, or in few, or in many. But how sovereignty itself—the supreme power—can be divided,—how the people of the several States can be partly sovereign, and partly *not* sovereign—partly supreme, and partly *not* supreme, it is impossible to conceive. Sovereignty is an entire thing;—to divide, is,—to destroy it' (ibid 146, italics in original). See also Charles E Merriam, 'The Political Theory of Calhoun' (1902) 7 American Journal of Sociology 577, 588.

United States constituting one nation: 'There is, indeed, no such community, *politically* speaking, as the people of the United States, regarded in the light of, and as constituting one people or nation', Calhoun argued forcefully.[46] For that reason, the citizens of the United States ultimately owed their allegiance to the States and not the Union.[47] The States, Calhoun maintained, had as an essential attribute of their sovereignty the right to judge the constitutionality of federal law and, if necessary, to nullify it.[48] In this way, the States would have an effective veto power regarding federal legislation.[49]

Calhoun further argued that the states had a right to dissolve their relationship with the Union—the right to secede—rather than submitting themselves to federal law which they deemed to be unconstitutional.[50] The right of secession was the ultimate right of constitutional defence of the States. In a response to his adversary, the Senator of Massachusetts, Daniel Webster, Calhoun thus argued:

> I rest the right of a State to judge of the extent of its reserved powers, in the last resort, on higher grounds – that the constitution is a compact, to which the States are parties in their sovereign capacity; and that, as in all other cases of compact between parties having no common umpire, each has a right to judge for itself. To the truth of this proposition the Senator from Massachusetts has himself assented, if the constitution be a compact – and that it is, I have shown, I trust, beyond the possibility of doubt. Having established that point, I now claim, as I stated I would do in the course of discussion, the admissions of the Senator, and among them, the right of secession and nullification, which he conceded would necessarily follow if the constitution be indeed a compact.[51]

Calhoun's ideas and arguments influenced American history both during the 'nullification crisis' of 1832–33 and the Civil War. His controversial legacy, however, is not merely American. The doctrine of states' rights was appropriated by the so-called Bavarian Calhoun: the German constitutional theorist Max von Seydel. Inspired by Calhoun's writings, Seydel argued that the German *Länder* had merely

[46] Calhoun (n 44) 162.

[47] ibid 122.

[48] See, for example, Calhoun's South Carolina Exposition of 1828, reprinted in the special issue by AB Hart and E Channing (eds), *Constitutional Doctrines of Webster, Hayne and Calhoun* in *American History Leaflets: Colonial and Constitutional* (Harvard University 1896); John C Calhoun, 'Speech in Support of the Veto Power', delivered in the United States Senate (28 February 1842); Calhoun (n 44) 236ff, 277–78; Merriam (n 45) 589–90.

[49] See eg, Merriam (n 45) 584–85.

[50] Calhoun (n 44) 277–78; Merriam (n 45) 584–85.

[51] John C Calhoun, 'Speech in Reply to Mr. Webster, on the Resolution Respecting the Rights of the States, Delivered in the Senate, Feb. 26th, 1833' in Richard K Crallé (ed), *The Works of John C. Calhoun Volume II: Speeches of John C. Calhoun delivered in the House of Representatives and in the Senate of the United States* (D Appleton and Company 1881) 301–2.

delegated certain powers or functions to the federal government but that this delegation did not entail a transfer of sovereignty itself.[52]

As was the case for the doctrine of federal intervention and federal execution, the doctrine of states' rights is founded on the principles of federalism. Since the states have created the Union through a compact between them in order to preserve themselves politically, they have a right, as a last resort, to nullify federal laws and to dissolve this same compact as a means of constitutional self-defence if the constitution has been breached. Nevertheless, this form of constitutional guardianship creates as many constitutional guardians as there are Member States. It therefore presents a fundamental threat to the unity, stability, and order of a federation and can ultimately lead to its collapse.

This was Webster's argument in response to Calhoun: 'could anything', Webster declared, '[be] more preposterous, than to make a government for the whole Union, and yet leave its power subject, not to one interpretation, but to thirteen or twenty-four interpretations?'[53] Constitutional defence by Member States, as is the case for constitutional defence by Union institutions, can, sooner or later, be a fundamental threat to the federation by breaking it apart. The doctrine of states' rights is therefore also confronted by the conundrum of federal constitutional defence by bringing the logic of the state into the federation.

D. Competing Claims to Constitutional Guardianship

In contrast to the authority of a state that has as its ultimate source the unitary political existence of the state expressed in the will of the people (or the prince), the federation, being a double political existence, has twin sources of public power: the political existence of the Union and the political existence of its Member States (*Chapter 1:IV*). Governmental authority in a federation can therefore be wielded legally, and ultimately extra-legally, in the name of the security of the individual states and for the wellbeing of their citizens, *and* in the name of the security of the Union and for the wellbeing of its citizens.[54] That is, authority can be wielded in the name of the people as one or the peoples as many; in the name of the '*union* of states' or in the 'union of *states*'. Because of the multiple constitutional orders of the federation that stand in a heterarchical relationship to one another of relative autonomy, there is no unequivocal answer to the question of who has the authority

[52] Karl Kössler and Francesco Palermo, *Comparative Federalism Constitutional Arrangements and Case Law* (Hart Publishing 2017) 87. A line of argument that today is manifest in the doctrine of the German Constitutional Court on the relationship between Germany and the EU. See, eg, BVerfG, Judgment of the Second Senate of 30 June 2009—2 BvE 2/08 (*Lisbon Ruling*).

[53] Speech by Daniel Webster as cited by Thomas C Fischer, 'Federalism in the European Community and the United States: A Rose by Any Other Name' (1994) 17 Fordham International Law Journal 389, 431. For an introduction to the debate between Webster and Calhoun, see Forsyth (n 18) 117–32.

[54] Huber (n 14) 54–55.

to act as the guardian of the constitution, what or which constitution(s) should be saved, and in the name of whom the emergency powers are authorized. It is in the power of the Union to suspend the political autonomy of one or more of its Member States to defend the constitution and security of the Union as a whole. At the same time, the Member State can suspend or nullify the constitutional order of the federation in whole or in part within its territory in order to protect its own constitutional order or stability, welfare or security.

The conflict between these forms of constitutional defence, the doctrine of federal execution and federal intervention versus the doctrine of states' rights, are manifest both in the case of the American Civil War, where the Southern States' attempt at secession was crushed by the Union army, and in the case of the Austro-Prussian War, which led to the collapse of the German Confederation after the Union failed to prevent Prussia seceding.[55] Both sides, in both conflicts, could present strong and valid arguments founded on the principles of federalism and their respective constitutional orders.[56] The Member States had a right to secede as a means of constitutional defence, whereas the Union had a right to intervene to preserve the order and stability of the Union. Both of these actions, though based on the logic of federalism, will, however, bring the federation to the brink of collapse by introducing the logic of the state into the federation. This is the most fundamental paradox of constitutional defence in a federal union of states. The federation as a discrete political form relies on the suspension of sovereignty and therefore on the question of who decides remaining unanswered. Emergency government has the potential to lead to a definite answer to this question: 'Sovereign is she who decides upon the exception'.[57]

The government of the Eurozone has posed this question twice: judicially in *Weiss*[58] and in a more 'political' manner in the 'Greek crisis', or so it will be argued. Nevertheless, perhaps the question can remain open for the time being, or at least without a final and decisive answer. Like other federations, the EU relies on an equilibrium between the political forces it unites. This can only be done as long as the question of sovereignty—the question of who ultimately decides—can remain open. Only then can the Union and its Member States coexist as two equal political entities in a state of 'constitutional tolerance'. As we shall see, the emergency government of the Eurozone has introduced a strong element of reason of state into the Union that threatens the constitutional balance of the EU by eroding the political autonomy of the Member States, *de facto* if not *de jure*.

[55] ibid 46, 55–56.

[56] ibid 52–56.

[57] Schmitt, *Political Theology* (n 11) 5, amended translation ('Souverän ist, wer über den Ausnahmezustand entscheidet').

[58] BVerfG, Judgment of the Second Senate of 05 May 2020—2 BvR 859/15 and Case C-493/17 *Weiss and Others* [2018] ECLI:EU:C:2018:1000. See section II:C of this chapter. The 'Greek crisis' is discussed in section II:D.

II. European Emergency Government

A. Eurocrisis Law

Prior to the Eurozone crisis, constitutional defence was primarily a judicial matter in the EU. The unity, stability, and order of the EU has been secured by the preliminary reference procedure[59] and the infringement procedure.[60] The annulment procedure, furthermore, has provided a possibility for judicial review of EU law.[61] When the importance of the federal balance for the stability of the federation is taken into account, judicial constitutional defence is in many ways preferable to executive constitutional defence because it presents a comparatively minor threat to the political autonomy of the Member States. As Madison realized, the enforcement of the federal constitution by force would look more like a declaration of war and might lead to the dissolution of the federal union.

Unfortunately, judicial constitutional defence is limited regarding the kinds of crises it can deal with. War, secession, subversion, insurrection, natural catastrophes, and economic depressions might all demand an *immediate response of executive measures.* A court can retrospectively authorize, legalize, or otherwise justify executive acts of emergency politics, but it cannot act.[62] Judicial constitutional defence alone is therefore incapable of dealing with fundamental internal threats to the constitutional order and stability of a federal union. Or, in the words of Rossiter: 'If a situation can be dealt with judicially, it is probably not a crisis'.[63] For example, with the outbreak of the Civil War, judicial constitutional defence could no longer preserve the constitution and public order of the United States; executive constitutional defence was employed by President Lincoln to repress the rebellious Southern States. However 'valuable and important it is for the defence against subversions and constitutional disorder', judicial constitutional defence, in the words of Huber, is 'incapable of safeguarding the Union as a whole against the area of conflict between the fundamental political existences and vital powers of the Union'.[64] With the unfolding of the Eurozone crisis, the EU's lack of executive constitutional defence became apparent. Europe found itself in the most serious economic crisis since the Great Depression with few, if any, real emergency powers at the Union level. If executive constitutional defence was not deemed necessary earlier, it quickly became so.

[59] Article 267 of the Consolidated Version of the Treaty on the Functioning of the European Union [2016] OJ C202 (hereafter TFEU).

[60] Article 258 TFEU.

[61] Article 263 TFEU.

[62] In contrast, the constitutional dictator acts. He is, Schmitt writes, 'the commissar of action; he is the executive, in contrast to merely decision-making process or judicial verdict – in contrast to deliberare and consultare' (*Dictatorship* (n 11) 8).

[63] Rossiter (n 8) 9.

[64] Huber (n 14) 1, my translation.

Executive constitutional defence is not straightforwardly employed in the EU for a number of reasons. As we saw earlier (*Chapter 5:I:A*), emergency government is often made possible either by having a direct provision for emergency government *or* by giving the governmental institutions the flexibility necessary to exercise emergency government within the scope of the law. During the Eurozone crisis, the EU governmental institutions could only to a limited extent avail themselves of any of these options. Prior to the crisis, there were no legal bases, or sparse at best, in the Treaties for economic emergency politics beyond the scope of Articles 122(2) and 143 TFEU.[65] Moreover, because of the rigidity and detailed nature of the EU Treaties, the narrow constitutional mandates of the governmental institution of the EU and the complex process of Treaty revision, the flexibility of the EU's executive branch of government is highly restricted. In contrast to systems of parliamentary sovereignty where emergency government can be exercised within the boundaries of the constitution because of the lack of a strict separation between legislative and executive powers and the relative flexibility of cabinet,[66] the governmental institutions of the EU are not constituted with the flexibility that would allow them, in an unproblematic manner, to exercise emergency powers without going beyond their legal mandate.

Because of the limited possibility for the use of executive constitutional defence provided by the EU Treaties, emergency politics in the EU must be authorized on more *political* grounds. The EU is not unique in that regard. Executive constitutional defence must sometimes go beyond the constitution in order to save the political community. No one expressed this better than Lincoln. To critiques of his employment of emergency measures to repress the rebellious Southern States, his response was this:

> Every man thinks he has a right to live and every government thinks it has a right to live. Every man when driven to the wall by murderous assailants will override all laws to protect himself, and this is called the great right of self-defence. So every government, when driven to the wall by a rebellion, will trample down a

[65] Article 122(2) TFEU reads: 'Where a Member State is in difficulties or is seriously threatened with severe difficulties caused by natural disasters or exceptional occurrences beyond its control, the Council, on a proposal from the Commission, may grant, under certain conditions, Union financial assistance to the Member State concerned. The President of the Council shall inform the European Parliament of the decision taken'. In May 2010, the Council was able to extend help to the Greek financial authorities via Article 122 thus interpreting the financial crisis of 2008–9 as an exceptional occurrence beyond the control of the Greek government, see Waltraud Schelkle, *The Political Economy of Monetary Solidarity: Understanding the Euro Experiment* (OUP 2017) 212, 141. Article 143 TFEU allows for the Union to provide assistance to a non-Eurozone Member State that is experiencing balance of payments difficulties that 'jeopardise the functioning of the internal market or the implementation of the common commercial policy'. The three non-Eurozone bailouts—Hungary, Latvia, and Romania—were all based on Article 143 TFEU, see Claire Kilpatrick, 'Are the Bailouts Immune to EU Social Challenge Because They Are Not EU Law?' (2014) 10 European Constitutional Law Review 393, 400.

[66] Rossiter (n 8) 135–36, 139, 154–58.

constitution before it allows itself to be destroyed. This may not be constitutional law, but it is fact.[67]

The *extension* of executive powers is arguably of greater importance in federal systems than in unitary states because of the division of powers between the Union and the Member States.[68] The division of powers in a federation can have the implication that no one, neither the Union nor the Member States, can address the problem within the scope of the law. Centralized states merely have to *concentrate* the powers already granted to government on fewer hands or *transfer* powers from civil authority to military authority,[69] whereas federal systems will have to *extend* the powers available to government as such. A good historical example of this is the New Deal that led to a profound change to the US Constitution and significantly altered and enlarged the powers of the US government.[70]

Whether this can be upheld as a general rule or not, it has definitely been the case in the Eurozone crisis. Following the 'no-bailout clause' (Article 125 TFEU), the Union was not allowed to bail out a Member State on the brink of default and the European Central Bank (ECB) was forbidden to act as a lender of last resort to sovereigns (Article 123 TFEU).[71] However, seeing that the Member States had given up their old national currencies, they had lost one of their most important policy tools to deal with the crisis, namely, an independent monetary policy.[72] The possibility of devaluation and (internal) quantitative easing (QE) and large scale fiscal investment based on deficit spending no longer existed for the Member States who had adopted the euro. At the beginning of the Eurozone crisis, neither the EU nor the Member States had adequate powers available to them to deal with a recession of this scale.

Despite these constraints, a permanent European governmental emergency apparatus has been instituted during the Eurozone crisis with a view to governing

[67] Lincoln to Hodges, as cited by Rossiter (n 8) 11.

[68] 'If successful constitutional dictatorship involves either a union of the ordinarily separated powers or a simple disregard of that hoary principle of constitutionalism, then it would seem axiomatic that the less rigidly a government conforms to the theory of the separation of powers, the more easily it can adapt itself to the rigors of any particular crisis' (Rossiter (n 8) 154).

[69] In France, the 'state of siege' is characterized by the transfer of powers from civil administration to military commanders. Similarly, martial law in Britain is characterized by the extension of military government to domestic areas and civil persons (ibid 79–90, 140).

[70] Bruce Ackerman, *We the People II: Transformations* (The Belknap Press of Harvard University Press 1998) pt III; Gary Gerstle, *Liberty and Coercion: The Paradox of American Government from the Founding to the Present* (University Press 2018) pt III; Rossiter (n 8) ch 17.

[71] Paul de Grauwe, 'The European Central Bank as Lender of Last Resort in the Government Bond Markets' (2013) 59 CESifo Economic Studies 520.

[72] Paul de Grauwe, 'The Governance of a Fragile Eurozone' (2012) 45 The Australian Economic Review 255. As has been pointed out by Schelkle (n 65) 128–29, 181–82, the *de facto* constraint on the Member States' monetary sovereignty predates the euro. Notwithstanding that the Member States *de jure* had more policy tools available to them under the ERM system, the ERM crisis of 1992–93 made it clear that they could not make use of them effectively: 'The ERM crisis had shown most governments how little monetary sovereignty they had'.

not only the crisis but also the future developments of the Eurozone and the EU. This governmental apparatus relies on a patchwork of legal instruments and governmental agreements of a contested legal nature: the 'Six Pack', the 'Two Pack', and the 'European Semester' (all three formally EU law); the European Stability Mechanism (ESM)[73] and the 'Fiscal Compact'[74] (both formally international law); the 'Memorandas of Understanding' (MoUs) specifying loan conditionality (the legal status of which is 'liminal' or contested[75]); the Banking Union[76]; and, finally, the 'non-standard monetary policy instruments' of the ECB, importantly the Outright Monetary Transactions programme (OMT) and QE. Following Claire Kilpatrick, I refer to this body of (legal) instruments as 'Eurocrisis law'.[77]

The emergency apparatus allows EU institutions both to exercise emergency powers *on behalf* of a Member State 'loyal to the Union' that is incapable of dealing with an internal crisis, and it allows EU institutions to act *against* a Member State that breaches EU law and threatens the stability of the Union. Both forms of emergency rule entail a significant interference in the 'internal affairs' of the Member State in question. In this way, significant parts of Eurocrisis law emulate the structure of executive constitutional defence of the German Confederation: the federal intervention and the federal execution.

Before the Eurozone crisis, there was a legal ban for a Member State, 'loyal to the Union' but in a crisis beyond its command, to ask for help from the Union or the other Member States beyond the limited scope of Articles 122 and 143 TFEU. There was, in short, only a limited possibility for a federal intervention. With the creation of the ESM in 2012, a permanent legal structure was put into place that allows for a federal intervention. Following the conclusion of the ESM Treaty, an ESM Member State that finds itself in a financial crisis beyond its control may request financial assistance in the form of a loan from the ESM.[78] When a request is made, the ESM Board of Governors will entrust the Commission and the ECB with the task of assessing the emergency situation. In the ESM, the link between a threat to a Member State and a threat to the Union that always exists implicitly for federal interventions is made explicit. The ESM can only provide stability support if 'indispensable to safeguard the financial stability of the euro area as a whole and of its Member States'.[79] A federal intervention based on the ESM is therefore always linked to a 'Eurozone-wide state of exception' (ie, a *Bundes-Ausnahmezustand*).

[73] And early in the crisis the European Financial Stability Facility (EFSF).

[74] Formally the Treaty on Stability, Coordination and Governance in the Economic and Monetary Union.

[75] Claire Kilpatrick, 'The EU and Its Sovereign Debt Programmes: The Challenges of Liminal Legality' (2017) 14 EUI Working Papers LAW 1.

[76] Stefaan de Rynck, 'Banking on a Union: The Politics of Changing Eurozone Banking Supervision' (2016) 23 Journal of European Public Policy 119; Schelkle (n 65) 217–22.

[77] Claire Kilpatrick, 'Constitutions, Social Rights and Sovereign Debt States in Europe: A Challenging New Area of Constitutional Inquiry' 34 EUI Working Papers Law 1.

[78] Article 13 of the Treaty Establishing the European Stability Mechanism (hereafter ESM Treaty).

[79] Article 12 of the ESM Treaty.

The ESM was (formally) created outside EU law. Nevertheless, as most other forms of emergency politics, the ESM is anchored in public law and administered by public law institutions. The legal basis for the ESM is Article 136 TFEU, amended *ex-post facto* to allow for the establishment of 'a stability mechanism to be activated if indispensable to safeguard the stability of the euro area as a whole'.[80] Furthermore, the Commission and the ECB 'perform the tasks provided for' in the ESM Treaty.[81] The ESM is thus outside the public law structure of the EU but at the same time firmly anchored in it. It is a true, albeit unconventional, emergency regime: it suspends the public law norm but operates with the force of law through public law institutions. It is a form of 'liminal legality' existing in the 'contested border zone between law and non-law ... and EU law and non-EU law'.[82] The narrative that the bailout programmes formally fall outside EU law—and in case of the MoUs their formal a-legal nature—has been used by EU institutions as well as Member State courts to immunize bailout conditionality from fundamental rights challenges, or so it will be argued. It allows for the creation of a zone where the law is suspended but where public power can still be exercised with the force of law.[83]

The ESM works differently to the German federal intervention because *de jure* an EU 'federal commissioner' can neither (partially) suspend the targeted Member State's constitution nor rely on 'forced administration'. Nevertheless, the ESM does *de facto* allow for just that because the price of an ESM loan is the 'strict conditionality' specified in an MoU negotiated between the ESM and the Member State concerned.[84] With the constant threat of cutting off funds, a Member State government and/or parliament requesting an ESM intervention is thus caught, paraphrasing Huber, between the Scylla of defaulting and the Charybdis of the Troika (the Commission, the ECB and the International Monetary Fund (IMF)).[85]

The loss of political autonomy is of course *material* rather than *formal* since the ESM is a 'requested intervention'. For that reason, the current President of the

[80] European Council Decision 2011/199/EU of 25 March 2011 amending Article 136 of the Treaty on the Functioning of the European Union with regard to a stability mechanism for Member States whose currency is the euro [2011] OJ L91/1.

[81] Preamble (10) and (17) of the ESM Treaty.

[82] Kilpatrick (n 75) 3.

[83] In Case T-680/13 *Chrysostomides, K. & Co. and Others v Council and Others* [2018] ECLI:EU:T:2018:48, paras 113–14, the General Court recognizes that this presents a problem for the rule of law, which the EU, following Article 2 of the Treaty on European Union [2016] OJ C 202 (hereafter TEU) is founded upon. The Court argues that the Euro Group is a 'body of the Union' and that its acts and conduct 'in the exercise of its powers under EU law are therefore attributable to the European Union. Any contrary solution would clash with the principle of the Union based on the rule of law, in so far as it would allow the establishment, within the legal system of the European Union itself, of entities whose acts and conduct could not result in the European Union incurring liability'. This case was appealed to the ECJ and it is currently pending, see Case C-597/18 P *Council v K. Chrysostomides & Co and Others Case*.

[84] ESM Treaty, Article 13(3) and 13(4).

[85] Huber (n 14) 10.

European Court of Justice (ECJ), Koen Lenaerts, can apparently without irony write the following:

> a national parliament may, where the constitution requires its approval, reject the conditions attached to ESM financial assistance. Of course, in so doing, national parliaments must strike the right balance between the risks associated with default and the adoption of austerity measures that will inevitably give rise to discontent among the electorate.[86]

Setting aside the question of whether a Member State (or which Member States!) in actual fact would have been allowed to default,[87] seeing that a sovereign default might have led to contagion across the Eurozone, Lenaerts is correct in his analysis of the *formal* political autonomy of a Member State to reject ESM conditionality. Being 'free to default', the Member State's governmental apparatus stays in place and submits itself 'freely' to the conditionality programmes attached to the ESM programme. That being said, from a more material perspective, voting in favour of defaulting is not a viable choice for most Member State parliaments. *De facto*, if not *de jure*, the Troika acting on behalf of the ESM therefore becomes a 'protector' for the bailout Member States as the federal commissioner did under the federal intervention in the German Confederation.

The role of the ECB and the Commission as 'protectors' is further strengthened by the 'stricter version' of the Stability and Growth Pact created during the crisis with the Six Pack, the Two Pack, and the Fiscal Compact. The Two Pack, for example, created the possibility for strengthening the economic and budgetary surveillance of Eurozone Member States who receive *either* external financial assistance under the European Financial Stabilisation Mechanism (EFSM),[88] the EFSF, the ESM, the IMF or another bilateral basis *or* who 'experience or are threatened with serious difficulties with respect to their financial stability or to the sustainability of their public finances, leading to potential adverse spill-over effects on other Member States in the euro area'.[89] It is for the Commission, not the Member

86 Lenaerts (n 2) 766.

87 Damian Chalmers, 'European Restatements of Sovereignty' in Richard Rawlings, Peter Leyland and Alison L Young (eds), *Sovereignty and the Law: Domestic, European and International Perspectives* (OUP 2014) 210–11, has argued that 'The President of the Commission has indicated that overcoming the crisis represented "a fight for European integration itself". Alongside this, the crisis is presented as one of systemic risk whereby the whole European political economy could collapse as a consequence of the ripple effects from either a sovereign debt default or a bankruptcy of a large commercial bank. To refuse aid or to default is to be an enemy not simply of the euro but, presented like this, of Europe itself. It is not clear what possibility for membership of the Union exists for States who default'.

88 The EFSM was established by Regulation 407/2010/EU of 11 May 2010 establishing a European Financial Stabilisation Mechanism [2010] OJ L118/1 (hereafter EFSM).

89 Regulation 472/2013/EU of the European Parliament and of the Council of 21 May 2013 on the strengthening of economic and budgetary surveillance of Member States in the euro area experiencing or threatened with serious difficulties with respect to their financial stability [2013] OJ L140/1, Article 1, 1(b) and 1(a).

State concerned, to decide when the latter is the case.[90] If the formal request for assistance is what preserves the political autonomy of the Member States from a legal perspective, the Two Pack undermines this autonomy. Because of the potential spill-overs of a crisis internal to a Member State, the Two Pack allows European institutions to intervene in the internal fiscal affairs of EU Member States and subject them to 'enhanced surveillance' without a formal Member State request. Whereas the ESM is a form of '*requested* federal intervention', the Two Pack creates the possibility for a form of '*unrequested* federal intervention'. The Two Pack, therefore, allows the Commission *to declare a form of 'state of exception' on behalf of its Member States.*

A Member State subjected to 'enhanced surveillance' shall, in cooperation with the Commission and the ECB, 'adopt measures aimed at addressing the sources or potential sources of difficulties'.[91] This is done by directing recommendations at the Member State, such as a macroeconomic adjustment programme. If the Member State concerned is 'experiencing insufficient administrative capacity or significant problems in the implementation of the programme' it is *obligated* to seek 'technical assistance from the Commission'.[92] A Member State subjected to 'enhanced surveillance' thus has a legal obligation to inform the Union if it is not capable of implementing the ECB's and the Commission's recommendations itself. In that case, the ECB and the Commission will supply 'technical assistance' which 'may include the establishment of a *resident representative and supporting staff* to advise authorities on the implementation of the programme'.[93]

In this way, the Two Pack creates the possibility for the Commission and the ECB, through their resident representative, to exercise emergency public powers directly in and on the Member States subjected to 'enhanced surveillance'. That is, the Two Pack creates the possibility of a form of 'forced administration'. Similarly, if the Council, on a proposal by the Commission, decides that a Member State has an 'excessive deficit',[94] the Member State has a duty to present to the Council and the Commission 'an economic partnership programme', which specifies 'the policy measures and structural reforms that are needed to ensure an effective and lasting correction of the excessive deficit'.[95] The implementation of the programme will be monitored by the Commission and the Council.[96]

[90] Regulation 472/2013/EU, Article 2, 1(a).

[91] Regulation 472/2013/EU, Article 3, 1.

[92] Regulation 472/2013/EU, Article 7, 8.

[93] Regulation 472/2013/EU, Article 7, 8, italics added.

[94] Article 126(6) TFEU and Regulation 1176/2011/EU of the European Parliament and of the Council of 16 November 2011 on the prevention and correction of macroeconomic imbalances [2011] OJ L306/25, Article 7.

[95] Regulation 473/2013/EU of the European Parliament and of the Council of 21 May 2013 on common provisions for monitoring and assessing draft budgetary plans and ensuring the correction of excessive deficit of the Member States in the euro area [2013] OJ L140/11, Article 9, 1.

[96] Regulation 473/2013/EU, Article 9, 6.

In the case of serious non-compliance with the recommendations made in the different 'adjustment programmes' for the Member States, the Stability and Growth Pact has established a link between a federal intervention and a federal execution under Article 126(9)–(11) TFEU and strengthened by the 'stricter' Stability and Growth Pact. A Member State that persistently fails to take action in response to the recommendations by the relevant EU institutions—a Member State that *resists* a federal intervention—can be required to lodge a deposit with the Commission amounting to 0.2 per cent of its gross domestic product (GDP) in the preceding year,[97] or it can have a fine imposed on it by the Commission amounting to 0.2 per cent of its GDP in the preceding year.[98] The federal intervention blends into the federal execution because, owing to the mutualization of risk, there are no internal affairs of the Member States that cannot become a Union matter.

As is generally the case for emergency politics in the federation, in the concrete praxis of the government of the Eurozone crisis, it is not always clear who authorizes the extended use of executive powers and for the sake of whom. In a federal union of states, emergency rule is 'mixed'. For example, within the framework of the ESM, stability support can be granted only to a crisis-ridden state if necessary to safeguard the Eurozone and its Member States.[99] The European governmental emergency apparatus is a form of 'executive federalism' that has strengthened the executive branch of government of the Union and, in many cases, the executive branches of the Member States. This is manifest in a widespread use of 'rule by decree' by Member State governments and the granting of wide-ranging powers to government ministers.[100] Like other forms of 'executive lawmaking', Eurocrisis law has worked as a kind of enabling act transferring legislative powers from parliaments to the European and Member State executives. In this way, the structure of the federal intervention allows a Member State government to repress internal

[97] Regulation 1173/2011/EU of the European Parliament and of the Council of 16 November 2011 on the effective enforcement of budgetary surveillance in the euro area [2011] OJ L 306/1, Article 4. See also, Regulation 1174/2011/EU of the European Parliament and of the Council of 16 November 2011 on enforcement measures to correct excessive macroeconomic imbalances in the euro area [2011] OJ L306/8, Article 3.

[98] Regulation 1173/2011/EU, Article 6.

[99] ESM Treaty, Article 12.

[100] Afroditi Marketou, 'Greece: Constitutional Deconstruction and the Loss of National Sovereignty' in Thomas Beukers, Bruno Witte and Claire Kilpatrick (eds), *Constitutional Change through Euro-Crisis Law* (CUP 2017) 190; Leticia Díez Sanchez, 'Spain: Dealing with the Economic Emergency through Constitutional Reform and Limited Parliamentary Intervention' in Thomas Beukers, Bruno de Witte, and Claire Kilpatrick (eds), *Constitutional Change through Euro-Crisis Law* (CUP 2017) 204–9; Leonardo Pierdominici, 'Constitutional Change through Emergency Decrees: The Abolition of Provinces in Italy' in Thomas Beukers, Bruno de Witte, and Claire Kilpatrick (eds), *Constitutional Change through Euro-Crisis Law* (CUP 2017) 222–28; Stephen Coutts, 'Ireland: Traditional Procedures Adapted for Economic Emergency' in Thomas Beukers, Bruno de Witte, and Claire Kilpatrick (eds), *Constitutional Change through Euro-Crisis Law* (CUP 2017) 233ff; Diletta Tega, 'Welfare Rights in Italy' in Bruno Witte and Claire Kilpatrick (eds), *Social Rights in Times of Crisis in the Eurozone: The Role of Fundamental Rights' Challenges* (EUI Working Paper Series Law 2014) 53.

opposition and enforce unpopular programmes.[101] The princes in the German Confederation could use the mechanism of the federal intervention to rely on the force of the collected armies of all the *Länder* to repress a national-liberal uprising in an individual *Land*, so has Eurocrisis law been employed by some Member State governments to cut public finances and enforce labour law reforms that would have been difficult to get through Member State parliaments in 'normal times'.[102]

B. The End of Constitutional Tolerance?

Compared to other young federations, the history of the EU, until the outbreak of the Eurozone crisis, has been characterized by relative internal stability and surprisingly little contestation of Union authority.[103] Until recently,[104] Member State courts have in general accepted the authority of EU law and have for the most part only insisted on their right to act as the guardian of the constitution as a theoretical possibility. The EU was celebrated for this achievement of 'constitutional tolerance',[105] even after the end of the 'permissive consensus'[106] where the doctrine of constitutional pluralism was widely adopted and celebrated by EU lawyers.[107] Some scholars have argued that the relatively sparse constitutional contestation

[101] See, eg, the account by Marketou (n 100) 180–81 of how the 'anti-MoU forces' were repressed in the Greek Parliament during the 2010 bailout.

[102] For example, Maria Luz Rodríguez, 'Labour Rights in Crisis in the Eurozone: The Spanish Case' in Bruno De Witte and Claire Kilpatrick (eds), *Social Rights in Times of Crisis in the Eurozone: The Role of Fundamental Rights' Challenges* (EUI Working Paper Series Law 2014) 11 argues that 'the anti-crisis decisions are a mix of EU recommendations and/or impositions and national policies. This is the case because European authorities and the current Spanish Government, whether they state it or not, share the same political vision, the same economic ideology, and the same strategy to overcome the crisis ... This mix between EU demands and contributions from the Spanish Government has led to a more authoritarian labour relations model'. For a similar analysis of Portugal, see Miguel Nogueira de Brito, 'Putting Social Rights in Brackets? The Portuguese Experience with Welfare Challenges in Times of Crisis' in Bruno de Witte and Claire Kilpatrick (eds), *Social Rights in Times of Crisis in the Eurozone: The Role of Fundamental Rights' Challenges* (EUI Working Paper Series Law 2014) 68.

[103] Goldstein (n 35).

[104] For a discussion of the recent decision by the German Constitutional Court in *Weiss*, BVerfG, Judgment of the Second Senate of 05 May 2020—2 BvR 859/15, see section II:C of this chapter. See also the case from the German Constitutional Court on the European Arrest Warrant, BVerfG, Order of the Second Senate of 15 December 2015—2 BvR 2735/14; the 'Slovak Pension' case (Case C-399/09 *Marie Landtová v Česká správa socialního zabezpečení* [2011] OJ C 232/6). For a summary, see Jan Komárek, 'Playing with Matches: The Czech Constitutional Court's Ultra Vires Revolution' *Verfassungsblog* (22 February 2012). See also Case C-441/14 *Dansk Industri (DI), acting on behalf of Ajos A/S v Estate of Karsten Eigil Rasmussen* [2016] ECLI:EU:C:2016:278 and the Danish Supreme Court 15/2014 *Dansk Industri (DI) Acting for Ajos A/S v The Estate left by A.* For a summary of the case, see Mikael Rask Madsen, Henrik Palmer Olsen, and Urška Šadl, 'Competing Supremacies and Clashing Institutional Rationalities: The Danish Supreme Court's Decision in the Ajos Case and the National Limits of Judicial Cooperation' (2017) 23 European Law Journal 140.

[105] Weiler (n 6) 13.

[106] Lisbeth Hooghe and Garry Marks, 'A Postfunctionalist Theory of European Integration: From Permissive Consensus to Constraining Dissensus' (2009) 39 British Journal of Political Science.

[107] For an overview, see Matej Avbelj and Jan Komárek, *Constitutional Pluralism in the European Union and Beyond* (Hart Publishing Limited 2012).

in the EU can be explained by the institutionalization of a form of Member State veto, the Member States could retain control of politically sensitive issues and were therefore less likely to rebel against EU authority, as Calhoun recommended.[108] Moreover, the ECJ's interlocuters at the domestic level, most importantly the 'empowered' domestic courts acting in the capacity of European courts together with private litigants, are generally understood to be important factors for acceptance of the authority of EU law.[109]

If, in earlier times, the EU could maintain a strong degree of constitutional tolerance by allowing the Member States to control politically sensitive issues, this is no longer the case since the Eurozone crisis. The demand for fiscal consolidation attached to the bailout programmes has led to *de facto* micromanagement of deficit Member States and to significant cuts to the public sector, pensions, and social benefits, and to a large degree dismantled collective bargaining. The austerity measures imposed have led to drastic changes in the political and social fabric of the bailout Member States: record high long-term unemployment, homelessness, poverty, labour exploitation, hereunder child labour and human trafficking, and restricted access to basic needs such as clean and affordable water.[110] The effects of austerity have not been spread evenly within the bailout states but have disproportionately been borne by the low-income families who depend more on public services and spend a higher proportion of their income on basic services and food.[111] The effects of austerity have, furthermore, disproportionately hit the marginalized and disadvantaged groups of society, importantly ethnic minorities, women, and the young.[112] The austerity programmes have had significant consequences not only for social rights and workers' rights, but also political rights and civil rights. The emergency government of the Eurozone has bypassed the ordinary channels of government and has thereby enforced executive decisions without the usual scrutiny at the Member State level.[113] With regard to civil rights, the large-scale

[108] Joseph HH Weiler, 'The Transformation of Europe' (1991) 100 The Yale Law Journal 2403, 2428 describes this 'equilibrium' as a combination of federal legal order combined with a confederal political order. As has been argued throughout this book, the distinction between 'confederal' and 'federal' is flawed, see, eg, Chapter 1:I:A.

[109] Karen J Alter, *Establishing the Supremacy of European Law: The Making of an International Rule of Law in Europe* (OUP 2001) ch 2; Anne-Marie Burley and Walter Mattli, 'Europe Before the Court: A Political Theory of Legal Integration' (1993) 47 International Organization 41, 63–64; JHH Weiler, 'A Quiet Revolution: "The European Court of Justice and Its Interlocutors"' (1994) 26 Comparative Political Studies 510; Weiler (n 108) 2425ff; Goldstein (n 35) 43–44, 63.

[110] Council of Europe, 'Safeguarding Human Rights in Times of Economic Crisis' (2013) Issue Paper from Council of Europe Commissioner for Human Rights 15.

[111] ibid 16.

[112] ibid 7, 22–25; Kilpatrick (n 65) 393–94; Aoife Nolan, 'Welfare Rights in the Eurozone: Ireland' in Claire Kilpatrick and Bruno De Witte (eds), *Social Rights in Times of Crisis in the Eurozone: The Role of Fundamental Rights' Challenges* (EUI Working Paper Series Law 2014) 39–40; Leticia Díez Sánchez, 'Deconstitutionalisation of Social Rights and the Quest for Efficiency' in Bruno De Witte and Claire Kilpatrick (eds), *Social Rights in Times of Crisis in the Eurozone: The Role of Fundamental Rights' Challenges* (EUI Working Paper Series Law 2014) 117.

[113] Council of Europe (n 120) 16.

protests against austerity in Greece, Portugal, and Spain have been violently repressed leading to concerns about the excessive use of force against demonstrators and infringements of the right to freedom of assembly and expression.[114] The austerity measures have, moreover, led to a diminished access to justice, for example by cutting legal aid and increasing court fees.[115] During the crisis, the EU has significantly extended the scope of its powers and its capacity to intervene in the 'internal affairs' of its Member States. The Troika has intervened in most, if not all, core 'politically sensitive' Member State competences: taxation, healthcare, education, pensions, labour law, unemployment benefits, and military spending.

As we saw earlier in the chapter (Chapter 5:I:D), the authority of the federal level to exercise emergency powers and intervene in the internal affairs of the Member States is inherently contested. Following the 'doctrine of Calhoun', it is the Member States who are the rightful guardians of the constitutionality and boundary of federal law. In line with this, the emergency government of the Eurozone has led to a wave of contestations and resistance of the authority of EU institutions and the new 'Eurocrisis law'. These new manifestations of opposition have taken many different forms: an avalanche of court cases, the formation of new social movements and the rise of parties whose core political programme includes the abolition of the euro or a significant reform of the EU. Compared to earlier EU history, the magnitude of this wave of contestation is unprecedented. That being said, in comparison to the early history of the United States in particular, the actual resistance has been surprisingly modest. The instances of direct contestation of EU emergency authority are relatively few and none of them has succeeded in their aim, at least not yet.

European courts (the ECJ and Member State courts acting in their dual capacity as national and European courts) have been an important site for the constitutional contestation of the emergency government of the Eurozone. European courts are the main *legal route* available through which the constitutionality of 'Eurocrisis law' can be contested. In the early history of European integration, the authority of the EU was not contested by its Member States in any significant manner when compared to, for example the early history of the United States.[116] Nevertheless, the contestation of EU authority that *has* taken place has to a large degree manifested itself in the 'judicial dialogues', famous among EU law scholars, between Member State courts and the ECJ.

On a fundamental level, these debates are about the question of ultimate legal authority, or *Kompetenz-Kompetenz*, claimed both by the ECJ and the highest Member State courts (*Chapter 1:IV:B*). On the one hand, the ECJ, with reference to the authority granted to it in the Treaties, has asserted its right to decide on the validity of EU law and the legality of all acts of the EU institutions. On the other

[114] ibid 21.
[115] ibid.
[116] Goldstein (n 35).

hand, referring to the principles of conferral, Member State courts have claimed ultimate jurisdiction over the question of the constitutionality of EU law stating that only they can determine whether the EU acts *ultra vires*. These positions highlight different aspects of the nature of the foundation of EU authority. While the Member State courts will ultimately understand the foundations as *treaty*, the ECJ will ultimately insist on it as *constitution*. From the perspective of the theory of the federation, there is nothing new in the overall issue of these debates. They emulate similar debates in the German Confederation and the United States, for example the debate between Webster and Calhoun. On a fundamental level, they reflect the heterarchical relationship between the dual political existences of the federation as a political form.

Nonetheless, the concrete issues contested are always unique to an actual federation. One of the most important 'judicial dialogues' in the EU involves the protection of fundamental rights that make up the core of the 'value order' constitutionalism to which a majority of the EU Member States belong. Following EU law doctrine, EU law takes primacy over Member State law,[117] even constitutionally protected fundamental rights protected by Member State constitutions.[118] Several Member State courts, however, have contested the ECJ's claim of the unequivocal primacy or supremacy of EU law over Member State law, with reference to concerns relating to fundamental rights protected by Member State constitutions.[119] They have therefore insisted on their right to submit EU law to constitutional review and, ultimately, to void EU law in the case it breaches the core fundamental rights that lie at the heart of many of the constitutions of the Member States. The ECJ has not accepted the right of Member State courts to void EU law on this basis. However, the ECJ has pledged itself to review EU law on the basis of analogous rights at the EU level.[120]

As has been discussed extensively in this book, the EU has, by many of its Member States, at least to some extent, been understood as an integral part of the realization and consolidation of their own constitutional orders centred on fundamental rights and the notion of human dignity (*Chapters 3:II* and *4:II*). It is therefore in no way surprising that the protection of fundamental rights has been one of the important reasons for the delineation of EU authority by Member State courts.

[117] Case C-6/64 *Flaminio Costa v E.N.E.L.* [1964] ECR 585.

[118] Case C 11/70 *Internationale Handelsgesellschaft mbH v Einfuhr- und Vorratsstelle für Getreide und Futtermittel* [1970] ECR 1125.

[119] And later also the protection of democratic legitimacy (see Case 2134/92, *Brunner v The European Union Treaty* (1994) 1 CMLR 57 and Member State constitutional identity (see *Lisbon Ruling* (n 51) and BVerfG, Order of the Second Senate of 15 December 2015—2 BvR 2735/14 (*EAW order*)). For the contestation of EU authority with reference to fundamental rights, see the Solange cases of the German Constitutional Court (Solange I, BverfGE 37, 291, 29 May 1974; Solange II, BverfGE 73, 339, 22 October 1986).

[120] *Internationale Handelsgesellschaft* (n 118).

Following the theory of the federation, the EU Member States, after all, come together in a union to preserve their constitutional orders, not to destroy them.

The prominent position of not only political and civil rights but also social rights in both the Charter of Fundamental Rights of the European Union (EUCFR) and in the constitutional orders of many bailout Member States[121] means there is a clear possibility of judicial contestation of bailout conditionality with reference to fundamental rights breaches. And many cases have come before the Member State courts. Nevertheless, despite the strong probability that the bailout conditionality actually breaches both the EUCFR and the social rights protected in many of the bailout Member States, surprisingly little contestation of EU authority has resulted from the Eurocrisis social rights jurisprudence. Despite the magnitude of cases lodged in front of Member State courts contesting the constitutionality of austerity measures, these cases have not led to any manifest contestation of the supremacy of EU law or the EU's authority to exercise emergency rule.

The primary reason for this is that the Member State courts and the European institutions have tacitly agreed to treat bailout conditionality as a matter internal to the Member States despite the obvious contradictory evidence. This has been done by treating the austerity conditionality attached to the bailouts as *non-EU law*. For example, in a series of cases, the supreme administrative court in Greece, the Council of State, argued that pension cuts in Greece, implemented as part of the bailout conditionality, did not breach Article 34 EUCFR on social security and social assistance. The reason given by the Council of State was that the Charter was binding on Member States only when they are implementing EU law[122] and not in cases of purely domestic measures, to which it considered the cases at hand to belong.[123] This formalistic argument allows the domestic courts not to make a preliminary reference to the ECJ on the question of whether the bailout conditionality is in conformity with the EUCFR.

That being said, a few cases on the compatibility of bailout conditionality with the EUCFR have been referred to the ECJ by Portuguese[124] and Romanian courts.[125] In most of these cases, however, the ECJ maintained that it was without

[121] See the Portuguese Constitution (1976), especially Chapter III: 'Workers rights, freedoms and guarantees' and Title III: 'Economic, social and cultural rights and duties'; the Greek Constitution (1975) Articles 22–23, providing for especially workers' rights; the Romanian Constitution (1991) Articles 32, 34, 40, 43, 47, and 135; and the Constitution of Latvia (1922) Articles 106–22.

[122] Article 51(1) of the Charter of Fundamental Rights of the European Union [2012] OJ C326/391 (hereafter EUCFR): 'The provisions of this Charter are addressed to the institutions, bodies, offices and agencies of the Union with due regard for the principle of subsidiarity and to the Member States only when they are implementing Union law'.

[123] Evangelia Psychogiopoulou, 'Welfare Rights in Crisis in Greece: The Role of Fundamental Rights Challenges' in Bruno De Witte and Claire Kilpatrick (eds), *Social Rights in Times of Crisis in the Eurozone: The Role of Fundamental Rights' Challenges* (EUI Working Paper Series Law 2014) 11.

[124] Case C-128/12 *Sindicato dos Bancários do Norte and Others* [2013] ECLI:EU:C:2013:149 and Case C-264/12 *Sindicato Nacional dos Profissionais de Seguros e Afins* [2014] ECLI:EU:C:2014:2036.

[125] Case C-434/11 *Corpul Național al Polițiștilor* [2011] ECLI:EU:C:2011:830 and Case C-134/12 *Corpul Național al Polițiștilor* [2012] ECLI:EU:C:2012:288.

jurisdiction because it was not clear that the domestic laws in question were in fact implementing EU law.[126] In *Sindicato dos Bancários do Norte and Others*, for example, the ECJ argued that it clearly lacked jurisdiction because the request from the Portuguese Labour Court 'did not contain any concrete element allowing to infer that the Portuguese law was aiming to apply Union law'.[127] Similar lines of argument have been put forward by other EU institutions, including the Commission[128] and the ECB, leading the European Parliament's Economic Committee to state that it 'Regrets that the programmes are not bound by the Charter of Fundamental Rights of the European Union, the European Convention of Human Rights and the European Social Charter, due to the fact that they are not based on Union primary law'.[129]

As shown by Claire Kilpatrick, the argument that the bailouts are not subject to legal challenges within the EU legal order because they are not EU law is not convincing. Since the crisis, seven EU Member States have been bailed out. Three of these Member States (Hungary, Latvia, and Romania) are non-Eurozone states and they have all, from a formal perspective, received assistance purely under EU law.[130] The loan conditions for Portugal and Ireland relied partly on the EFSM (established under EU law) and the EFSF (the precursor to the ESM established under international law).[131] These bailouts are therefore of a 'mixed legal parentage'[132] and as a consequence, even from a formal perspective, at least in part subject to EU law. Only the bailouts of Greece and Cyprus are based entirely on non-EU law sources: bilateral agreements, the ESFS, and the ESM.[133] Even in these cases, however, there is still an indirect link to EU law. The link is the Two Pack regulation, which empowers the Commission and the ECB to subject a deficit Member State that receives external financial assistance under, for example, the ESM, to 'enhanced surveillance' (linking the federal intervention with the federal execution).[134] It is conceivable that, in this way, these bailouts are brought within the

[126] In Case C-258/14 *Florescu and Others* [2017] ECLI:EU:C:2017:448, however, the ECJ *did* claim jurisdiction but ruled that there was no breach of EU law including the EUCFR.

[127] Júlio Gomes, 'Social Rights in Crisis in the Eurozone. Work Rights in Portugal' in Bruno De Witte and Claire Kilpatrick (eds), *Social Rights in Times of Crisis in the Eurozone: The Role of Fundamental Rights' Challenges* (EUI Working Paper Series Law 2014) 80. The same argument is put forward by the ECJ in *Sindicato Nacional* (n 124) paras 17–22 and in the two Romanian cases C-434/11 *Corpul Național al Polițiștilor* (n 125) para 16 and C-134/12 *Corpul Național al Polițiștilor* (n 125) para 13.

[128] In the case of Greece 'whenever the Troika's requirements were contested, the creditors have claimed that the particular measures were the Greek Government's political choice under its exclusive competence for the implementation of obligations resulting from the economic adjustment programmes' (Marketou (n 100) 185).

[129] EP Committee on Economic and Monetary Affairs: 'Report on the enquiry on the role and operations of the Troika (ECB, Commission and IMF) with regard to the euro area programme countries' (28 February 2014) as cited by Kilpatrick (n 65) 395.

[130] Kilpatrick (n 69) 400.

[131] ibid; Kilpatrick (n 75) 2.

[132] Kilpatrick (n 65) 400.

[133] Kilpatrick (n 75) 2–3.

[134] Kilpatrick (n 65) 400.

scope of EU law. 'Eurocrisis law' makes up a comprehensive emergency apparatus operating with the force of law.

The different legal instruments used to govern the Eurozone crisis are in their concrete use completely interrelated and it is therefore impossible to separate the obligations incurred by a bailout Member State under EU law and non-EU law.[135] Furthermore, the bailout conditionality is enforced by EU institutions, which also brings them within the scope of EU law.[136] As we have seen, the Commission and the ECB become *de facto* 'protectors' of deficit Member States and they can simultaneously enforce Eurocrisis law *against* and *on behalf* of a Member State with reference to a variety of legal sources; some of them EU law (eg the Two Pack) and some of them formally international law (eg the ESM).

The use of international law is therefore better understood as the creation of something similar in structure to Ernst Fraenkel's theory of the 'dual state'.[137] It is a system that allows for the 'norm' (eg the 'no bailout clause' and the EUCFR) and the 'exception' (eg bailouts and austerity) to coexist within the European constitutional order. The 'normative state' of EU law has never been (fully) suspended, but by its side there now exists the 'prerogative state' of 'Eurocrisis law', enabling the exercise of governmental power through measures and decrees not subject to the constraints of the Treaties.[138] The severing of the ties between the bailout conditionality and EU law, as fanciful as it may be, has worked as a legal justification for the immunization of emergency politics from fundamental rights' challenges under EU law. It has allowed the European institutions not to take (unwanted) responsibility for the political and social implication of the emergency government of the Eurozone and to maintain the logic, however illusory, of market discipline.

This might be understandable on grounds of political expediency, but it is a little surprising, at least prima facie, that the tale of the non-EU law nature of the bailouts has generally also been adopted by Member State courts. Having disregarded the possibility that the Member State courts have taken this position because of a limited grasp of EU law, Kilpatrick presents another theory as to why that has been the case: the insulation of the bailouts from EU law served the purpose of avoiding

[135] For how this applies in the Portuguese case, see Roberto Cisotta and Daniele Gallo, 'The Portuguese Constitutional Court Case Law and Austerity Measures: A Reappraisal' in Bruno Witte and Claire Kilpatrick (eds), *Social Rights in Times of Crisis in the Eurozone: The Role of Fundamental Rights' Challenges* (EUI Working Paper Series Law 2014) 87–88.

[136] As pointed out by Kilpatrick (n 65) 405, in contrast to the Member States, there is no reason to believe that EU institutions are only bound by the EUCFR when they are implementing EU law. Kilpatrick (n 75) 13]. In the Joined Cases C-8/15 P and C-10/15 P *Ledra Advertising v Commission and ECB* [2016] ECLI:EU:C:2016:701, the Court confirmed this view.

[137] Fraenkel (n 11).

[138] Another example of this is demonstrated in what the Eurogroup secretariat allegedly told the Greek Finance Minister, Yanis Varoufakis, at a pivotal meeting in the summer of 2015: 'The Eurogroup does not exist in law, as it is not part of any of the EU treaties. It is an informal group of finance ministers of the Eurozone member states. Thus there are no written rules about the way it conducts its business, and therefore its president is not legally bound' (Yannis Varoufakis, *Adults in the Room: My Battle with Europe's Deep Establishment* (Penguin 2017) 447).

'what promised to be an open and highly charged conflict with the EU institutions and legal order, including the Court of Justice'.[139] By not recognizing bailout conditionality as EU law, the Member State courts have avoided an '*undesired EU judicialization* of the conflict between bailout sources and national constitutional rights'.[140] In other words, the Member State courts have gone out of their way to avoid challenging federal authority despite having ample opportunity and perhaps even a legal obligation to do so. They have done what they could to avoid adding a constitutional crisis to the economic crisis. Instead of triggering something akin to the US nullification crisis of the 1830s, Member State courts have, by treating bailout conditionality as the implementation of international agreements or purely domestic measures, tacitly agreed to treat the question of the constitutionality of bailout conditionality as an 'internal affair'.

In reviewing the constitutionality of the bailouts against domestic constitutional standards, most Member State courts have upheld their constitutionality. Politically, this is understandable since declaring the bailout conditionality unconstitutional would presumably endanger the continuation of the bailout, hence creating the possibility of a sovereign default. The emergency situation alone makes it difficult for Member State courts to strike down bailout conditionality. For example, this has come out in Greek cases in which the Council of State has upheld the constitutionality of austerity measures with reference to the doctrine of the state of exception.[141] Similarly, the Irish Supreme Court has justified domestic austerity measures with reference to the constitutional mandate of the government to protect the national interest in the face of the most serious economic crisis in Ireland's history.[142] Only the Portuguese Constitutional Court has in any significant way contested the constitutionality of national bailout measures leading to Portugal's relatively swift exit from its bailout programme. [143] Nonetheless, even in this case, the Portuguese Court has not contested the necessity of austerity *per se* but only questioned the fairness of the distribution of the burden.[144] Notwithstanding the significant critique raised by EU institutions in response to the Portuguese cases, it would have been a qualitatively different problem if the Portuguese Constitutional

[139] Kilpatrick (n 77) 23.

[140] ibid 24. See also Cisotta and Gallo (n 135) 89.

[141] Matina Yannakourou, 'Challenging Austerity Measures Affecting Work Rights at Domestic and International Level. The Case of Greece' in Bruno Witte and Claire Kilpatrick (eds), *Social Rights in Times of Crisis in the Eurozone: The Role of Fundamental Rights' Challenges* (EUI Working Paper Series Law 2014) 23.

[142] Nolan (n 112).

[143] Nogueira de Brito (n 102) 71ff; Gomes (n 127) 79–84. See also Kilpatrick (n 77) 8, 18. Together with the more sustained resistance of the Portuguese Constitutional Court, a smaller number of austerity measures have been struck down by the Italian Constitutional Court and by the Romanian Constitutional Court. See Antonio L Faro, 'Fundamental Rights Challenges to Italian Labour Law Developments in the Time of Economic Crisis: An Overview' in Bruno Witte and Claire Kilpatrick (eds), *Social Rights in Times of Crisis in the Eurozone: The Role of Fundamental Rights' Challenges* (EUI Working Paper Series Law 2014) 61.

[144] Nogueira de Brito (n 102) 75; Cisotta and Gallo (n 135) 91.

Court had treated the bailout conditionality as EU law and thereby openly contested EU authority.[145]

C. Who Decides?

The only Member State court to have openly contested the authority of Eurocrisis law and insisted on its ultimate right to void EU acts as a means of constitutional defence is the German Constitutional Court. The challenge to EU authority mounted by the German Constitutional Courts targets aspects of the ECB's 'non-standard monetary policy instruments', the OMT and QE programmes, which have been some of the most important manifestations of emergency rule in the Eurozone crisis, and remain of critical importance for the EU's response to the Covid-19 crisis of 2020.

These programmes have allowed the ECB to act as a lender of last resort to sovereigns and buy government securities in order to lower the interest rate and increase the money supply. These unconventional policy instruments were employed because the crisis measures already discussed proved insufficient to deal with the Eurozone crisis.[146] By 2012, the markets had started seriously to call into question the irreversibility of the euro within the crisis-ridden Member States and to price in the likelihood of sovereign defaults. On this background, it was deemed necessary for someone to step in to relieve the fiscal authorities of the Member States and guarantee the survival of the Eurozone as a whole. When no other actor appeared on the stage, the ECB took up the slack and provided relief for Member State fiscal authorities 'through the monetary back door', as Waltraud Schelkle put it.[147] The announcement of the OMT programme by Mario Draghi was prefaced by the 'whatever it takes' speech that famously calmed the markets: 'Within our mandate, the ECB is ready to do whatever it takes to preserve the euro. And believe me, it will be enough'.[148]

Both the OMT and the QE are controversial because the ECB arguably did not act within its mandate but went well beyond it in an attempt to safeguard the EU and the Eurozone as a whole. The exercise of this form of governmental power tends to be authorized with reference to the survival of the political community as a whole. This authority is derived from the very source of the law—*salus populi*—the safety and welfare of the people. In a public lecture at the London School of

[145] Kilpatrick (n 77) 23–24.

[146] Schelkle (n 65) 214–15.

[147] Waltraud Schelkle, 'European Fiscal Union: From Monetary Backdoor to Parliamentary Main Entrance' (2012) 13 CESifo Forum 28.

[148] Speech by Mario Draghi, President of the European Central Bank at the Global Investment Conference in London 26 July 2012 <https://www.ecb.europa.eu/press/key/date/2012/html/sp120726.en.html> accessed 9 January 2018.

Economics in May 2020, assessing among other things the ECB's response to the 2020 Covid-19 crisis, this was expressed by one of the pre-eminent economists of the Eurozone, Paul de Grauwe, in the following way:

> Of course, as you know, there is a legal issue: '*Das ist verboten*'; it is not permitted; the Treaties say that monetary financing is not permitted. My response is with Cicero: *Salus populi suprema lex [esto]*. Cicero, a great Senator, and also a philosopher, realised more than 2000 years ago, that when you are experiencing an existential crisis, you have to be willing to set aside rules that you have imposed on yourself. These rules may serve you in normal times but can become extremely counter-productive when we experience an existential crisis, and then we should be willing to set these self-imposed rules aside'.[149]

What Cicero referred to, of course, was the office of the dictator in the Roman Republic, the constitutional guardian and defender of the Republic in times of crisis.[150] In this chapter, this form of emergency authority has been discussed primarily in terms of executive constitutional defence. Throughout the crisis, the ECB has claimed this form of extraordinary governmental authority and thereby introduced a strong element of reason of state into the Eurozone. That is, the ECB has claimed authority on the basis of 'the socio-politico maxim that stands above the dualism legality/illegality and is derived only from the necessities of the assertion and extension of political power'.[151] This is the authority to go beyond the law in order to ensure a future state of legality; the authority of the guardian of the constitution and the defender of the political community. In this way, the constitutional authority that the ECB can rely on is the classical definition of the 'defender of the republic', the constitutional dictator, namely, someone who in 'being independent of any other institution, was able to issue orders and to execute them immediately, that is, without having to obey other legal remedies'.[152]

It is always controversial for a government to go beyond the law in order to save the constitution, but it is arguably more so for a central bank. The ECB cannot rely on political foundations of authority beyond the Treaties in an unproblematic way. The ECB is commissioned by the Treaties to ensure *price stability* and it is granted more or less complete independence in achieving this aim, but it is not appointed as a general 'guardian of the constitution' or 'defender of the Union'. Following this logic, in some of its rhetoric, the main aim of the ECB's emergency measures is

149 LSE Public Lecture, 'Assessing the Economic Impact of COVID-19', Thursday 7 May 2020 <http://www.lse.ac.uk/Events/2020/05/202005071600/assessing-the-economic-impact>.

150 Rossiter (n 8) ch 2; Andreas Kalyvas, 'The Sublime Dignity of the Dictator: Republicanism and the Return of Dictatorship in Political Modernity' in Peter Wagner (ed), *African, American and European Trajectories of Modernity: Past Oppression, Future Justice?* (Edinburgh University Press 2015).

151 Schmitt, *Dictatorship* (n 11) 8.

152 ibid 4.

therefore downgraded from ensuring the survival of the Eurozone and the EU to a mere precondition for the ECB to fulfil the legal mandate it has been given by the Treaties and by 'the people in its jurisdiction', namely, securing price stability.[153] And it is on that ground that the ECJ defended the legality of the OMT programme in *Gauweiler*.[154] The ECB's exercise of governmental power has to be tied to the constitutional foundations of its 'commissarial mandate' of securing price stability. It is self-evidently correct that the continued existence of the euro is a precondition for price stability in the Eurozone. Nevertheless, it is less plausible that the right to act as constitutional guardian of the Eurozone is part of the 'technical mandate' of price stability.

The ECB is a non-representative and unelected technocratic institution and it can therefore, at best, rely on an informal representation of the people(s) of Europe. In contrast to the US presidency, the ECB is not invested with a strong 'political' mandate grounded in the principle of political representation. The ECB's authority is based in *commission* and not *representation*, at least for the time being. It has the power and authority necessary to execute its constitutional mandate, but it has no authority to give itself a new one. For that reason, the ECB can more credibly act as a 'commissarial dictator' than a 'sovereign dictator', in Schmitt's terms.[155] Originally, however, the US presidency was not meant to be the plebiscitarian office it is today, as discussed in Chapter 3.[156] The power and authority of the presidency has, in important part, been expanded through the extraordinary governmental authority claimed in times of profound crisis, be that civil war, world war, or economic recession. The US President is still not directly elected by the American people but by the Electoral College. Nevertheless, through the leadership of presidents such

[153] See speech by Benoît Cœuré, Member of the Executive Board of the ECB: 'Restoring Trust in Economic and Monetary Union' (the Forum Eco Libération ESCP, Paris, 1 December 2012).

[154] The ECJ had to construct its version of this argument in a more convoluted manner because in *Pringle* it had defined the aim of safeguarding the Eurozone as 'economic policy' belonging to the reserved competence of the Member States (*Thomas Pringle v Government of Ireland and Others* [2012] ECLI:EU:C:2012:756 para 56). To justify the OMT programme, the ECJ argued that the OMT programme was within the scope of the ECB's competence of 'monetary policy' because the programme aimed to rectify the 'disrupted monetary policy transmission mechanism' (Case C-62/14 *Gauweiler and Others* [2015] ECLI:EU:C:2015:400 para 50). However, following the ECB, this 'disruption' was caused 'by the demand for excessive risk premia for the bonds issued by certain Member States, such premia being intended to guard against the risk of a break-up of the euro area' (ibid para 72). Thus the ECB had to save the euro, ie, to 'dispel unjustified fears about the break-up of the euro area' (ibid para 76), in order to correct the disrupted 'monetary policy transmission mechanism' so it, in turn, could provide the constitutional mandate of price stability. Where there's a will there's a way.

[155] Schmitt, *Dictatorship* (n 11) chs 1 and 4. The constitutional guardian, or constitutional dictatorship, Schmitt argues, remained more or less unchanged until, in the nineteenth century, it was fused with the authority of the constituent power in what Schmitt called 'sovereign dictatorship' (ibid 4). With this combined authority, the sovereign dictator can reconstitute the political community in an emergency situation. In contrast to the sovereign dictator, the commissarial dictator cannot create new constitutional norms. The commissarial dictator 'is entitled to do everything that is appropriate in the actual circumstances'—except making new laws (ibid 8). Mandated directly by the constituent power, the sovereign dictator knows no such limits.

[156] Bruce Ackerman, *We the People*, vol I: Foundations (The Belknap Press of Harvard University Press 1991) 67ff.

as Abraham Lincoln, Woodrow Wilson, and Franklin D Roosevelt, the presidency has unquestionably come to be invested with the authority of the nation.

During the Eurozone crisis, the ECB has availed itself of extraordinary authority and granted itself new powers, as governmental institutions often do in times of crisis. Perhaps this is why the ECB in recent years has started to appeal directly to 'the people of Europe' in speeches and in its online self-descriptions, that is, the source of (potential) 'European sovereignty'.[157] Similar appeals have been made by the Commission in the 2018 'State of the Union: The Hour of European Sovereignty'.[158] As Lincoln realized during the Civil War, an appeal to the people of the Union, the federal nation, can provide the necessary authority to act, even against the will of several of the Member States.[159] In times of crisis, federal institutions can find it necessary to insist on an interpretation of the foundation of governmental authority not in a federal compact between the Member States but in the political will of the people of the Union. This 'refounding' of authority is unitary and statist. It signifies a shift from a 'federal' to a 'national' foundation of governmental authority. Ultimately, it insists, the survival of the Union is of greater importance than the political autonomy and will of the Member States. In the EU, this means prioritizing the will and welfare of 'the people of Europe' over that of the individual peoples of France, Italy, Germany etc. To paraphrase Lincoln: it might not be EU law, but it is fact.

This is the kind of authority the ECB has relied on throughout the economic crisis in a manner similar to the authority invoked by President Roosevelt during the Great Depression, notwithstanding the difference between the respective economic policies of the New Deal and the Eurozone crisis.[160] This form of emergency government, however, goes beyond the mixed emergency rule that characterizes the federation. Much of Eurocrisis law tends to target the government of the individual Member States, whereas the emergency government of the ECB targets a state of emergency of the Union as a whole, independently from any particular Member State. The ECB's emergency measures are meant to stabilize and save the Eurozone, and more broadly the EU as a whole.[161] The emergency rule of the ECB

[157] Hjalte Lokdam, 'We Serve the People of Europe': Reimagining the ECB's Political Master in the Wake of Its Emergency Politics' (2020) 58 Journal of Common Market Studies 978. See also Hjalte Lokdam, 'Is the European Central Bank Becoming a Central Bank for the People of Europe?' *Verfassungsblog* (24 April 2016).

[158] The European Commission, 'State of the Union 2018: The Hour of European Sovereignty' (Strasbourg, Speech 12 September 2018).

[159] See, eg, President Lincoln's 1863 Gettysburg Address.

[160] For a discussion of the New Deal in the context of constitutional dictatorship, see Rossiter (n 8) ch XVII.

[161] In more material terms, the unconventional monetary policies of the ECB have, of course, benefitted some classes, groups, and states more than others. According to Mark Blyth, 'Policies to Overcome Stagnation: The Crisis, and the Possible Futures, of All Things Euro' (2016) 13 European Journal of Economics and Economic Policies: Intervention 215, the 'rescue' has in that sense been thought within a regime of 'deflation, high profitability, and inequality', and for that reason Blyth maintains that it has been ineffective.

has been undertaken as if the EU were a *state* and the Member States were mere regions or other *subordinate entities*. In a speech by a Member of the Executive Board of the ECB, Benoît Cœuré, the emerging 'statist nature' of the Eurozone as a governmental unit was openly stated in the following way: 'the notion that the euro is a currency without a state is in my view misguided. The euro is a currency with a state—but it's a state whose branches of government are not yet clearly defined'.[162]

The ECB's exercise of extraordinary governmental authority has generally been accepted by the Member States and their institutions, except by the German Constitutional Court. In the now famous OMT case, the German Constitutional Court argued that, subject to the ECJ's interpretation, it considered the OMT programme to be *ultra vires* on the grounds that it was in breach of EU law[163] and that it transgressed the 'principle of democracy' central to the constitutional identity of Germany.[164] The reason given by the German Constitutional Court for the possible violation of German constitutional identity is that the OMT might constrain the budgetary autonomy of the German *Bundestag* so that it would no longer remain 'master of its decisions', and nor could it any longer 'exercise its budgetary autonomy under its own responsibility'.[165] Following the reasoning of the German Constitutional Court, the possible implication of the OMT programme is that it is not only an infringement of the constitutional and political autonomy of Germany but a deprivation of the right of the German people to elect their own representatives in a meaningful manner.

It is somewhat ironic that the only direct judicial challenge to the EU institutions' exercise of emergency powers has been sustained by one of the Member States *least* affected by the Eurozone crisis and 'European emergency rule'. Whatever the merits of the argument of the German Constitutional Court, it is certainly the case that the parliaments of bailout Member States have been deprived to a much more significant degree of the possibility of 'exercising their budgetary autonomy under their own responsibility'. For the Member States governed by emergency measures, the only real question for the electorate has been who should implement the predefined austerity measures;[166] that is, if the people were even granted the right to elect their own representatives.[167] The implications of the emergency government of the Eurozone for the political autonomy and democratic rights of 'deficit' Member States and their peoples are much graver than they are for Germany. The

[162] Speech by Benoît Cœuré (n 153).

[163] Specifically of Articles 119 and 127(1)–(2) TFEU and Articles 17–34 of the Consolidated version of the Treaty on the Functioning of the European Union, Protocol (No 4) On the Statute of the European System of Central Banks and of the European Central Bank [2016] OJ C202/230 (ESCB Statute) and possibly also Article 123 TFEU, see BVerfG, Order of the Second Senate of 14 January 2014—2 BvR 2728/13 (hereafter *OMT case*) paras 55, 101.

[164] *OMT case* (n 163) paras 51–53.

[165] *OMT case* (n 163) para 102.

[166] Marketou (n 100) 194.

[167] Both Italy and Greece have had non-elected technocratic governments.

constitutional courts of the bailout Member States, where almost all political autonomy was lost *de facto* if not *de jure*, have gone out of their way to avoid a constitutional conflict, whereas only the constitutional court of a relatively unscathed surplus Member State has dared to contest the authority of the emergency powers employed by EU institutions.

There are several possible explanations as to why this is the case. First, in contrast to the bailout Member States it was possible for the German Constitutional Court to contest EU emergency authority because the political consequence of voiding the OMT programme would (arguably) not be a collapse of the German economy. Second, the German economy is by far the most important of the Eurozone and without Germany's support the OMT programme would not be credible. The purpose of the OMT case, as has been argued by Michael Wilkinson, can therefore be interpreted as a way for Germany to exercise its influence over the shape of the OMT programme.[168] When compared with the situations of the Constitutional and Supreme Courts of the bailout Member States, an open contestation of EU emergency politics must have appeared to be a politically viable possibility for the German Constitutional Court.

Be that as it may, the German Constitutional Court did not nullify the OMT programme, nor did it forbid the German *Bundesbank* from partaking in the programme. Following its own doctrine of conducting *ultra vires* review of EU law only on the basis of the principle of 'openness towards European law',[169] the German Constitutional Court sent a reference to the ECJ in January 2014 on the question of whether the OMT programme is compatible with EU law[170] if it complied with the 'implementation framework' set out by the German Constitutional Court.[171] In contrast to the Portuguese and Romanian cases discussed above, the ECJ did not declare itself to be without jurisdiction on the grounds of the 'liminal legality' (non-law/non-EU law) of the crisis measures.[172] The reason for that might be that the German Constitutional Court insisted on the possibility of taking preventive

[168] Michael A Wilkinson, 'The Euro Is Irreversible! … Or Is It?: On OMT, Austerity and the Threat of "Grexit"' (2015) 16 German Law Journal 1049; Michael A Wilkinson, 'Constitutional Pluralism: Chronicle of a Death Foretold?' (2017) 23 European Law Journal 213.

[169] BVerfG, Order of the Second Senate of 06 July 2010—2 BvR 2661/06 (*Honeywell*) para 111; *Lisbon Ruling* (n 51) paras 225, 240.

[170] *OMT case* (n 163) para 101.

[171] Following the German Constitutional Court, 'This requires, in light of Art. 123 TFEU, that the possibility of a debt cut must be excluded (cf. n. 86 and 87), that government bonds of selected Member States are not purchased up to unlimited amounts (cf. n. 81), and that interferences with price formation on the market are to be avoided where possible (cf. n. 88 et seq.). Statements by the representatives of the European Central Bank in the proceedings before the Constitutional Court concerning the framework for the implementation of the OMT Decision (limited volume of a possible purchase of government bonds; no participation in a debt cut; observance of certain time lags between the emission of a government bond and its purchase; no holding of the bonds to maturity) suggest that such an interpretation in conformity with Union law would also most likely be compatible with the meaning and purpose of the OMT Decision' *OMT case* (n 163) para 100.

[172] Despite challenges of admissibility from the European Parliament, the Commission, the ECB and eight Member States, see *Gauweiler* (n 110) paras 11–31.

measures independently of an ECJ preliminary ruling.[173] These measures might have endangered the OMT programme and hence the stability of the Eurozone. As is well known, the ECJ ruled that the OMT programme was not in breach of EU law and that it did not have to live up to the 'implementation framework' set out by the German Constitutional Court.

The German Constitutional Court accepted the interpretation of the ECJ and the legality of the OMT. This, however, did not stop the German Constitutional Court from referring a very similar case to the ECJ on the constitutionality of the ECB's deployment of QE during the crisis.[174] The German Court focused specifically on one aspect of the ECB's QE programmes, the Public Sector Purchase Programme (PSPP).[175] Relying on the reasoning of *Pringle* and *Gauweiler*, the ECJ ruled that the ECB, also with regard to QE, had acted within its mandate.[176] As remarked by two *Weiss* commentators, 'ultimately the ECJ will do, and appears to have done, whatever it takes to save the euro'.[177] The most direct judicial contestations of EU governmental authority came to nothing—or so it seemed for a while.

In contrast to its submissive response to the ECJ's OMT ruling, the German Constitutional Court did not accept the ECJ interpretation of the constitutionality of QE.[178] To the shock of the legal academic community, the German Constitutional Court declared both the ECB's programme and the ECJ's judgment to be *ultra vires*.[179] The ECJ's decision was 'arbitrary', the German Constitutional Court argued, because its judgment rendered the principle of proportionality 'meaningless'[180] and the ECJ therefore manifestly exceeded its constitutional mandate 'resulting in a structurally significant shift in the order of competences to the detriment of the Member States'.[181] The ECJ's approach ultimately entailed, the German Constitutional Court stated, 'that the ECB is free to choose any means it considers suitable'.[182] Following the judgment of the German Constitutional Court, the ECJ acted *ultra vires* and therefore *Weiss* has no binding force in Germany.[183]

173 *OMT case* (n 163) para 103; Wilkinson, 'The Euro Is Irreversible! … Or Is It?' (n 168) 1051 n 12.

174 German Constitutional Court, Press Release No 70/2017, Proceedings on the European Central Bank's expanded asset purchase programme are stayed—Referral to the Court of Justice of the European Union (15 August 2017).

175 For an overview, see ECB, 'Implementation aspects of the public sector purchase programme (PSPP)' <https://www.ecb.europa.eu/mopo/implement/omt/html/pspp.en.html> accessed 11 May 2020.

176 *Weiss* (n 58).

177 Mark Dawson and Ana Bobić, 'Quantitative easing at the Court of Justice – Doing whatever it takes to save the euro: *Weiss and Others*' (2019) 56 Common Market Law Review 1005, 1040.

178 BVerfG, Judgment of the Second Senate of 05 May 2020—2 BvR 859/15.

179 ibid paras 116–19; para 155; para 164; para 178.

180 See especially ibid paras 138–42.

181 ibid para 119. The German Constitutional Court's argument is that the ECJ's application of the principle of proportionality rendered the principle meaningless with regard to the difference between the ECB's exclusive competence within monetary policy and its limited competences within economic policy (ibid paras 127–38).

182 ibid para 140.

183 ibid para 163.

German institutions, including the German *Bundesbank*, are therefore constitutionally bound to resist the PSPP programme.[184]

At the time of writing (August 2020), it is not yet clear whether this judgment will be the beginning of a full-blown nullification crisis in the EU or whether it can be avoided by 'muddling through'. The German Constitutional Court declared the ECB's QE programme unconstitutional largely on formal and procedural grounds (with reference to a breach of the principle of proportionality) and not with reference to a breach of monetary financing (Article 123 TFEU).[185] Specifically, the German Constitutional Court argues that, as of yet, it is not ascertainable whether the ECB 'did in fact consider and balance the effects that are inherent in and direct consequences of the PSPP'.[186] The German Court is especially concerned by the fact that QE allows for the circumvention of the austerity that was otherwise attached to bailouts.[187] It is this break with austerity that may render the programme 'disproportionate'.[188] It granted the German *Bundestag* and the *Bundesbank* three months before the decision comes into effect to negotiate with the ECB in order to bring its QE programme in line with the German Basic Law.[189] In this way, the case can be understood as an attempt by the German Constitutional Court to exercise control over the substantial policies of the Eurozone and, at the same time, check the authority of both the ECB and the ECJ.

Within this three-month deadline, the ECB has not yielded to the pressure of the German Constitutional Court and has insisted that it is 'exclusively subject to the jurisdiction of the Court of Justice of the European Union and accountable to the European Parliament'.[190] Nevertheless, the *Bundesbank*—simultaneously a branch of the European System of Central Banks (ESCB) and the central bank of Germany—has made an attempt to evade the crisis. The President of the *Bundesbank*, Jens Weidman, has requested the ECB's authorization of the disclosure of some of its internal documents relating to the ECB's 'proportionality assessment' of the PSPP to the German Federal Government, which they can share

[184] 'In the exercise of their responsibility with regard to European integration (*Integrationsverantwortung*), the Federal Government and the *Bundestag* are obliged, in their capacity as constitutional organs, to take suitable steps to ensure adherence to the European integration agenda (*Integrationsprogramm*). Moreover, they have an obligation to monitor the further execution of the PSPP to ensure timely action countering any risks regarding adherence to the European integration agenda (*Integrationsprogramm*) and/or the overall budgetary responsibility of the German Bundestag . . . The Bundesbank may in principle not participate in the implementation and execution of Decision (EU) 2015/774 and the subsequent Decisions (EU) 2015/2101, (EU) 2015/2464, (EU) 2016/702 and (EU) 2017/100' (ibid para 116). See also paras 229–30.

[185] ibid para 116; paras 165–67.

[186] ibid para 169.

[187] See especially ibid paras 170–71.

[188] ibid paras 170–71.

[189] ibid para 235

[190] ECB Speech, 'In the spirit of European cooperation: Introductory remarks by Yves Mersch, Member of the Executive Board of the ECB and Vice-Chair of the Supervisory Board of the ECB, at the Salzburg Global webinar' (Salzburg Global webinar, 2 July 2020) <https://www.ecb.europa.eu/press/key/date/2020/html/ecb.sp200702~87ce377373.en.html> accessed 8 August 2020.

with the *Bundestag*.[191] The ECB granted this authorization, and the *Bundestag* passed a resolution accepting the proportionality assessment of the ECB as per the requirement of the judgment of the German Constitutional Court in *Weiss*.[192]

Nevertheless, even if this particular nullification crisis is successfully evaded, it is doubtful whether the ECB's large Pandemic Emergency Purchase Programme,[193] put in place in April 2020 in order to tackle the Covid-19 crisis, would clear the hurdle of 'proportionality' in the eyes of the German Constitutional Court. And indeed, a case against it was lodged on 17 June 2020 by the Alternative für Deutschland.

D. The Greek Crisis

Beyond the German Constitutional Court's contestation of the ECB's OMT and QE programmes, the outcome of which remains to be seen, all judicial contestation of 'Eurocrisis law' and the EU's emergency government of the Eurozone has been neutralized or defeated. This applies particularly to the contestation of austerity in bailout Member States where bailout conditionality has been treated as an 'internal affair'. The contestation of the emergency government of the Eurozone, however, has not been dealt with merely by courts. Austerity and emergency politics have been widely contested in bailout Member States in a more 'political manner' by political parties, labour unions, and social movements.[194]

This broader contestation of the emergency government of the Eurozone has been united around being not merely against austerity but also the 'post-political' and 'post-democratic'[195] manner through which the Eurozone crisis has been governed in the eyes of the protestors.[196] These movements have primarily understood the crisis as a *political crisis* manifest in the erosion of the legitimacy of the current democratic regimes.[197] The outrage has been directed against both domestic

[191] Ibid.

[192] 'ECB Stimulus Plan Meets Court Requirements: German Finance Minister' *Reuters* (29 June 2020) <https://www.reuters.com/article/us-ecb-policy-germany-idUSKBN2401OX> accessed 8 August 2020; Birgit Jennen, 'German Parliament Backs ECB Bond-Buying After Court Standoff' *BloombergQuint* <https://www.bloombergquint.com/politics/german-parliament-backs-ecb-bond-buying-ending-court-standoff> accessed 8 August 2020.

[193] See ECB, Press Release, April 7 2020 'ECB announces package of temporary collateral easing measures' <https://www.ecb.europa.eu/press/pr/date/2020/html/ecb.pr200407~2472a8ccda.en.html> accessed 7 May 2020.

[194] Cristina Flesher Fominaya, 'European Anti-Austerity and pro-Democracy Protests in the Wake of the Global Financial Crisis' (2016) 16 Social movement studies 1.

[195] Colin Crouch, *Post-Democracy* (Polity 2004); Peter Mair, *Ruling the Void: The Hollowing of Western Democracy* (Verso 2013).

[196] Christian Scholl and Annette Freyberg-Inan, 'Imagining another Europe: Building a Pan-European Counter-Hegemonic Bloc Around an Anti-Austerity Master Frame' (2018) 16 Comparative European Politics 103, 118; Donatella Della Porta, 'Mobilizing Against the Crisis, Mobilizing for 'Another Democracy': Comparing Two Global Waves of Protest' (2012) 4 Interface 274, 276.

[197] Mary Kaldor and Sabine Selchow, 'The "Bubbling Up" of Subterranean Politics in Europe' (2013) 9 Journal of Civil Society 78, 84–89.

elites[198] and European elites.[199] The central demand of these protestors has been to *reclaim* 'real democracy'[200] primarily on a domestic level but also to some extent on a European scale.[201] The language of these movements is that of popular sovereignty and the primacy of the political (democracy) over the economy. Their fundamental demand is an end to necessity politics.[202]

To begin with, the anti-austerity movement was primarily manifest in the 'indignant citizens' movements, such as the Spanish *Indignados* and the Greek *Aganaktismenoi* who adopted classical anarchist anti-statist tactics manifest in horizontal politics of occupations and public assemblies.[203] Over time, however, the anti-austerity movements have mostly broken with the anti-statist view and adopted a more radical reformist strategy, combining electoral politics and referenda aiming for a radical political change through the ballot box and the recuperation of state democracy.[204] The European pro-democracy and anti-austerity movements have had a significant electoral impact in several Member States. The rise of the Podemos party, for example, brought an end to the traditional two-party system in Spain when the party, barely two years old, won 21 per cent of the vote in the 2015 election making it Spain's third largest party.[205] While its vote share has fallen in subsequent elections, Podemos (now under the Unidas Podemos umbrella) entered government in January 2020, thus introducing the first national coalition government in Spain since the fall of the Franco regime.

Another significant case of a Member State government formed by an anti-austerity party is the Greek Syriza-led government elected in January 2015. Like Podemos, the election of Syriza into government also defied the bipartisan system that had prevailed since the transition to democracy.[206] The Syriza-led government, and the 'Greek crisis' of 2015, is of special interest because it is one of the

198 Both Podemos and the 5 Star Movement famously describe the national elites as '*La Casta*'.

199 For example, the umbrella organization Blockupy that directly contests EU imposed austerity and emergency politics in Frankfurt in front of the ECB and the Alter-Summit. Alter Summit's 2013 Manifesto: 'Roll Back Austerity and Claim Real Democracy!' <http://www.altersummit.eu/manifeste/article/the-manifesto> accessed 1 February 2018.

200 The slogan of the massive 2011 demonstrations (estimated participation 0.8–1.5 million) was 'Real Democracy Now' (*¡Democracia Real YA!*), see Kaldor and Selchow (n 197) 79.

201 See DiEM25's Manifesto: 'The European Union will be democratised. Or it will disintegrate!' <https://diem25.org/manifesto-long/> accessed 1 February 2018.

202 See the DiEM25 manifesto and Podemos' 2014 Manifesto *Mover Ficha*, [Eng. *'Making a Move'*] available in unofficial English translation <https://hiredknaves.wordpress.com/2014/01/20/podemos-translated-manifesto/> accessed 1 February 2018.

203 Dario Azzellini and Marina Sitrin, *They Can't Represent Us! Reinventing Democracy from Greece to Occupy* (Verso 2014) 5–7.

204 Paolo Gerbaudo, 'The Indignant Citizen: Anti-Austerity Movements in Southern Europe and the Anti-Oligarchic Reclaiming of Citizenship' (2017) 16 Social Movement Studies 1: Special Issue: Resisting Austerity: Collective Action in Europe in the Wake of the Global Financial Crisis 36, 37–38, 45–48.

205 Graeme Hayes, 'Regimes of Austerity' (2017) 16 Social Movement Studies 21, 27.

206 Emmanouil Tsatsanis and Eftichia Teperoglou, 'Realignment under Stress: The July 2015 Referendum and the September Parliamentary Election in Greece' (2016) 21 South European Society and Politics 427, 431.

few Member State governments that has attempted to openly and directly contest the authority of the emergency government of the Eurozone on states' rights grounds.[207] The OMT and QE cases are the main manifestation of a Member State court claiming the right to judicial constitutional defence against the EU, whereas the Syriza-led government is the most significant case of a Member State government contesting the EU's authority to govern the Eurozone crisis. The Syriza government is the only government that has put the bailout conditionality to a vote with the so-called referendum on austerity on 5 July 2015.

In a structurally similar manner to the German Constitutional Court's position in *Gauweiler* and *Weiss*, the Syriza government contested EU authority with a reference to a breach of both EU constitutional values and to Greece as a sovereign democratic state. In the address Prime Minister Tsipras gave when the referendum was called, he argued that the deal presented by the Eurogroup contravened 'the founding principles and values of Europe. The value of our common European structure'. The proposals, Tsipras continued, directly violated 'European social rules and fundamental rights' and proved that the Eurogroup was not interested in reaching 'a viable and beneficial agreement for all sides, but the humiliation of the entire Greek people'. The referendum was called on the basis of both the Greek Constitution and Europe's democratic tradition and clearly aimed at guarding both: 'Greece is, and will remain an indispensable part of Europe and Europe an indispensable part of Greece. But Greece without democracy is a Europe without identity or a compass', Tsipras declared.[208]

In response to Tsipras's announcement that a referendum on the bailout conditions was to be held, the EU employed a different kind of force on Greece than earlier economic sanctions. In what was widely interpreted as a deeply political move, the ECB decided to freeze the Emergency Liquidity Assistance (ELA) to the Greek banking sector, on which the sector had relied since 11 February 2015, resulting in the need for the Greek government to declare a bank holiday and impose capital controls.[209] Had the ECB cut ELA off completely, it would have had enormous political consequences for Greece, effectively forcing it to adopt its own currency and exit the Eurozone.[210] Even before this, however, the ECB had responded to the election of Syriza by lifting the waiver it had introduced in 2010 to allow Greek banks to make use of Greek sovereign bonds as collateral in its dealings with the ECB. Effectively, the ECB thus first forced Greek banks to make use of the significantly more expensive ELA in response to political developments in

207 Another example is the 2019 spat over the Italian budget, see 'EU Rejects Italian Draft Budget, Setting up Standoff with Defiant Italy' *Reuters* (23 October 2018) <https://www.reuters.com/article/us-italy-eu-budget-rejection-idUSKCN1MX20K> accessed 23 July 2020.

208 Reporting by Michele Kambas, 'Text: Greek Prime Minister Tsipras announces bailout referendum' *Reuters* (27 June 2015).

209 Pawel Tokarski, 'Die Europäische Zentralbank als politischer Akteur in der Eurokrise: Mandat, Stellung und Handeln der EZB in einer unvollständigen Währungsunion' (2016) 14 SWP-Studie 1, 27.

210 ibid.

Greece, before then freezing their access to ELA also in response to political developments.[211] The ECB thereby acted as a 'federal executioner' in the Greek crisis and was in possession of means that could have destroyed the Greek economy and forced it out of the Eurozone.

As is well known, to the outrage of European leaders and institutions, the Greek people voted an overwhelming 'no' to the bailout conditionality. Nevertheless, in a desperate attempt to keep Greece in the Eurozone, the Syriza government acceded to the Eurogroup's demands. On 13 July 2015, Syriza committed to the harshest austerity programme Greece has yet seen.[212] That the bailout measures were even harsher than those decided on in the referendum has widely been interpreted as a 'punishment' of Greece for daring to contest the emergency government of the Eurozone or an attempt to force Greece to leave the Eurozone, something the Syriza government was not willing to let happen.

In this way, this direct 'popular' contestation of the emergency government of the Eurozone was defeated. Together with the potential nullification crisis sparked by *Weiss*, the Greek crisis is the clearest example of the contradictory nature of constitutional defence and the fragility of authority in a federal union of states. In the contest between the political rights of the European institutions and Greece to act as the guardian of the constitution and decide on the exception, Greece lost and submitted itself to the will of the Eurogroup. That being said, this vindication of the rights of European institutions is incredibly fragile and it might be a pyrrhic victory. The growth of the executive power of the Union has introduced an unstable equilibrium bringing the Union at once closer to statehood and to collapse. In this way, the government of the Eurozone crisis, and the new institutional arrangements it has given birth to, presents a threat to the constitutional balance of the EU.

[211] Hjalte Lokdam, 'Banking on Sovereignty: The Political Theory of Central Bank Independence and the European Central Bank' (PhD, London School of Economics and Political Science 2020) ch 6.

[212] 'Greek Debt Crisis: Deal Reached after Marathon All-Night Summit - As It Happened' *The Guardian* (London, 13 July 2015).

Conclusion

What type of political association is the EU? From the start of the European integration process, this question has puzzled scholars. Because of its lack of a monopoly on violence and its limited competences, the EU is clearly not a new state. However, the EU has gone far beyond what was considered normal for organizations of international law by making laws that are directly binding in and on its Member States. Many different answers have been offered, but in the absence of an agreed response, most scholars implicitly avoid the issue by suggesting that the EU is *sui generis*. Because the EU cannot be made sense of either on the basis of international law or on the basis of domestic public law, they conclude that it must be something new and unique. This book demonstrates that this conclusion is mistaken. It argues that, in contrast to what is commonly maintained, the EU is not an association *sui generis*. Rather, the EU belongs to the political form of the *federation*: a discrete form of political association on a par with, though differentiated from, the two other forms of political modernity, namely, the *state* and the *empire*. *The federation is a political union of states founded on an interstate agreement of a constitutional nature, a federal compact, that does not absorb the Member States into a new state.* The argument of the book is advanced in five chapters, each dealing with a central aspect of the constitutional theory of the federation that is of importance to a proper understanding of the contemporary constitutional order of the EU.

Chapter 1 identifies a number of reasons why the federal constitutional nature of the EU has generally been overlooked in the literature. The main reason is that the EU is arguably the only federal union of states founded since the nineteenth century. As a consequence, constitutional debates about the federation have been overlooked by constitutional theorists and the theory of the federation forgotten. The federation as a concept has consequentially taken on the new meaning of the federal state. For that reason, the federation as a political form is mistakenly conceptualized as a species of the state and the EU is wrongly described as an 'incomplete federation'. In contrast with the federal state, the federation is a political union of states that, on a free basis, constitute a common governmental structure and a common public law but that do not unite to the degree that they form a fully fledged federal state.

The conceptualization of the federation as a species of the state leads to a misunderstanding of the constitutional foundations of the federation. In contrast to a state constitution, the federal constitution is not founded on a unilateral act of

The Constitutional Theory of the Federation and the European Union. Signe Rehling Larsen, Oxford University Press (2021).
 DOI: 10.1093/oso/9780198859260.003.0007

a sovereign people but on a federal compact or federal treaty (*Bundesvertrag*) between the Member States. The federation is founded on compact rather than command; the federal founding is a contractual agreement between the federating states. This interstate agreement (compact or treaty), however, is also a constitution because it gives birth to the political existence of the Union and leads to a political change in the constitution of its members by giving them the new status of member-statehood. The federal compact is therefore always a constitutional contract (*Verfassungsvertrag*), a secular 'covenant', independent of whether it is conceptualized as such. Chapter 1 is thus concerned with the enigma of the EU, namely that it does not conform to the model of the state, and demonstrates how the theory of the federation can solve the mystery of its legal and political form. Central to this chapter is the problem of sovereignty, that is, the question of where and whether sovereignty persists in a federation and specifically in the EU. In contrast to the state, the federation and the structure of federal public law is not organized around the concept of sovereignty. As Chapter 1 demonstrates, there is an antinomy between the concept of sovereignty and the concept of the federation. For that reason, scholars tend to trivialize or deny the existence of either sovereignty or the federation.

On the one hand, the 'sovereignty hunters' will attempt to make sense of the concrete political associations of the federation by reducing them to the political form of the state: either one federal state (*Bundesstaat*) or the composite states (*Staatenbund*). The problem with this approach is that in protecting the distinction between public law and international law on which the theory of the state relies, it fails to account for the actual workings of concrete political associations. In order to preserve the public law theory of the state, two categories—*Staatenbund* ('state federation' or 'confederation') and *Bundesstaat* ('federal state')—are created that cannot account for the public law of any historical examples of federations. The desire for jurisprudential clarity leads to the oversimplification of reality. This way of thinking dominates the debate on the constitutional nature of the EU and contributes to the widespread idea of its uniqueness.

On the other hand, there are scholars whose point of departure is the intricate governmental structure that regulates the exercise of public power in the EU, both by the Union institutions and its Member States, and on that basis conclude either that sovereignty is a myth conjured up in the minds of nineteenth-century lawyers or that sovereignty can be reduced to the question of a bundle of competences. The latter approach has resulted in the widespread use of meaningless categories, at least from the perspective of public law, such as 'monetary sovereignty' and 'fiscal sovereignty'. For these scholars, sovereignty no longer has the connotation of legal and political autonomy and final authority but is reduced to the question of capacity. In order to account for the day-to-day workings of the EU, these scholars have to deny or trivialize the concept of sovereignty.

In Chapter 1, I argue that rather than taking either of these two unsatisfactory routes, the federation, and the EU as a manifestation thereof, must be recognized as a discrete political form. It is so precisely because it cannot be made sense of on the basis of sovereignty. In order to comprehend the federation and the EU we have to conceptualize political and public law orders without sovereignty. This means that we should treat the federation, and thus the EU, as an autonomous political form characterized by its own vices and virtues without having recourse to the prejudices of the state.

The argument presented in Chapter 2 is that as actual constitutional projects, federations come into existence because of the impotence and instability of the state as a political form. States decide to come together in a federation because, for one reason or another, they are incapable of maintaining their own political autonomy and existence. The medieval and early modern federations were constituted between smaller states and free cities, pledging themselves to common and mutual defence against a strong (neighbouring) empire. They were, therefore, 'defence federations'. Common military defence, however, is not the only reason why states decide to come together and constitute among themselves a federal union. To ensure their autonomy and survival, states around the time of the industrial revolution needed to be able to govern and control larger internal markets. By allowing for the creation and expansion of internal markets, the 'economic federation' evolved historically as an alternative to the empire. Whereas the empire relies on imperial conquest for the expansion of internal markets, the federation creates an internal market by mutual promises and pledges, and not by acts of domination.

Chapter 2 demonstrates that the project of European integration, as with other federations, originates in the impotence of the state as a form of political association in the post-WWII era. The project of European Union was born out of a shared understanding among the political elites of the Original Six—with De Gaulle as the main, if not only, exception—that the nation-state was an unviable political form associated with past atrocities. After WWII, projects of both 'defence federation' and 'economic federation' were launched. However, only the latter was successfully established with the Treaty of Rome. The European Economic Community (EEC) therefore emerged as an 'economic federation', with defence added later as a subordinate aim. That the EEC/EU emerged as an almost 'pure' economic federation is arguably an important reason why the federal constitutional nature of the EU has generally not been recognized in the literature. Despite the importance of the government of welfare for most if not all historical federations, the aim of welfare is not widely discussed in the literature and the 'economic federation' is not commonly recognized as a federal subspecies.

Having discussed the origins of federal unions of states (the question of why states decide to come together in a federation), Chapter 3 lays out the main principles of federal public law: a public law structure which is not organized around the concept of sovereignty. In contrast to the state, the federation has a dual governmental structure consisting of the institutional structures of both the Union and the Member States, and a dual source of authority: the political existence of the Union and the political existence of the Member States. Because of this duality, the federation is fundamentally different from the unity of the state, which always has the relationship between people and government as the foundation for its authority. Moreover, the dual structure of the federation (the Union and the Member States) are not parallel and fully autonomous orders vis-à-vis one another. Rather, they are characterized by a 'mixed autonomy' or the principles of independence and interdependence. When states come together in a federation, they give birth to a new legal and political order (the Union) that is independent from the constitutional orders of the Member States. This new legal and political order, however, encompasses the Member States in their entirety at the same time as it is a component of the constitutional orders of the Member States. The constitutional order of the federation is in this way a new legal order and yet it is internal to its Member States. The internal multiplicity of the federation characterized by mixed autonomy relativizes the relationship between people and government that lies at the heart of the theory of the state.

Neither of the component parts of the public law structure of the federation (the institutional structures of the Union and the Member States), exercises public power in accordance with the theory of the state. Union institutions are, importantly, not indicative of a new 'super-state'. In contrast to a state, the federation is constituted to achieve the enumerated aims that the Member States came together to secure. The powers of the Union institutions are therefore always limited to these pre-given constitutional aims. Union authority is in this way governed by the principles of teleology and specialization.

Becoming a Member State signals a radical transformation of the constitution of the Member State. The constitutional change of the Member States is not necessarily manifest in the change of any constitutional laws but rather in the transformation of the Member States' constitutions in the positive sense, that is, the fundamental characteristics of how they govern themselves as political associations. The federal compact between the Member States on which all federations rely is a 'status contract' (*Statusvertrag*) that, like marriage, transforms the contracting parties by giving them a fundamental new status. Member-statehood, Chapter 3 explains, is in this way a distinct form of statehood, which means that the Member States cannot be conceptualized as 'states' in the classical sense of the term. A federation is thus characterized not merely by the birth of the new federal existence, the Union, but also by a process of state transformation. In a federation, the legal order of the Union makes up a part of the Member States' own constitutions. 'Member-statehood' therefore entails the *constitutional internalization* of the constitutional order of the Union by the Member States. Notwithstanding that the constitutional orders of the Union and the Member States are autonomous they are also interrelated and interdependent.

The emergence and transformation of the constitutional settlements of the EU Member States is intimately linked to their membership in the EU and the constitutional order of the Union, albeit in different ways. For the founding Member States, EU member-statehood signals a form of 'constrained statehood' that should be understood as an integral part of the post-WWII political project of 'constrained democracy'. The founding Member States, albeit to different degrees, all wanted to protect themselves from 'political extremism', manifest in fascism and communism, and European integration became an important means of doing that. A similar argument for a relative 'constitutional synthesis' between the constitutional orders of the Union and the Member States can be advanced with regard to the acceding Member States of the Mediterranean enlargements (Spain, Portugal, and Greece) in the 1980s. For these states, member-statehood in the EU has been understood as an important protection against the return of fascism and authoritarianism. It provides a means of realizing their own understanding of constitutional autonomy by protecting themselves, via membership of the EU, from the return of dictatorship. This, however, is less the case for the other states that have acceded to the EU.

For the 'continuous democracies' of the UK and Scandinavia (Denmark and Sweden), constrained democracy was never entrenched to any significant extent. In contrast to the 'core' Member States, the 'continuous democracies' experienced neither the collapse of their constitutional orders in the interwar period nor saw WWII as a significant constitutional watershed. Not being marked by a fear of the political power of the people, these Member States retained parliamentary sovereignty as the bedrock of their constitutional orders. The internalization of the demands of member-statehood (eg judicial review of parliamentary legislation to ensure conformity with EU law) has therefore entailed a process of 'constitutional modernization' that brought these three states broadly, but not unproblematically, in line with the original Member States of the EU. The 'continuous democracies', however, are not the only states for which the demands of member-statehood have not been easily internalized.

Despite constituting themselves as liberal democracies after the collapse of communism, the post-communist countries are also not heavily influenced by the doctrine of constrained democracy. The watershed for these Member States is not the internal collapse of their constitutional orders but the collapse of the foreign empire or super-power (the Soviet Union) they were ruled by for decades. These states are therefore not afraid of their own people and accordingly gave themselves constitutions with a strong accentuation of sovereignty. The constitutional internalization of the demands of EU member-statehood for these states was achieved through the employment of the idea of 'the return to Europe' as a political myth allowing the Member States to give themselves radically new constitutional orders in the guise of a return to their somewhat fictitious past of democratic nation-states.

For these states, European integration was therefore perceived simultaneously as a path and a threat to democracy.

The Member States of the EU are therefore characterized by a strong degree of constitutional heterogeneity. This constitutional heterogeneity, Chapter 4 argues, constitutes a significant challenge for the EU because all federations rely on the capacity to strike a balance between the two contradictory aims and forces that characterize all federations. These contradictory aims and forces are born of the curious sentiment that lies at the origin of all federal unions of states. On the one hand, the states come together in a federation because they want to preserve their own political identity and autonomy, that is, they want to remain who they are. On the other hand, the states come together in a federation as a rejection of the status quo and out of a desire to form an 'ever-closer union' with their future fellow Member States. This double telos of the federation is inherently contradictory and pulls the federation in two opposing directions. The federation is simultaneously directed towards unity and diversity, transformation and conservation, the past and the future. The only way the federation can balance these contradictory forces is via the persistence of a fundamental political homogeneity among Member States. This homogeneity among Member States is relative to their own legal and political orders and self-perception. Member States need to be homogenous with regard to what they perceive to be politically salient and for that reason the content of the political homogeneity of the Member States will be specific to any given federation. In the case of the EU, the political homogeneity professed by the constitutional order of the Union lies in the principles of 'value order constitutionalism' and 'constrained democracy'.

The EU, Chapter 4 explains, has attempted to govern this homogeneity by allowing Member States to accede to the Union only via the application of accession criteria. The purpose of accession criteria for a federation is to mould the acceding states in accordance with the self-image and aspirations—in short, the ideology—of the Union. It is a highly intrusive set of legal and political mechanisms that, for the duration of the accession period, reduce the acceding state to a dependency of the Union. Nevertheless, this process is not imperial because it is instigated on the basis of the free decision of the acceding state to join the Union with the promise of political equality after accession. Despite the intrusiveness of the EU accession process, especially in the case of the post-communist countries, it is not clear that the constitutional order of the Union and the values it claims to promote have been genuinely internalized by the post-communist Member States.

Another way in which the EU attempts to govern the constitutional homogeneity of its Member States is by a mechanism of constitutional defence manifest in Article 7 of the Treaty on European Union (TEU) procedure.[1] This procedure is

[1] Article 7 of the Consolidated version of the Treaty on European Union [2016] OJ C202/13.

meant to allow the Union to sanction Member States in which there is a fundamental threat to the values enshrined in Article 2 TEU on which the Union professes to be founded. The limited scope of Article 7 TEU together with the high political threshold for its triggering, however, means that it does not provide the EU with any legal possibility of intervening in the internal constitutional affairs of its Member States in order to prevent the rise of authoritarian constitutionalism. The EU therefore has limited legal possibilities of intervening in the internal constitutional affairs of Poland and Hungary, which in recent years have undergone radical constitutional changes that arguably put them at odds with the constitutional identity of the EU as defined by Article 2 TEU. But Chapter 4 concludes that the legal limitations cannot be the only reason for the lack of exercise of constitutional defence by the Union. In response to the Eurozone crisis, the EU has to a large degree made use of extra-legal instruments of emergency politics that have allowed the Union, *de facto* if not *de jure*, to take more or less full control over the state apparatus of deficit Member States.

The problem of constitutional defence in the EU is further discussed in the context of the emergency government of the Eurozone in Chapter 5. The argument presented is that the government of the Eurozone crisis is a manifestation of a particular kind of emergency rule, namely, federal emergency politics or federal constitutional defence. In contrast to the state, the federation is a double political existence. This means that emergency politics can be exercised by a variety of different constitutional actors (Union institutional actors and Member State institutional actors) and wielded on behalf of different units (the Union and the Member States). In this way, the federation allows for a contest not merely between different institutions but also between the Union and its Member States. Although this contest can lead to intense conflicts, federal emergency politics is, more often than not, a collaboration of the executive branches of government at the Union and Member State levels. Federal emergency politics is a form of 'mixed emergency rule' that generally involves multiple actors and multiple claims to emergency authority. Chapter 5 lays out two theories of federal emergency politics and demonstrates in what ways they apply to the government of the Eurozone crisis. One is the doctrine of 'federal intervention' (*Bundesintervention*) and 'federal execution' (*Bundesexecution*) based on the theory and constitutional praxis of the nineteenth-century German Confederation, and the other the 'doctrine of states rights' that was influential in the early history of the United States and was most clearly expressed in the writings of John Calhoun.

In the German Confederation, the federal execution authorized the use of executive measures *against* a non-complying Member State, whereas the federal intervention authorized the use of executive measures on *behalf* of a Member State incapable of dealing with an internal crisis. These constitutional mechanisms gave German princes the possibility of relying not merely on their own military capacity but also on that of all their fellow Member States to repress the national liberal uprisings characterizing the history of the German Confederation. In this way, they were an important means for the preservation of the monarchical constitutional order in the German Confederation and the power and authority of the German princes. Nevertheless, these mechanisms simultaneously gave the Union the authority to take over the complete control of the administration of the crisis-ridden Member State in question and *de facto* if not *de jure* reduce it to a mere administrative dependency.

Chapter 5 demonstrates that central legal instruments employed by the EU in order to govern the Eurozone crisis conform to the theory of federal intervention and federal execution. The emergency politics of the Eurozone crisis, and federal emergency politics in general, has provided Member State elites with the possibility to rely not only on their own executive apparatus but also that of the Union at large to enforce unpopular decisions that would have been difficult to get through parliaments in ordinary times. As was the case in the German Confederation, the employment of this kind of emergency politics tends to have the consequence that the Member State in which federal emergency politics is employed, *de facto* if not *de jure*, is reduced to an administrative dependency. Federal execution and federal intervention as instruments of federal constitutional defence are in this way a consolidation of the Union's right to act as the guardian of the constitution and a significant source of federal power against the Member States.

The doctrine of states' rights, in contrast, maintains that it is not the Union but the Member States that have the ultimate right to act as the guardian of the constitution. If a Member State deems that there has been a breach of the constitution, it has a right to nullify federal law on its territory and ultimately to secede as a means of constitutional defence. This doctrine provides strong ammunition for Member States who wish to contest federal authority. It was widely used in the early history of the United States, such as in the 'nullification crisis' of the 1830s and later in the Civil War.

In May 2020 the German Constitutional Court surprised legal academics across Europe by declaring both the European Central Bank's (ECB's) Public Sector Purchase Programme (PSPP) together with the European Court of Justice's (ECJ's) defence of its constitutionality *ultra vires*. The programme in question is part of the ECB's broader Quantitative Easing (QE) programme. This case followed another challenge by the German Constitutional Court of the ECB's Outright Monetary Transactions programme (OMT), announced with the famous 'whatever it takes' speech by former ECB President Mario Draghi. With regard to the OMT, the German Constitutional Court in the end submitted itself to the will of the ECJ. For a while, EU scholars savoured the victory of the legal monism that they hoped had finally been achieved. The submission of the German Constitutional Court, however, turned out to be temporary. Unless the crisis can be evaded by a combination of the conceptual gymnastics of lawyers and concerns for political expediency, the EU will enter its first proper nullification crisis. Whether the EU manages to muddle through despite this conflict, as the United States ultimately did during the 1830s nullification crisis, remains to be seen.

The constitutional implications of the crisis, however, run much deeper than current high politics between Europe's most powerful courts. Underneath the battle of judges and central bankers lies a more serious predicament that has received much less attention from constitutional scholars and EU lawyers alike: the problem of damage incurred on the political balance in the EU. In material terms, it is clear that the political autonomy of especially the *deficit* Member States has been eroded. It is therefore somewhat ironic that it is the constitutional court of one of the Member States least affected by the crisis that has mounted a direct constitutional challenge to EU authority with reference to the 'principle of democracy'. If any of the 'peoples of Europe' have been deprived of the right to elect their own representatives, it is the peoples of the Member States that have been subjected to federal interventions and federal executions under 'Eurocrisis law' (importantly the 'Fiscal Compact', the European Stability Mechanism (ESM), the European Semester, the 'Six Pack', and the 'Two Pack').

Despite the ample opportunity of Member State courts to contest the legality of Eurocrisis law (either with reference to a breach of the EU Charter of Fundamental Rights or a breach of the fundamental rights protected by the constitutions of many 'deficit Member States'), little judicial contestation has taken place. Instead, both the ECJ and Member State courts have to a large degree attempted to avoid an open constitutional conflict in the EU and the question of who ultimately decides that has now been raised with *Weiss*.[2] Evading the question has been done, for instance, by treating bailout conditionality as an 'internal affair' of the Member States.

In the Member States most affected by the Eurozone crisis, judicial constitutional defence, which could have been pursued with reference to fundamental rights breaches, has been conspicuous mostly in its absence. Nevertheless, EU authority and the austerity that the emergency government of the Eurozone imposed *have* been contested in the deficit Member States. There has been widespread political contestation by social movements and political parties, mostly in southern Europe. That being said, there are few examples of direct 'political' challenges to the emergency government of the Eurozone by Member State governments. The clearest example is the 2015 'Greek crisis' where the governing party Syriza mounted a direct challenge to the emergency government of the Eurozone crisis with reference both to the constitutional and political values of Greece and the EU at large. At the height of the Greek crisis, the Greek people voted overwhelmingly 'no' to the bailout conditionality in the so-called referendum on austerity. However, before a direct conflict between the will of the Greek people and the EU could show itself, Syriza conceded to the Eurogroup's demands and committed to

[2] Case C-493/17 *Weiss and Others* [2018] ECLI:EU:C:2018:1000; BVerfG, Judgment of the Second Senate of 05 May 2020—2 BvR 859/15.

the harshest austerity programme Greece has yet seen. In the case of the Greek crisis, the question of ultimate authority was in the end not raised, preserving, at least formally, the idea of the political balance between the Union and the Member States on which the EU, as all federal unions of states, relies.

Even in cases where emergency politics can be successfully employed without major contestation of Union authority on the part of the Member States, it nevertheless presents a threat to the survival of the federation as a political form. Emergency politics introduces a strong element of reason of state that *de facto* if not *de jure* erodes the political autonomy of its Member States by reducing them to administrative dependencies. This is a highly centralizing force that brings the EU, and especially its core Eurozone states, closer to statehood, something that is recognized by officials of the European Central Bank.

Finally, if previous federal unions of states can be invoked for the purpose of seeking to understand the future of the EU, the emergence of a European federal *state*, if it comes about, will not be a peaceful and unproblematic process. The establishment of constitutional hierarchy and legal monism is likely to be born not out of superior legal arguments but out of the exercise of political power. The three most important modern federations—Switzerland, Germany, and the United States—all had civil wars on the path to statehood. The constitutional theory of the federation put forward in this book is in that sense a cautionary tale. Political domination is rarely a promising route to ensure the survival of a political association. In the case of the EU, it would be a direct betrayal of its founding promise of 'peace and prosperity' in Europe.

Index

For the benefit of digital users, indexed terms that span two pages (e.g., 52–53) may, on occasion, appear on only one of those pages.